Faith in Democracy?
Religion and Politics in Canada

Faith in Democracy?
Religion and Politics in Canada

Edited by

John Young and Boris DeWiel

CAMBRIDGE
SCHOLARS

P U B L I S H I N G

Faith in Democracy? Religion and Politics in Canada, Edited by John Young and Boris DeWiel

This book first published 2009

Cambridge Scholars Publishing

12 Back Chapman Street, Newcastle upon Tyne, NE6 2XX, UK

British Library Cataloguing in Publication Data
A catalogue record for this book is available from the British Library

ISBN (10): 1-4438-0117-8, ISBN (13): 978-1-4438-0117-1

TABLE OF CONTENTS

LIST OF TABLES AND FIGURES

ACKNOWLEDGEMENTS

Earlier drafts of these papers were presented at a seminar held at the University of Northern British Columbia. The authors wish to thank the participants of this seminar and UNBC for its support of such inquiry. We also thank Tara Rogers and Clarence Hofsink for their research and editorial assistance.

INTRODUCTION

FAITH AND POLITICS IN CANADA

JOHN F. YOUNG

The title of this collection of essays, *Faith in Democracy?,* questions the capacity of Canadian democracy to embrace religious belief and disparate faith groups as legitimate players on the political stage. This is more than a rhetorical question, as issues and public policies in contemporary Canada reflect an increasing concern that religion and religious belief ought not to intrude in political debate and matters of governance. Faith risks relegation to the private sector. An example is the tempest that followed Pope Benedict's initial incursion into Canadian politics. In the immediate aftermath of the parliamentary decision to change the legal definition of marriage, Pope Benedict declared that Canada's laws allowing same-sex marriage were evidence of God's exclusion from the public sphere. Speaking to Canadian bishops, the Pope was critical of Catholic politicians in Canada who ignore the teachings of the Church, and yield to "ephemeral social trends and the spurious demands of opinion polls." He further declared, "In the name of tolerance your country has had to endure the folly of the redefinition of spouse, and in the name of freedom of choice it is confronted with the daily destruction of unborn children."[1] The Pope's statements caused no small stir. One proponent of same sex marriage responded by pointing out that Canada does not have a state religion, and that politicians "have a responsibility to not be proponents of a particular faith when making decisions that affect everyone."[2] Such a solution suggests that religious beliefs have only diminished status in the pantheon of ideas. They are private matters and have no role to play in the theatre of public policy. Religious leaders who engage in ongoing political debate ostensibly violate the separation of church and state.[3] All beliefs may be equal, but some beliefs are more equal than others.

Yet religion is nothing new to the Canadian public square, and has intersected with politics throughout Canadian history. When Lord Durham responded to the rebellions of 1837 and famously described Canada as "two nations warring in the bosom of a single state," he had in mind much more than a dispute over language. Religious tension and conflict between friends and foes of Catholicism were fundamental to early Canadian politics. This tension was manifest not only in the pursuit of responsible government, but also in other subsequent policy arenas such as education and immigration. Such involvement was not considered trespass, but part of the play of politics. As John Webster Grant described, the representation of interests connected with organized religion helped establish religious pluralism as an important part of Canadian identity.[4] Grant also highlighted that it was not the conflict itself, but the dynamics of that pluralism that had the most telling impact on society. Writing in the 1970s, he declared,

> Undoubtedly, we have entered an era of religious pluralism. The future is likely to belong, however, neither to a static pluralism of inherited denominational traditions, nor to a polarized pluralism of competing claims to religious control, but rather to a dynamic pluralism of cells acting as leaven in the lump of society.[5]

How dynamic is religion in Canadian politics today? Is it now leaven in the lump linked to change and development in Canada or is it a reactionary force intent to defend and perpetuate the traditions of yesterday?

Canada's connection with religious pluralism is certainly one source of its commitments to tolerance and multiculturalism. Yet these commitments also invite study of the consequences of axiological heterogeneity. Whether we refer to value pluralism, splendid isolationism, public morality, or moral relativism, ultimately we focus on the influence of moral perspectives within society, and the authoritative allocation of values that politics determine. Despite any efforts to set religion aside as an active ingredient, religious belief has played, and should continue to play, an important role in this contestation. To suggest it ought not to be part of public discussion and debate or influence public policy is to diminish democracy–not because the Bible or the Koran are superior political texts, but because democracy is, at its core, a debate.[6] As the boundaries of public debate have broadened over past generations to include a multiplicity of perspectives, including ideas and beliefs previously considered socially unacceptable, it now seems odd to encourage the exclusion of values and beliefs that so recently were fancied as mainstream. Efforts to push such beliefs outside the public square set a dangerous precedent, provide rationale for further exclusion rather than inclusion, and logically culminate in monism rather than pluralism.[7] At the same time, as the arena admits greater disparity in values, it may be natural to question whether a Babel like confusion of disparate values and beliefs can foster not only passive tolerance of conflicting beliefs, but civic commitment, engagement, and responsibility. Grant's leaven presupposes not only contrasting values but also common commitments.

An introduction to the study of religion and politics in Canada must highlight that the country is hardly a single entity or in possession of a single identity. It may be more appropriate to suggest that there are many different Canadas. As a federal state, there are significant differences across the ten provinces and three territories, something taken as a given by Canadians, but sometimes poorly understood outside Canada. There are different solitudes between the Canada found in large urban settings and the Canada of rural communities and small cities. Inter and even intra provincial variations might explain why Canadian efforts to define itself tend more towards what Canada is *not* (i.e. not the United States of America) than what Canada is. Those few federal planks that extend, however thinly, across the provinces and connect all Canadians support heavy loads. Thus, the Medical Care Act is regarded by some as a supporting beam of our national identity. Efforts to reform the Act are thus perceived as a dismantling of Canada, as if prior to the Act in 1966 there was no Canada, only too much territory and not enough population or government. In order to profile some of these differences across Canada, we provide here a snapshot of religious pluralism in Canadian society. This pluralism is manifest not only through the multi denominational beliefs of Canadians, but also through federalism and public policy. We then review some of the recent flashpoints in Canadian politics to illuminate the challenges inherent in balancing competing values and beliefs.

According to the 2001 census, Canada is still a predominantly Christian country, even if it is reluctant to identify itself as such. The census suggests that three out of four Canadians identify themselves as Christians: including Catholic (43%), Protestant (29%), Orthodox (1.6%) and self identified "other" Christian faiths (2.6%).[8] There are more than a dozen different Christian denominations in Canada with membership greater than 100,000 adherents, and so religious pluralism is well engrained in Canadian society. Yet to even loosely describe Canada as Christian requires specific qualifications. The declaration of religious affiliation or identity, for example, is a poor measure of religiosity, defined by the degree to which religious beliefs are considered important to the individual and measured by the frequency of religious practice and attendance. Only 32% of all Canadians attend religious services at least monthly, while 54% of Canadians engage in monthly or more frequent religious practices such as prayer.[9] Perhaps more relevant are data that reveal trends across time. The data in Table 1 suggest that while the Christian population is still a majority, it is also a diminishing proportion of the Canadian population. Most noticeable is the persistent decline of Protestants.

Table 1-1: Protestant and Catholic identification as a percentage of total population of Canada

	Protestants	Catholics	Percent of Total Population
1901	56	42	98
1971	44	46	90
1991	35	45	80
2001	29	43	72

Source: Statistics Canada

Why the marked and consistent Protestant decline? One explanation is change in immigration policy. Protestants comprised about 40% of the immigrant population prior to 1961, but fell to just 10% of all immigrants in the decade between 1991 and 2001.[10] Immigration also accounts for rapid increases in the numbers of Islam, Hindu, Buddhist and Sikh believers in Canada. The rates of growth in Canada for each of these religions are dramatic. Between 1991 and 2001 the Muslim population in Canada grew by 129%; Hindu 89%; Sikh 89%; and Buddhist 84%.[11] Immigration can also help to explain some continuity in the proportion of Catholics in Canada. Although the percentage of immigrants who identify themselves as Catholics has declined (from 39% prior to 1961 to 23% in the decade ending in 2001), Catholics continue to be the largest religious group among all immigrants to Canada in each decade since 1961.[12] However, immigration can only explain part of Protestant decline. Although the population of non Christian religions has doubled over the previous decade, they still collectively account for only 5% of the total Canadian population.[13]

Two further explanations for Protestant decline are examined more closely in the next chapter of this volume by Kuipers and Kanji. Over the last decade, there has been an increase of almost 1.5 million Canadians without any religious affiliation. This growth means that one in every six Canadians now has no religion, a proportionate increase from 12% of the population in 1991 to 16% one decade later. On first analysis, the standard modernization thesis seems to hold: the more urban, industrialized and educated the population, the weaker the demand for religious association.[14] The growth of the state, particularly in such realms as health and social services and public education, has clearly undermined some traditional roles of the church, and thus contributes to this diminution of demand. Reginald Bibby argues, however, that the decrease in religious affiliation does not confirm any increase in atheism or secularism. He suggests that many individuals still entertain religious beliefs but do not associate with specific religious groups or identities.[15] Be that as it may, the non religious find their largest share (35%) of any age cohort among adults between the ages of 25 and 44 and their smallest share (6.2%) in the age cohort over 65 years. These data may indicate future declines in religious affiliation, although not directly connected to Protestantism.

Table 1-2: Number of Religious Believers as Percentage of Provincial Populations in Canada (2001)

Province Territory	Population	Catholic	Protestant	Other Christian	Non Christian	No Religion
	thousands		Percentage of population			
Newfoundland	508	36.9	59.7	0.6	0.2	2.5
Prince Edward Island	133	47.4	42.8	2.6	0.2	6.5
Nova Scotia	898	36.5	48.8	1.5	0.9	11.6
New Brunswick	720	53.6	36.6	1.2	0.5	7.8
Quebec	7,126	83.2	4.7	2.2	3.8	5.6
Ontario	11,286	34.3	34.9	5.0	8.7	16.0
Manitoba	1,104	26.5	43.1	5.4	3.0	18.3
Saskatchewan	963	29.8	46.6	4.3	0.9	15.4
Alberta	2,941	25.7	38.9	5.7	4.5	23.1
British Columbia	3,869	17.2	31.4	6.1	8.5	35.1
Yukon	29	21.0	33.2	4.0	1.2	37.4
Northwest Territories	37	45.7	31.3	2.9	1.3	17.4
Nunavut	27	23.3	66.7	3.2	0.2	6.0

Source: Statistics Canada

Kuipers and Kanji also point out that the decline in Protestantism may have much to do with choices that mainstream Protestants have made concerning their practices and doctrines. Some mainstream Protestant churches have abandoned some of the traditionalism that helped define their faith.[16] This "supply side" explanation, encouraged by Rodney Stark and other scholars,[17] carries some weight when we compare the real number decline among mainstream Protestant churches in Canada (770,000 adherents in the 1990s) with the increase in membership among "other" Christian congregations (427,000 during the same period).[18] More than half of those who left the four main Protestant Churches - the United Church of Canada, the Anglican Church, the Presbyterian Church or the Lutheran Church - were compensated by increases to Baptist, Evangelical, Mormon, Adventist, and other Christian faiths.[19]

All these explanations not only help explain the decline of mainstream Protestantism, but also help illuminate the changing contours of the religious landscape in Canada. Further detail of this landscape is also provided when we focus on specific regions, which help us recognize the different Canadas. When we look at provincial populations, for example, there are very noticeable differences. Table Two summarizes some of the most identifiable characteristics. Newfoundland, which joined Canada in 1949, is the only province with a Protestant majority, while Quebec is the only province with a Catholic majority. British Columbia, on the other hand, has a plurality of those who profess no religion. And the three northern territories each have different religious landscapes.

Certainly, historical and cultural factors are a large part of the explanation for such provincial variation. Thus, Quebec maintains an enduring identification with Catholicism, although this affiliation in no way suggests high levels of commitment to Catholic doctrine or to regular attendance. In fact, Quebec has among the lowest levels of religiosity to complement the highest levels of religious affiliation in Canada.[20] Additionally, immigration patterns facilitate the emergence of ethnic and cultural neighbourhoods, particularly in large metropolitan areas, such as Toronto and Vancouver. Yet historical and cultural factors again reveal only part of the story. There are also important institutional and structural explanations that are part of these provincial differences. One example is the difference in education policy across the provinces. For better or worse, the Federal Government in Canada plays no meaningful role in the delivery of public education. Provincial jurisdiction has meant that the curriculum and financing of schools are determined at the provincial level, which has led to a variety of distinct models across Canada. While all provinces provide full funding for public schools, four provinces (Alberta, Saskatchewan, Ontario and Quebec) provide similar funding for "separate schools," a designation that has reference to Catholic schools in the first three provinces and to English speaking schools in Quebec.[21] Separate boards are not recognized in the other six provinces, including Manitoba, which first abandoned Catholic schools in 1890 and provoked a national crisis. Just as relevant as the existence of separate school boards is the policy in five provinces (British Columbia, Alberta, Saskatchewan, Manitoba and Quebec) to provide public money to independent schools, in some cases as high as 60% of comparable funding to public schools. Since the majority of these schools have strong religious identities, the pursuit of government funding has led to a series of court challenges when such funding is denied, and, in the case of Ontario, even to investigations by the United Nations Human Rights Commission.

At issue is why the provincial government in Ontario provides full funding for Catholic schools and no public money for independent schools with other religious identities and curriculum. UNHRC ruled that Canada was under obligation to provide an effective remedy to eliminate discrimination in the allocation of public funding to schools, and implied that either public funding should be extended to all religious groups, or that public funding for Catholic schools should be terminated.[22] Yet the Canadian government protected the status quo with reference to the constitutional division of powers between federal and provincial governments and the historical political bargain that protected enumerated school financing within the Constitution. Eliminating public funding for Catholic schools would require a constitutional amendment, a ridiculously difficult challenge in the Canadian context. Alternatively, extending full funding to other denominational schools in Ontario alone would cost that province up to 700 million dollars per year, an expense best left to political, rather than judicial, decision making.[23] Although UNHRC reaffirmed its concerns in November 2005, the decision continues to be ignored by the governments of Canada and Ontario, suggesting some limits to tolerance do exist. This issue of public funding to religious schools flared most recently in the Ontario provincial election in 2007. The election platform for the leading opposition party included promises to extend full funding to religious schools, which became a dominant issue of the campaign and became a strong factor in the re election of the government.[24]

While we will not investigate any correlation between such religious funding and religious identity here, such policy choices not only attract political attention and controversy, but also help define and shape the religious profiles of each province. Together with the overall dynamics of religious identification, federalism is another important context for the study of religion in Canada. Public policy is determined nationally and provincially, and each of the provinces has its own unique constellation of religious identities and political forces. This helps explain why some of the issues discussed in subsequent chapters reflect provincial decisions and politics and how religious pluralism impacts national identity.

A further feature of the religious landscape in contemporary Canada is that there is now little viability for political parties with overt religious platforms. As mentioned above, this has not always been the case, and both the Cooperative Commonwealth Federation (CCF) and the Social Credit Party were good examples of 20th century religious-political movements.[25] Both of these parties came to power at the provincial level and left their marks on Canadian politics. Since the CCF reorganized itself in 1961 and entered into closer relationships with organized labour, the successor New Democratic Party has shed much of its Christian identity. While it maintains a social gospel mindset, the party's positions on contemporary issues tend to reflect post Christian and post materialist interests. It is more likely that political influence has had a larger impact on the doctrine of the United Church of Canada than religious doctrine has shaped the New Democratic Party.[26] The Social Credit Party has not played any significant role since the 1970s, although the Reform Party of Canada that rode a populist wave in national politics in the 1990s was viewed by many as a second coming of Social Credit. Certainly the Reform Party relied on religious believers for support both at the ballot box and within the organization. But the party itself was a populist movement without an overt religious platform and Reform remnants eventually merged with remnants of the Progressive Conservative Party to form the Conservative Party of Canada in 2003. It is clear the articulation of traditional religious interests in Canada is *within* parties rather than *by* political parties. One particular exception is the Christian Heritage Party, which seeks to apply inerrant biblical principles to Canadian politics. The party has been running in national elections for 20 years, but has never elected a candidate. In the January 2006 Federal election, the CHP ran only 45 candidates in the 308 ridings throughout Canada and won 28,000 votes, or 0.2% of the total vote. In this instance, the exception proves the rule. While groups of believers can influence candidate and leadership selection, parties that pursue success at the ballot box have been careful to downplay references to religion.

Also missing in Canada is an organized and influential religious lobby. Much has been made of the political influence of the religious right in the American context. But despite some consternation among the political left in Canada and some hope among religious interests, religious groups have little clout in Canada's corridors of power. Canada has not sanctioned established religion since 1854, and neither does it enjoy the civil religion tradition that has been cultivated in the United States.[27] While Canadians implore God to keep their land glorious and free as they sing their national anthem, traditional religion finds few examples of public expression in daily life in Canada. The United States, in contrast, has promoted a consciousness of a redeemer nation in pursuit of a divine purpose. The specifics of religious belief may vary, but patriotism presupposes trust in God. The United States also has a political system that possesses multiple points of access, with checks and balances among the judiciary, Congress, and the President. It includes citizen sponsored initiatives and referenda and greater expectations of elected representatives voting in the legislatures according to constituent rather than party interests. Such access improves the prospects for organizations, religious or not, to influence legislation. The emergence of a religious right in America was also a consequence of judicial decisions and political initiatives from four decades ago. Reactions to such national level decisions as *Roe v. Wade* and the campaign for an Equal Rights Amendment fuelled greater awareness of the need for national action. Political participation among religious groups followed, as did cross denominational political organizations. This participation was directed towards federal politics rather than local or state policy. Canada as a nation has had no such crystallization of a religious right. Or at least not yet. More recent debates behind the redefinition of marriage and perceived secularism of the Supreme Court of Canada and various Human Rights Commissions have spurred stronger reactions from religious leaders and believers in Canada. In this volume, John von Heyking explores the emergence of a secularist civil faith and inerrant Charter, while Boris DeWiel studies the theology of secularism relevant to the Canadian context.

The number of issues that have surfaced over the past decade suggests not only a conflict of values, but also an intensifying struggle to define the boundaries of debate in Canada. The disputes are many, and connect directly with the allocation of values and rights and the persistence of religion in the public square. Can a Catholic social organization, the Knights of Columbus, refuse to rent their hall to a lesbian couple for their marriage celebration? Might a born again Christian require patrons of his copy services shop to take their business elsewhere? Can a school teacher write letters to the editor of a local newspaper opposing gay rights without losing his teaching certification? Can a student attend school with a ceremonial dagger? Can a news magazine publish cartoons with religious content considered newsworthy to some and offensive to others? As marriage is redefined, can a fundamentalist sect legally practice polygamy?

Managing and resolving such contestation are not easy tasks. Some of this contestation is correctly identified as the politics of universality in conflict with the politics of difference.[28] Yet within such disputes we also find efforts to suggest that public policy choices must be value neutral. Religious belief is increasingly perceived as a particular identity and not in the universal interest, which threatens to overshadow the more established embrace between religious pluralism and Canadian identity. Canada thus appears willing to yield to the temptation to recognize an absence of religion as a foundation for the promotion of tolerance and a common identity. In contemporary Canada, secularism thus auditions for the role of neutral adjudicator for democratic government, even if secularism lacks neutrality and is but a variation on a religious theme.

Tolerance is a much simpler value and not much of a virtue when it can also be confused with indifference. I am mostly indifferent to my neighbour's passion for the accordion, for example, especially when his practice is unheard and within the confines of his own walls. But when he practices into the night outdoors on his patio, my commitment to tolerance is tested. So it is with contemporary Canada, as changes in the relative commitment to religious beliefs in society influence and shape Canadian law. How tolerant is Canada is tested as substantial change is introduced in public policy. The last three chapters in this volume address consequences and tensions connected to Canada's commitment to religious pluralism. The attention to Islam is less centered on the specifics of Muslim faith than on the challenges of reconciling universal and particular interests. Although Muslims are a small minority in Canada, global events and dramatic rates of growth combine to foster some measure of alarm, possibly misguided. Paul Rowe looks at Muslims in Canada and the degree to which the Canadian context shapes Muslim communities and political behaviour. John Soroski studies the difficulty in reconciling both universal and particular perspectives in liberalism and in Canadian law. Barry Cooper asks whether addressing the threat of extremist groups might reshape civil liberties in Canada.

Collectively, these essays address John Webster Grant's assessment that religious pluralism provides leaven for Canadian society. Secularism as an ersatz religion is now part of that leaven. With the displacement of traditional religious values, however, it remains to be seen whether secularism can strengthen the vitality of religious pluralism. Additionally, whether or not Canada's commitment to pluralism can embrace Islam and encourage Islam's embrace of pluralism will help determine the endurance of faith in democracy and heavily influence Canadian politics in the future.

Notes

---

[1] "Pope Scolds Canada on Gay Marriage, Abortion," Associated Press, September 8, 2006. http://www.cbc.ca/world/story/2006/09/08/pope-canada.html. For the text of the speech, see "Address of His Holiness benedict XVI to the Bishops of the Episcopal Conference of Canada-Ontario on their 'Ad Limina' Visit," http://www.vatican.va/holy_father/benedict_xvi/speeches/2006/september/docume nts/hf_ben-xvi_spe_20060908_canada-ontario_en.html.

[2] "Pope Scolds Canada."

[3] Another case in point would be then Federal Minister Pierre Pettigrew's criticism of the Catholic Church's position on the redefinition of marriage more than one year before the Pope's statement. Pettigrew claimed that the Church had no right to engage in such a political debate, declaring that "the separation of Church and state is one of the most beautiful inventions of modern times." See "Church Told to Butt Out: Same Sex Debate No Place for Religion," *National Post* (January 28, 2005), A1. Oddly, some proponents of this separation have argued the state has an obligation to establish guidelines for the enforcement of moral relativism, compliance to which would coerce churches to alter their religious doctrine. This would supposedly strengthen the separation of church and state. See *CBC's Radio Commentary,* July 18, 2005, http://www.cbc.ca/insite/COMMENTARY/2005/7/-18.html.

[4] John Webster Grant, "Religion and the Quest for a National Identity: The Background in Canadian History," in Peter Slater, ed., *Religion and Culture in Canada* (Waterloo, Canadian Society for the Study of Religion: Wilfred Laurier Press, 1977), 7-22. Quote on pp 19-20.

[5] Grant, pp. 19-20.

[6] See, for example, Boris DeWiel, *Democracy: A History of Ideas* (Vancouver: University of British Columbia Press, 2000).

[7] See William Galston, "Religion and the Limits of Liberal Democracy," in Douglas Farrow, ed., *Recognizing Religion in a Secular Society: Essays in Pluralism, Religion, and Public Policy* (Montreal: McGill-Queen's University Press, 2004), 41-50.

[8] Statistics Canada, "2001 Census: Analysis series, Religions in Canada" (May 13, 2003) Catalogue No. 96F0030XIE2001015.

[9] Warren Clark and Grant Schellenberg, "Who's Religious?" Statistics Canada: *Canadian Social Trends* (Summer, 2006) Catalogue No. 11-008. The data are from the General Social Survey from 2004. More tellingly, religiosity remains higher among immigrant populations than among Canadian born. See also Colin Lindsay, "Canadians attend weekly religious services less than 20 years ago," *Matter of Fact* (Statistics Canada, June 2008).

[10] Statistics Canada: Religions in Canada.

[11] Ibid.

[12] Ibid.

[13] Ibid.

---

[14] For more on the debate concerning secularization, see Pippa Norris and Ronald Inglehart, *Sacred and Secular: Religion and Politics Worldwide* (Cambridge University Press, 2004).

[15]Reginald W. Bibby, "Nevers, Nones, and Nots: Latent Life in Unexpected Places," unpublished paper, www.reginaldbibby.com.

[16] Roger O'Toole, "Religion in Canada: Its Development and Contemporary Situation," *Social Compass* 43:1 (1996), 119-134.

[17] Roger Finke and Rodney Stark, *The Churching of America, 1776-2005: Winners and Losers in Our Religious Economy* (Rutgers University Press, 2005).

[18] Statistics Canada: Religions in Canada.

[19] Ibid.

[20] See Warren Clark and Grant Schellenberg, "Who's Religious?"and Reginald Bibby, "Religion a la Carte in Quebec: A Problem of Demand, Supply, or Both?" published in French, "La Religion à la carte au Québec: Un problème d'offre, de demande, ou des deux?" in *Globe* 10:2 (2007-2008), 151-179. English version available at http://www.reginaldbibby.com/papers.html.

[21] This latter designation is only since 1996. Prior to that date, Quebec funded Catholic and Protestant school boards, after 1996, French and English language schools.

[22] United Nations, Human Rights Committee, 67th Session: Communication No. 694/1996, p.13.

[23] Larry Johnston and Susan Swift, "Public Funding of Private and Denominational Schools in Canada," Toronto: Ontario Legislative Library, 2000, p.3 http://www.ontla.on.ca/library/repository/mon/1000/10286133.htm.

[24] See Andrew Cardozo, "Ontario Election proved funding of religious schools too close to segregation…" *The Hill Times*, October 15, 2007.

[25] See Bruce L. Guenther, "Populism, Politics and Christianity in Western Canada," *Historical Papers: Canadian Society of Church History* (2000), 93-112.

[26] Roger O'Toole refers to criticism that the United Church of Canada is less a church than "the New Democratic Party at prayer." See O'Toole, "Religion in Canada."

[27] Robert Bellah, "Civil Religion in America," *Journal of the American Academy of Arts and Sciences* 96:1 (Winter, 1967) 1-21; Wilfred M. McClay, "Soul of a Nation," *The Public Interest* no. 155 (Spring, 2004) 4-19.

[28]See Charles Taylor, et al, *Multiculturalism: Examining the Politics of Recognition* (Princeton: Princeton University Press, 1994).

CHAPTER ONE

A COMPLICATED STORY: EXPLORING THE CONTOURS OF SECULARIZATION AND PERSISTING RELIGIOSITY IN CANADA

MEBS KANJI AND RON KUIPERS

I. Secularization: More than a "Subtraction Story"?

The "secularization thesis" has become a dominant theme in the contemporary academic study of religion. According to this thesis, the heady period of intellectual foment and ferment called the Enlightenment inaugurated historical processes of rationalization that would ultimately spell the end of religion as a publicly significant cultural phenomenon. José Casanova describes the way in which those holding this thesis would come to regard the prospects of religion after Enlightenment:

> Reduced to a pre-scientific and prelogical primitive form of thought and knowledge, religion necessarily had to disappear with the ever-progressive advancement of knowledge, education, and scientific worldviews. The "darkness" of religious ignorance and superstition would fade away when exposed to the "lights" of reason."[1]

In his monumental work, *A Secular Age*, Charles Taylor polemicizes against this account of religion's modern fate. He describes this narrative as a dubious "subtraction story," a story that seeks to explain modern secularization as nothing other than the result of a continuous process through which "human beings have lost, or sloughed off, or liberated themselves from certain earlier, confining horizons, or illusions, or limitations to knowledge." Such a subtraction story, he says, mistakenly encourages us to understand modern secularization as little more than a trimming process through which human beings discover "underlying features of human nature which were there all along, but had been

impeded by what is now set aside."[2] On this account, historical processes
of secularization follow a linear trajectory, along which a segment of
humanity can be seen to shed slowly the irrational accretions of myth,
religion and the sacred, in order to uncover a rational core of free thought
and autonomous science, which may finally come out from under the
stifling constraints of heteronomous religious authority.

Taylor finds this subtraction story unconvincing for several reasons.
First of all, he thinks it does little to explain how the historically emergent
secular alternatives to Western society's former religious orientation
"could become the necessary objective pole of moral or spiritual
aspiration, of 'fullness'." In order to explain the powerful attraction of
these emerging secular options, Taylor asks us to move beyond the
common subtraction story and also consider what additional *positive* story
must have been told about them. Only such a story, Taylor suggests, can
help us understand the historical shift from "a condition in which our
highest spiritual and moral aspirations point us inescapably to God, one
might say, make no sense without God, to one in which they can be related
to a host of different sources, and frequently are referred to sources which
deny God."[3]

A second and related reason for finding the subtraction story
unconvincing is that, in refusing to credit the operation of a more positive
narrative, it fails to help us appreciate the full complexity of the modern
social landscape. It fails to help us understand the way in which a plethora
of spiritual options today, of both sacred and secular varieties, have, in this
"age of authenticity," acquired the power to vie for the hearts, minds and
imaginations of those who inhabit it. According to Taylor, "Western
modernity, including its secularity, is the fruit of new inventions, newly
constructed self-understandings and related practices, and can't be
explained in terms of perennial features of human life."[4]

The empirical research and analysis we provide in this essay confirms
several of Taylor's suspicions concerning the adequacy of the secularists'
subtraction story. Using the data provided by the World Values Surveys
(WVS), we examine various dimensions of contemporary religious life, an
examination which reveals a much more complex picture than the typical
secularist subtraction story suggests.[5] In doing so, we focus particular
attention on the position Canada occupies with respect to global levels of
secularization and persisting religiosity. Do the levels of persisting
religiosity in Canada put it in league with the United States, which is often
considered to be the sole anomaly to the secularization thesis among
advanced industrial nations? Our research suggests an intriguing answer to
that question.

Finally, in telling what we consider to be a more complicated story about the effects of secularization processes in advanced industrial nations like Canada, we simultaneously challenge the thesis recently put forward by the political scientists Pippa Norris and Ronald Inglehart. In *Sacred and Secular*, they set out to defend (albeit in a somewhat mitigated fashion) the subtraction story implicit in the secularization thesis. According to Norris and Inglehart, this thesis retains explanatory force for those fortunate societies that have been able to provide a high level of material comfort and security for their members. As we shall see below, they think that the need for the consolation that religion supposedly provides decreases the day-to-day anxiety of people about issues concerning their material comfort and security. According to Norris and Inglehart, with the exception of the United States, the secularization thesis can in retrospect be understood to have enjoyed a high level of predictive accuracy, especially in predicting the fate of religion in these prosperous societies. Because they tie secularization to material prosperity in this way, they consider persisting and even rising levels of religiosity across the rest of the globe to be primarily due to the material insecurity experienced by members of less prosperous societies.[6] As the title of our paper suggests, however, we think that, even in advanced industrial nations, the situation is much more complicated than Norris and Inglehart believe. Yet before delving into this analysis of the World Values Survey data, we must first take a closer look at the secularization thesis itself to gain a deeper understanding of the story that Norris and Inglehart affirm, which we propose to complicate.

II. Secularization and Disenchantment: A Decline in Religious "Demand"?

According to Taylor, "a common 'subtraction' story attributes everything to disenchantment."[7] In introducing the word "disenchantment," Taylor referred to the influential work of the sociologist Max Weber, who famously described the result of modern processes of secularization and rationalization as "the disenchantment of the world."[8] According to this notion, once science provides us with a "naturalistic" explanation of the world, religious beliefs having to do with "God" or "transcendence" must come to be seen as the superfluous vestiges of the "magical" or "enchanted" thinking of a bygone age.[9] While Weber was aware that there may be losses inherent in this "eclipse of the transcendent" (to use Taylor's phrase), he remained resolute in describing the modern world as disenchanted. According to Taylor, for Weber "this sense of loss is inevitable; it is the price we pay for modernity and rationality.... [W]e must courageously accept this bargain, and lucidly opt for what we have inevitably become."[10]

For Weber, our disenchanted world, bereft of the consolations of transcendence once promised by religion, allows for a particularly modern form of thought that is distinctive precisely in its freedom *from* primitive, pre-scientific thought patterns. To this extent, his version of events can be read as a "subtraction story": in freeing itself from the primitive and the magical, modern thought becomes free *for* the pursuit of scientific discovery. What we are left with, said Weber, is a world which we now consider to be fundamentally "knowable." Rationalization, the path along which the world becomes disenchanted, implies that "principally there are no mysterious incalculable forces that come into play, but rather that one can, in principle, master all things by calculation." This calculability was, for Weber, precisely what it meant for the world to be disenchanted. It meant that "one need no longer have recourse to magical means in order to master or implore the spirits, as did the savage, for whom such mysterious powers existed. Technical means and calculations perform the service."[11]

Along with historical processes of rationalization, Weber also drew attention to processes of societal differentiation, through which such secular value spheres as the political, economic, aesthetic, erotic and scientific or intellectual have been freed from the authoritative dominance of the Medieval Christian Church to pursue autonomous developmental courses. As a result of such societal differentiation, the religious sphere shrinks in terms of both its scope and its influence.[12] According to the secularization thesis, then, particularly in Weber's version, we have subtraction on two fronts: rationalization (disenchantment) and societal differentiation (the shrinking public significance of the "sacred" sphere).

Today, however, sociologists and other scholars of religion are coming to terms with the fact that the predictions of religion's demise put forward in the classic secularization thesis appear to have been premature. Religious traditions and life patterns have not gone quietly into the private sphere, and various measures of demographic trends such as the WVS show that, if anything, the global population is becoming more rather than less religious.[13] The secularization thesis has nevertheless remained resilient and influential in the face of such countervailing historical trends in the sociology of religion as well as other intellectual disciplines. Such resilience has led contemporary sociologists of religion like Casanova, David Martin and Peter Berger to suspect the operation of ideological factors in a thesis that claims to be merely descriptive of historical developments.[14]

As we noted above, Norris and Inglehart respond to these criticisms of the secularization thesis by mounting what might be described as a "rearguard" action in its defense. In *Sacred and Secular*, they suggest that "talk of burying the secularization theory is premature."[15] In spite of the fact that WVS data show that, when viewed on a global scale, historical levels of religious participation not only persist but are increasing, they maintain that a qualified version of the secularization thesis can still be maintained and defended. According to their analysis, WVS data show that "the importance of religiosity persists most strongly among vulnerable populations, especially those living in poorer nations, facing personal survival-threatening risks." This aspect of global religiosity suggests to them that "feelings of vulnerability to physical, societal and personal risks" are a key factor driving its increasing levels.[16] In advanced industrial societies like Canada, where citizens enjoy a high level of material security, Norris and Inglehart predict that historical processes of secularization will continue apace.

Norris and Inglehart, then, would not be surprised to come across a news story like the one which ran in the *National Post* on September 13, 2006, in which journalist Dave Rogers reported the imminent closure of Ottawa-Hull's First Anglican Church (in whose cemetery Ottawa's founding fathers are buried) because of a severe decline in church attendance and enrollment.[17] Norris and Inglehart would likely view such a story as consistent with their prediction that *demand* for religion and religious services continues to decline in affluent societies such as ours, irrespective of the current state of the *supply* of such services.[18] The language of supply and demand suggests Norris and Inglehart employ a market model of religious trend analysis in their mitigated defense of the secularization thesis. This model, introduced by Rodney Stark and others,[19] claims that "the most influential strands of thought shaping the debate over secularization can be broadly subdivided into two perspectives"–demand-side and supply-side theories. Supply-side theories, such as those put forward by Stark and his colleagues, hold that the human demand for religion remains constant and stable and any observed fluctuations in human religious participation or activity can be explained by fluctuations in the supply of religious services by religious institutions. Demand-side theories, on the other hand, "suggest that as societies industrialize, almost regardless of what religious leaders and organizations attempt, religious habits will gradually erode." [20] That is, as industrialization progresses, the actual demand for religion declines in the affected population. Employing the same language, Norris and Inglehart maintain that "although the original theory of secularization was flawed in certain regards, it was correct in the demand-side perspective."[21]

In the analysis that follows, we wish to examine the merits and deficiencies of Norris and Inglehart's affirmation of the demand-side perspective. Their stance is clearly controversial, as many theorists still see merit in the supply-side perspective. Does a steady decline in a certain population's participation in and association with various aspects of institutional religious life mean that such people have become less religious or spiritual? We think that a simple yes or no answer to this question belies the complexity of the reality before us. Because the notion of religiosity is so complex, several different dimensions of *human* religious participation need to be considered. Consequently, we need to examine a variety of different aspects of religiosity (including support for mixing religion and politics) in order to confirm or reject any broad-gauged generalizations about secularization. The following data analysis tries to access and portray at least some of that complexity.

III. What Do the World Values Surveys Say?

1. Six Dimensions and Indicators of Religiosity

The World Values Surveys (WVS) provide several measures that deal in some way with the issue of religion. However, different indicators pertain to different aspects of religiosity. We begin our examination, therefore, by organizing the WVS data into six dimensions of religiosity (see Table 1).

Table 2-1: Dimensions and Indicators of Religiosity

I. Subjective religiosity
1. (v9) Indicate how important it is in your life: religion?
2. (v196) How important is God in your life?
3. (v186) Independently of whether you go to church or not, would you say you are: a religious person, not a religious person, a convinced atheist, or don't know?
II. Religious Involvement
1. (v185) Apart from weddings, funeral and christenings, about how often do you attend religious services these days?
2. (v40) Do you belong to religious or church organizations?
3. (v184) Do you belong to a religious denomination, if yes which one?

III. Prayer

1. (v198) Do you take some moments of prayer, meditation or
contemplation or something like that?
2. (v199) How often do you pray to God outside of religious services?
3. (v197) Do you find that you get comfort and strength from religion?

IV. Beliefs

1. (v191) Do you believe in God?
2. (v192) Do you believe in life after death?
3. (v193) Do you believe people have a soul?
4. (v194) Do you believe in hell?
5. (v195) Do you believe in heaven?

V. Confidence in Religious Institutions

1. (v147) How much confidence do you have in churches?
2. (v187) Generally speaking, do you think that the churches in your
country are giving adequate answers to the moral problems and needs of
the individual life?
3. (v188) Generally speaking, do you think that the churches in your
country are giving adequate answers to problems of family life?
4. (v189) Generally speaking, do you think that the churches in your
country are giving adequate answers to people's spiritual needs?
5. (v190) Generally speaking, do you think that the churches in your
country are giving adequate answers to social problems facing our
country today?

VI. Religion and Politics

1. (v200) How much do you agree or disagree with each of the following:
Politicians who do not believe in God are unfit for public office?
2. (v201) Religious leaders should not influence how people vote in
elections?
3. (v202) It would be better for (this country) if more people with strong
religious beliefs held public office?
4. (v203) Religious leaders should not influence government?

The first dimension considers people's *subjective evaluations* of the relevance that religion and God have in their lives. The second dimension measures people's *religious involvement* in religious services, religious organizations, and religious denominations. The third examines the role that *prayer* plays in people's lives, both in terms of practice and personal gain. The fourth taps people's religious *beliefs*, including their belief in God, life after death, the concept of the soul, and the opposing concepts of heaven and hell. The fifth assesses people's *confidence in religious institutions*, including their ability to give adequate advice on matters of morality, the family, spirituality, and social problems. The sixth and final dimension centers on *the link between religion and politics.* How much influence do people feel religion ought to have in politics?

2. Average Degrees of Religiosity in Various Societies

When we compare the average degree of religiosity on each of these six dimensions across various types of societies – agrarian, industrial and advanced industrial (see Appendix A for a complete listing of the countries included in each of these categories)–we do see, as Norris and Inglehart suggest, that people in advanced industrial societies tend to be less religious than people in agrarian states.

For example, Figure 1 shows that people in advanced industrial societies are less likely to have consistent broad-based religious beliefs and to place less stock in prayer than people in agrarian states. People in advanced industrial societies also have weaker subjective evaluations of their own religiosity and are less likely to place confidence in religious institutions and their advice. And lastly, people in advanced industrial states are less likely to be involved in religion and to support the mixing of religion and politics.

Notice however that not all citizens in advanced industrial states respond in exactly the same ways. Some are clearly more religious than others. Canadians, for example, may not be as religious as Americans, yet they are clearly more religious than average citizens in other advanced industrial states. Notice also that regardless of the type of society that we examine, the evidence consistently shows that the average degree of religiosity varies across different dimensions. For instance, measures pertaining to beliefs and prayer indicate higher average degrees of religiosity than do indicators of subjective religiosity and confidence in religious institutions across all three types of societies. Similarly, measures of subjective religiosity and confidence in religious institutions suggest higher average degrees of religiosity than do measures pertaining to religious involvement and the mixing of religion and politics. Some key points to draw from these data are that degrees of secularization can vary even among advanced industrial societies and they can also vary depending on the measures of religiosity that are employed. An important implication of these findings may be that particular aspects of religion in advanced industrial societies are more or less resilient to forces of industrialization and secularization than others. Any future predictions about secularization, therefore, need to take both of these considerations into account.

Figure 2-1: Average Degree of Religiosity in Various Societies

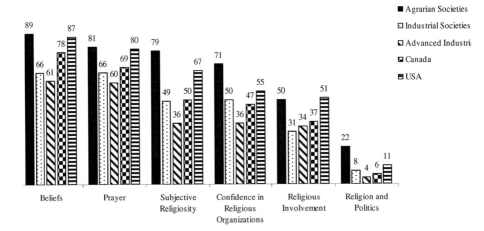

Note:

Beliefs: People's beliefs in God, life after death, the concept of soul, and the opposing concepts of heaven and hell.

Prayer: The role that prayer has in people's lives, both in terms of practice and personal gain.

Subjective Religiosity: People's subjective evaluations of the relevance that religion and God have in their lives.

Confidence in Religious Institutions: People's confidence in religious institutions' ability to give adequate advice on matters of morality, family, spirituality and social problems.

Religious involvement: People's involvement in religious services, religious organizations and religious denominations.

Religion and Politics: The influence people feel religion ought to have in politics.

Source: 2000 World Values Surveys.

For example, although people in advanced industrial states may appear generally not to be as religious as people in agrarian states, there is evidence to suggest that a strong majority still maintain certain core religious beliefs, and that a strong majority still value prayer, particularly in such countries as Canada and the United States. Secularization in advanced industrial states, however, may be having more devastating consequences for people's sense of subjective religiosity, their confidence

in religious institutions, their religious involvement and their support for
the idea of mixing religion and politics. Notice though, that according to
these aggregate results, people in advanced industrial societies are in fact
more inclined to be involved in religion (34%) than people in (generally
less wealthy) industrial societies (31%). This difference suggests the
possibility that some form of resurgence in religious involvement (either in
the traditional or some new unconventional sense) may be underway in
advanced industrial states, and this may have an affect on any future
prognostication concerning secularization processes in advanced industrial
states. At the very least, as the philosopher Jürgen Habermas reminds us,
"we must keep in mind that the dialectic of our own occidental process of
secularization has as yet not come to a close."[22] What is more, when we
unpack these dimensions into their individual components, we find even
more inconsistent results.

Table 2-2: Religiosity in Various Societies

Dimensions and Indicators of Religiosity	Types of Societies			
	Agrarian	Industrial	Advanced Industrial	Canada
I. Subjective religiosity				
1. Importance of religion (very important)	78%	36%	22 %	33%
2. Importance of God (very important)	75%	41%	22%	41%
3. Degree of religiosity (a religious person)	84%	71%	65%	77%
II. Religious Involvement				
1. Frequency of attending religious services (at least once a week)	27%	8%	5%	7%
2. Percentage belonging to religious organization	38%	11%	24%	30%
3. Percentage belonging to a religious denomination	86%	74%	72%	73%
III. Prayer				
1. Percentage indicating they take some moments for prayer	86%	64%	63%	82%
2. Percentage of prayer to God outside religious services (pray everyday)	63%	47%	39%	48%
3. Percentage indicating that they derive comfort and strength from religion (based on those who "take some moments for prayer")	95%	88%	77%	78%

IV. Beliefs				
1. Percentage indicating that they believe in God	95%	84%	78%	91%
2. Percentage indicating that they believe in life after death	82%	59%	59%	75%
3. Percentage indicating that they believe that people have a soul	93%	80%	85%	93%
4. Percentage indicating that they believe in hell	85%	50%	32%	52%
5. Percentage indicating that they believe in heaven	91%	58%	50%	77%
V. Confidence in Religious Institutions				
1. Degree of confidence in churches (a great deal)	64%	28%	15%	22%
2. Percentage indicating that churches give adequate answers to moral problems	75%	59%	41%	52%
3. Percentage indicating that churches give adequate answers to family problems	72%	53%	35%	49%
4. Percentage indicating that churches give adequate answers to peoples' spiritual needs	81%	76%	59%	73%
5. Percentage indicating that churches give adequate answers to the social problems facing country	65%	35%	30%	38%
VI. Religion and Politics				
1. Politicians who do not believe in God are unfit for public office (strongly agree)	45%	13%	5%	8%
2. Religious leaders should not influence how people vote in elections (strongly disagree)	5%	3%	3%	3%
3. It would be better if more people with strong religious beliefs held public office (strongly agree)	33%	14%	6%	8%
4. Religious leaders should not influence government decisions (strongly disagree)	6%	3%	4%	3%

Source: 2000 World Values Surveys

3. Religiosity in Various Societies, Compared Across Six Different Indicators

To begin with, consider people's *subjective evaluations* of the relevance that religion has in their lives. The evidence in Table 2 shows that people in advanced industrial societies attribute considerably less importance to both religion and God in their daily lives than do people in agrarian societies. In agrarian societies, for example, 78% of people indicate that religion is very important in their lives and 75% indicate that God is very important in their lives. Conversely, only 22% of people in advanced industrial societies indicate that religion and God carry the same importance. Does this mean, however, that people in more affluent societies no longer view themselves as being religious? There is evidence to suggest otherwise. Generally, we find that most people, regardless whether they live in vulnerable or affluent societies, consider themselves to be more religious than not. For instance, 65% of people in advanced industrial societies, 71% in industrial societies, and 84% in agrarian societies think of themselves as "a religious person." Notice too, that in all three measures, Canadians exhibit a greater degree of subjective religiosity than the average citizen of advanced industrial states. Furthermore, unlike the average citizens in advanced industrial states, Canadians emphasize the importance on God over that of religion.

Subjective assessments of religiosity are not the same as actual involvement in religious institutions and practices. When we look more closely at indicators of religious involvement, the evidence shows that people in agrarian societies attend religious services much more regularly than those in industrial and advanced industrial societies. Even in agrarian societies, only 27% of people indicate that they attend religious services at least once a week. In advanced industrial societies, however, the corresponding figure is a mere 5%. Should this be interpreted to mean that religious involvement, particularly in advanced industrial societies, is a thing of the past? The evidence is far from clear. Additional findings reported in Table 2 suggest that while people in advanced industrial societies may place very little emphasis on regularly attending religious services, the percentage of people in advanced industrial states indicating that they belong to religious or church organizations is more than double (+13%) that in industrial societies. In agrarian societies, 38% claim to belong to religious or church organizations. In industrial societies, that number drops to 11%. And in advanced industrial countries, 24% indicate that they belong to such organizations. At the very least, these non-linearities in results need to be considered when evaluating Norris and Inglehart's proposed link between secularization and material affluence.

While the cross-time evidence indicates that the proportion of citizens in advanced industrial states belonging to a religious denomination has declined relative to the frequency of attending religious services, differences in belonging to a religious denomination between advanced industrial and agrarian countries are not great.[23] In agrarian societies, the evidence from 1999/2000 suggests that 86% of people belong to a religious denomination compared to 72% in advanced industrial societies. On all three measures of religious involvement, Canadians stand out as being at least as involved, or in some cases even more involved, than average citizens in other advanced industrial states.

The evidence thus far indicates that although people in advanced industrial societies place less importance on religion and God than people in agrarian states, many still consider themselves to be religious and continue to belong to a religious denomination. What is more, even though very few people in advanced industrial societies attend religious services on a weekly basis, the proportion of people in advanced industrial societies indicating that they belong to religious organizations is more than double that in industrial societies. Is this clear evidence to suggest that secularization has occurred and continues to occur in advanced industrial societies? It is difficult to tell. In the case of Canada, the evidence supporting the secularization argument is even less conclusive than it is for other advanced industrial states.

Prayer is another aspect of religiosity that may be affected by increased human affluence and material security. Evidence shows that although the proportion of people who admit to taking some moments for prayer, meditation, contemplation and the like is lower in industrial and advanced industrial societies than it is in agrarian states, there is still a significant proportion of the public in advanced industrial states that takes the time to pray (see Table 2). 86% of citizens in agrarian societies indicate that they take the time to engage in such activities as compared to 63% in advanced industrial societies. And while less than a majority of these people indicate that they frequently engage in such activities (i.e., only 39% of people in advanced industrial states indicate that they regularly pray to God outside of religious services as compared to 63% of people in agrarian societies that report praying everyday), the proportion indicating that they derive benefits from partaking in such activity is relatively high. In agrarian societies, for example, more than nine in ten people (95%) who engage in activities such as prayer, meditation, contemplation, etc., indicate that they derive a sense of comfort and strength from religion. In advanced industrial states, nearly eight in ten people (77%) who participate in such activities indicate that they also derive such a sense of comfort and strength. This finding therefore suggests that even in advanced industrial societies, for those who still practice (albeit less frequently), prayer is still capable of serving as a coherent source of meaning. When we look at Canada specifically, the percentage of people indicating that they take some moments for prayer is virtually indistinguishable from that of average citizens in agrarian states. Moreover, Canadians are much more likely than average citizens in other advanced industrial states to pray outside of religious services. They are also at least as likely as their average counterparts in other advanced industrial states to derive comfort and strength from religion when they pray.

Turning now to the matter of religious beliefs, the evidence in Table 1 again indicates a complex picture that belies any simple prediction. The first point to note is that certain beliefs (such as the belief in God and the belief that people have a soul) tend consistently to be more widely held across different societies than other beliefs (such as the belief in hell, heaven or life after death). And here the differences between advanced industrial and agrarian states are not as great. The most recent evidence for example indicates that 78% of citizens in advanced industrial societies still believe in God, compared to 95% in agrarian societies. And 85% of people in advanced industrial societies believe that people have a soul, as compared to 93% in agrarian societies.[24] Indeed, Canadians in particular are virtually no different in either of these respects than average citizens of agrarian societies.

Significant majorities in advanced industrial countries also indicate that they believe in life after death (59%) and heaven (50%). However in this case the differences between agrarian and industrial/advanced industrial societies are much greater, although not as great as differences in the belief in hell. Only three in ten (32%) people in advanced industrial states believe in the notion of hell, as compared to 85% in agrarian countries. However, Canadians are more similar to average citizens in agrarian societies on each of these beliefs than are average citizens in other advanced industrial states.

It is conceivable that these findings may indicate more of a "supply-side" deficiency than a "demand-side" decline. At one time, beliefs such as these were crucial in sustaining the authority of the church. The promise of salvation made the church a very powerful institution in people's lives. The abuse of this power contributed to one of the great historical withdrawals of deference from religious institutional authority, the Protestant Reformation. Yet attitudes toward the ideas of salvation and damnation are changing radically within religious traditions themselves.[25] Religious institutions may yet prove themselves capable of flexibly adapting to contemporary contexts and avoid alienating the citizens of advanced industrial societies who may turn to them for spiritual guidance.

Additional evidence presented in Table 2 indicates that in advanced industrial societies, people's perceptions of religious institutions are not as strong as in agrarian societies. For example, sixty-four percent of people in agrarian societies indicate that they have a great deal of confidence in churches, compared to only 28% of people in industrial societies and 15% of people in advanced industrial societies. Even in Canada, confidence in churches, though above the average of other advanced industrial states, is still well below average confidence levels in agrarian societies.

Moreover, the evidence shows that people in advanced industrial societies tend to be more skeptical of the church's advice, not only on issues dealing with morality and the needs of the individual, family life and social problems, but also when it comes to issues of spirituality. Eight out of ten people (81%) in agrarian countries indicate that churches give adequate answers to people's spiritual needs, whereas only six in every ten people (59%) in advanced industrial states feel the same way. Note, however, that in Canada the proportion indicating that the church deals adequately with people's spiritual needs is somewhat higher than the average in advanced industrial states. When it comes to giving advice about moral problems and the needs of the individual, the differences are much more striking. Seventy-five percent of publics in agrarian societies feel that churches give adequate advice on such matters, while only 41% of people in advanced industrial societies feel the same way. In Canada, the proportion is somewhat higher but remains 20% lower than in agrarian societies. Likewise, 72% of the members of agrarian societies claim that churches give adequate answers to problems dealing with family life, but only 35% of people in advanced industrial societies agree that this is the case. In Canada, half of the respondents (49%) hold this view, which again is considerably less than agrarian states. Lastly, 65% of people in agrarian societies indicate that churches respond adequately to the social problems facing their countries, while only 30% of people in advanced industrial societies feel the same way. In Canada, only 38% of people feel that churches respond adequately to social problems, which is 30% lower than citizens in agrarian states. Declining confidence in religious institutions in advanced industrial societies, then, may also suggest an inability by religious institutions to respond to the religious needs of people in those societies, suggesting a supply-side concern and not just a demand-side decline. The challenge of maintaining religious traditions in advanced industrial societies, then, may be at least partly contingent on how well religious institutions can respond to the challenge of retaining continuity with their past while speaking relevantly to the ever-changing present.

To the extent that religion has become less relevant in advanced industrial societies, we would expect to find less of an inclination by citizens to apply religion in everyday affairs. With respect to the idea of mixing religion and politics, that expectation is confirmed. Forty-five percent of people in agrarian societies, for example, strongly agree that "politicians who do not believe in God are unfit for public office," whereas only 5% of people in advanced industrial states feel the same way. Also, 33% of people in agrarian societies strongly agree that "it would be better if more people with strong religious beliefs held public office," compared to only 6% of people in advanced industrial states. On both questions, the Canadian results are very similar to average citizens in other advanced industrial states. However, the findings show that people in advanced industrial states and agrarian societies are not that different when it comes to how much political influence they think should be held by religious leaders. There is only a 2% difference between advanced industrial and agrarian societies when it comes to whether religious leaders should have any influence on voting and government decisions. Only three percent of people in advanced industrial states strongly disagree that "religious leaders should not influence how people vote in elections," and 5% of people in agrarian societies feel that same way. Likewise, 4% of people in advanced industrial societies strongly disagree that "religious leaders should not influence government decisions," compared to 6% of people in agrarian societies. Thus, when it comes to religion and politics, there is some evidence to suggest that people in advanced industrial states are in fact not all that different from people in agrarian societies, at least not with regards to religious leaders' influence in politics.

When we step back from these various statistical measures and look at the overall results, the findings indicate that differences in religiosity between people in advanced industrial states and agrarian societies vary considerably across different dimensions of religiosity. On balance, the data concur with Norris and Inglehart's general claim that people in advanced industrial societies are not as likely to be religious as people in agrarian states. However, the evidence also presents a more complicated story of secularism in advanced industrial states. A closer look at the data indicates that there are many instances in which people in more affluent societies are still fairly religious compared to people in agrarian countries. This is especially true in the Canadian case. Moreover, to the extent that secularization may be taking place, the aggregate evidence seems to suggest that it may be both a supply-side as well as a demand-side issue. The major differences in religiosity between advanced industrial and agrarian states seems to be largely subjective and may be related more to confidence in religious institutions and traditional religious beliefs than to dimensions such as prayer, religious involvement, and the willingness to apply religion in politics. Moreover, when we limit our analysis exclusively to people who belong to a religious denomination, most of these differences become less striking (see Figure 2).

Figure 2-2: Average Differences in Religiosity between People in Advanced Industrial and Agrarian Societies

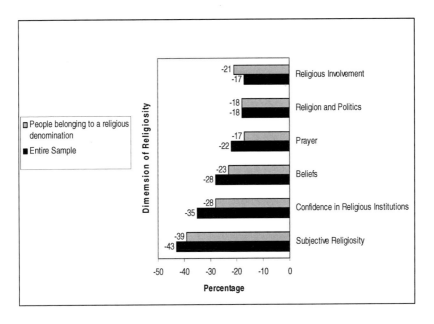

4. Average Differences in Religiosity in Advanced Industrial and Agrarian Societies by Generation and by Gender

An additional feature of Norris and Inglehart's analysis which we have not yet mentioned is that their qualified defense of the secularization thesis is also based on the notion of intergenerational change. This suggests that if there were one group among whom we should find clear and consistent evidence of a decline in religiosity, it would be among younger generations, particularly in advanced industrial states. But is this the case? The data in Figure 3 provide mixed results.

Figure 2-3: Average Differences in Religiosity between People in Advanced Industrial and Agrarian Societies by Generation

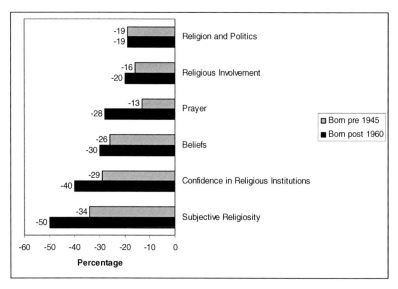

On one hand, the evidence consistently shows that people in advanced industrial societies are generally less religious than people in agrarian states and that in the great majority of cases such differences are much larger among younger generations than among older cohorts. On average, young people in advanced industrial societies express a lower degree of subjective religiosity (-50%) than young people in agrarian countries; they are also less involved in religion (-20%); they pray less (-28%); they believe less (-30%); they are less confident in religious organizations (-40%); and they are less willing to mix religion and politics (-19%). On the other hand, the magnitudes of these differences are not always consistent. Younger people in advanced industrial societies may be less religious than their counterparts in agrarian societies, but they differ more on certain aspects of religion than others. The largest discrepancies once again are on subjective religiosity and confidence in religious institutions, followed next by beliefs and prayer, and then by religious involvement and views on mixing religion and politics.

Furthermore, the evidence in Figure 4 indicates that young females in advanced industrial states typically share more similar perspectives on many religious issues with other females in agrarian societies than do their male counterparts, particularly when it comes to subjective religiosity, beliefs, prayer and religious involvement. These findings may also have implications for the continued prevalence and relevance of religion in advanced industrial states and deserve further research.

Figure 2-4: Average Differences in Religiosity between Young People in Advanced Industrial and Agrarian Societies by Gender

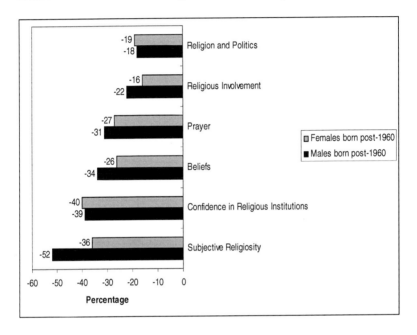

III. Summary

We believe this analysis paints a more complex and accurate picture of global religious patterns than that which Norris and Inglehart portray. While their analysis is not inaccurate, we think their affirmation of a demand-side interpretation of secularization in advanced industrial societies requires further investigation. Our analysis points to the existence of supply-side concerns as well, and our differentiated analysis of human religiosity also provides a better basis for explaining the persistence of religion in advanced industrial states such as Canada. Given the complexity of this story, we are of the view that Norris and Inglehart's prediction that further secularization will accompany increased human development is uncertain. Some aspects and dimensions of religiosity show themselves to be more resistant to secularization processes than do others. What might explain the persistence of those dimensions of religiosity which are not as affected by economic and material development as others seem to be? Might this persistence point to the existence of a basic spiritual hunger that many people share, which may or may not find expression in any particular array of traditional religious institutions? Our analysis does not confirm this possibility but it does show it exists. If we were to adopt a "supply-side" perspective while assuming that a basic need for religion remains across generations and cultures, then the future effects of secularization are unclear. Religious institutions may yet respond creatively to the present challenges they face and remain a relevant source of religious inspiration in advanced industrial societies.

Whether or not this will occur is uncertain. Whereas Norris and Inglehart predict, somewhat confidently, a steady erosion of religion in advanced industrial states (at least in those countries that continue to provide their citizens with high levels of material comfort and security), our analysis predicts neither an ongoing secularization nor its sudden reversal.

Our analysis concurs with certain conclusions Charles Taylor puts forward in *A Secular Age*. He agrees that many facets of life in advanced industrial societies are inhospitable to religious belief. Among these he includes an ongoing ideological fragmentation that is exacerbated by "expressive individualism," a decline in our "understanding of some of the great languages of transcendence," and "the individual pursuit of happiness as defined by consumer culture." In spite of this inhospitable environment, Taylor nonetheless insists, "The secular age is … deeply cross-pressured." That is, for many people in these societies, "the sense that there is something more presses in." For Taylor, this cross-pressure implies that "our age is very far from settling in to a comfortable unbelief." The frontiers of modernity are unquiet (to paraphrase the title of penultimate chapter of his book). Our analysis tends to support this view of the contemporary status of religion in advanced industrial states. That is, in these societies certain features of human religiosity appear to remain somewhat resilient to secular cross-pressures, a situation which complicates the secularist "subtraction story" in no small measure. As Taylor concludes, "Such are the strange and complex conditions of belief in our age."[26]

Works Cited

Ansell, Nicholas John. Forthcoming. *The Annihilation of Hell: Universal Salvation and the Redemption of Time in the Eschatology of Jürgen Moltmann.* Carlisle, UK: Paternoster Press.

Arendt, Hannah. *The Human Condition.* Second Edition. Chicago: University of Chicago Press, 1958.

Casanova, José. *Public Religions in the Modern World.* Chicago: University of Chicago Press, 1994.

Habermas, Jürgen. "Faith and Knowledge." In *The Frankfurt School on Religion: Key Writings by the Major Thinkers.* Edited by Eduardo Mendieta. New York: Routledge, 2005.

Inglehart, Ronald. *Human Values and Social Change: Findings from the Values Surveys.* Leiden: Brill, 2003.

Kuipers, Ronald A. and Mebs Kanji. Forthcoming. "The 'Secularization Thesis' Revisited: Using the World Values Surveys to Evaluate Levels of Secularization and Persisting Religiosity in Advanced Industrial Societies." In James K.A. Smith, ed. *Secularity and Globalization: What Comes After Modernity?* Waco, TX: Baylor University Press.

Martin, David. *On Secularization: Toward a Revised General Theory.* London: Ashgate, 2005.

Moltmann, Jürgen. "The Restoration of All Things." In *The Coming of God: Christian Eschatology.* Translated by Margaret Kohl. London: SCM Press, 1996.

Norris, Pippa and Ronald Inglehart. *Sacred and Secular: Religion and Politics Worldwide.* Cambridge: Cambridge University Press, 2004.

Rogers, Dave. 2006. "Ottawa's first Anglican church could be put up for sale." *National Post* (Sep 13, 2006): A8.

Stark, Rodney and Roger Finke. *Acts of Faith: Explaining the Human Side of Religion.* Berkeley: University of California Press, 2000.

Taylor, Charles. *A Secular Age.* Cambridge, MA: Harvard University Press, 2007.

Weber, Max. *From Max Weber: Essays in Sociology.* Ed. and Trans. H.H. Gerth and C. Wright Mills. New York: Oxford University Press, 1946.

Wittgenstein, Ludwig. *Remarks on Fraser's* Golden Bough. Edited by Rush Rhees. Nottinghamshire: Brynmill, 1971.

Notes

[1] José Casanova, 1994, *Public Religions in the Modern World* (Chicago: University of Chicago Press, 1994), 30-31.

[2] Charles Taylor, *A Secular Age* (Cambridge, MA: Harvard University Press, 2007), 22.

[3] Ibid., 26.

[4] Ibid., 22.

[5] The WVS data are drawn from coordinated face to face interviews conducted in multiple societies, collectively representing more than 80% of the world's population and all six inhabited continents (Inglehart 2003). Four rounds of the survey have been conducted thus far, covering a period from 1981-2000, thus making it possible to track changes in socio-cultural, political, and religious values across time.

[6] Pippa Norris, and Ronald Inglehart, *Sacred and Secular: Religion and Politics Worldwide* (Cambridge: Cambridge University Press, 2004).

[7] Taylor, *Secular*, 26.

[8] Taylor, *Secular*, 25.

[9] Weber borrowed this phrase from Friedrich Schiller. Max Weber, *From Max Weber: Essays in Sociology*, ed. and trans. H.H. Gerth and C. Wright Mills (New York: Oxford University Press, 1946), 155.

[10] Taylor, *Secular*, 307.

[11] Weber, *From Max Weber*, 139. Whether he shared this attitude or is merely describing it, Weber here effectively illustrates the rather presumptuous modern understanding of premodern ritual and intellectual practice as so many versions of the same *mistake*, that is, as so many forms of failed empirical science. For a criticism of this understanding, see Ludwig Wittgenstein, *Remarks on Fraser's Golden Bough*, ed. Rush Rhees (Nottinghamshire: Brynmill, 1971).

[12] See Weber, *From Max Weber*, 328. It is important to note here that both David Martin and Casanova accept the sociological analysis of societal differentiation as the "viable core" of what they otherwise take to be an ideologically-overdetermined secularization thesis. See David Martin, *On Secularization: Toward a Revised General Theory* (London: Ashgate, 2005), 17; Casanova, *Public Religions*, 20-25.

[13] As Norris and Inglehart suggest, however, a rise in the total level of global religious commitment and participation has been caused mainly by sharp increases among a certain segment of the world population, namely agrarian societies. We must be careful, then, about describing this rise as a universally human phenomenon. Admitting this need for caution, however, does not mean that the story Norris and Inglehart tell about secularization in advanced industrial societies is accurate or stands in no need of complication.

[14] Taylor, as we have already noted, explains this resilience as a feature of the 'positive' or 'spiritual' force these historically emerging secular options possess, i.e., their power to attract adherents with a positive vision of a substantive moral

order, a feature which the 'subtraction' story ignores or neglects. See, for example, Martin, *On Secularization*, 19.

[15] Norris and Inglehart, *Sacred and Secular,* 4.

[16] Norris and Inglehart, *Sacred and Secular,* 4 and 14.

[17] Dave Rogers, "Ottawa's first Anglican church could be put up for sale," *National Post* 13 Sep 2006, A8.

[18] Although, as the *National Post* story makes clear, the church's demise is also partly attributable to non-religious political factors, such as the migration of Anglophone Quebecers from the church's parish district following the election of the nationalist *Parti Québecois*. Still, one could still consider those in charge of this church to be incapable of replacing the religious 'demand' that existed prior to such migration. Norris and Inglehart, *Sacred and Secular.*

[19] Rodney Stark and Roger Finke, *Acts of Faith: Explaining the Human Side of Religion* (Berkeley: University of California Press, 2000), 36.

[20] Norris and Inglehart, *Sacred and Secular,* 7.

[21] Ibid.

[22] Jürgen Habermas, "Faith and Knowledge," in *The Frankfurt School on Religion: Key Writings by the Major Thinkers*, ed. Eduardo Mendieta (New York: Routledge, 2005), 328.

[23] See, for example, Ronald A.Kuipers and Mebs Kanji, forthcoming, "The 'Secularization Thesis' Revisited: Using the World Values Surveys to Evaluate Levels of Secularization and Persisting Religiosity in Advanced Industrial Societies," in James K.A. Smith, ed., *Secularity and Globalization: What Comes After Modernity?* (Waco, TX: Baylor University Press).

[24] It is also interesting to note in this respect advanced industrial states exhibit a higher proportion of belief in the soul than do their industrial counterparts.

[25] See Nicholas John Ansell, *The Annihilation of Hell: Universal Salvation and the Redemption of Time in the Eschatology of Jürgen Moltmann* (Carlisle, UK: Paternoster Press, 2006); Jürgen Moltmann, "The Restoration of All Things," in *The Coming of God: Christian Eschatology*, trans. Margaret Kohl (London: SCM Press, 1996).

[26] Taylor, *Secular*, 727.

CHAPTER TWO

THE CHARTER AND CIVIL RELIGION

JOHN VON HEYKING

"Human rights has emerged as the new secular religion of our time."[1] So said Canada's former Justice Minister, Irwin Cotler on numerous occasions. His view seems to be shared by a significant part of Canada's population, especially legal, journalist and academic elites. Canada's Charter of Rights and Freedoms, along with the Supreme Court, are the focal points for an evocation of civil religion. This claim contradicts the expectations of many, since Canada is an allegedly secular society. Commentators frequently locate the level of its secularity somewhere between that of the religious United States and the nonreligious European continent.[2] However, the manner in which important constituencies speak of the Charter, and the progressivist assumptions upon which their speech is based, reveal an attempt, intentional as well as inadvertent, to create a civil religion based upon the language of rights found in the Charter. This civil religion postulates that Canada participates in the unfolding of a progressive history toward a more democratic and egalitarian future in which individuals are thought to be unencumbered by history, nature, religion, tradition or community.[3] The "divinity" in which this civil religion cultivates worship is not the God of Abraham or any other ancient god, but "humanity" which has been the object of worship in the Enlightenment, and whose ideological exponents have included John Stuart Mill, Anne-Robert-Jacques Turgot, Auguste Comte, Karl Marx, and others.

The Endurance of Civil Religion

Civil religion is an enduring political, historical and philosophical problem. Despite, or because of, alleged secularization, civil religion persists, athough in forms we do not often recognize. Civil religion is frequently regarded as a product of premodern and preindustrial times before the rationalization of society. Premodern societies frequently made use of sacred symbols to invoke meaning and purpose for their societies, as well as to legitimate claims of rulers. For instance, the preamble of the Code of Hammurabi, the legal foundation of the Mesopotamian Empire, states that the sun-god Marduk (son of Enlil) is appointed ruler over all peoples, while his earthly analogue, Hammurabi, dispenses the essentials of just order. In ancient Greece, the polis was as much a religious cult as it was a political entity. Similarly, medieval European societies, guided by the central symbol of *sacrum imperium*, attempted to legitimate themselves under the auspices of the Christian symbol, *corpus mysticum* – the body of Christ. The Enlightenment consisted in large part of a struggle to detach political order from religious underpinnings, though frequently this meant replacing Christianity as the legitimating religion with secularism or historical progress as the legitimating religion.[4] Contemporary debates in Canada concerning the place of religion in public life can be seen as instances of this civilizational struggle for legitimacy that was fought among Western nations for more than three centuries.[5]

Civil religion has been a persistent concern for political philosophers, even for those of the Enlightenment. If one surveys the findings of philosophers including Plato, Machiavelli, Bacon, Hobbes, Rousseau and even Kant, perhaps the quintessential Enlightenment philosopher, one finds recognition that human beings need to connect their political societies to a divine source that legitimates their existence within a canopy of meaning broader than mere self-interest. They recognize the importance of civil religion even when some of them personally do not hold religious faith. Secularization, rationalization or industrialization of modern societies seems to promise a political society grounded on reason alone, but even Kant, the preeminent Enlightenment philosopher, thought civil religion was necessary because reason ultimately cannot ground itself. In more familiar terms, modern society seems to induce human beings to relate to one another in terms of instrumentality and self-interest, which prompts a countermovement to preserve particular traditions and ways of life. Modern society has difficulty fully satisfying human beings' longings for meaningful communal life, which also helps explain the persistence of civil religion.

More recently, the very notion of secularization has come under scrutiny. Scholars including Peter Berger have called attention to a resurgence of religious practice across the globe. Some have countered by arguing that what appears as a retreat of secularization is in fact due to greater fertility rates among people who do not hold those secular principles. Defenders of the secularization thesis argue that people feel they do not need religion when they have the basic necessities taken care of by a welfare state. Their argument is unconvincing because they fail to prove the direction of causation: people may prefer the welfare state because they are nonreligious, not the other way around. This, at least, was Tocqueville's fear when he warned about the democratic propensity to seek shelter in a paternalistic state.[6]

Secularization is a problematic category, but one central to numerous controversies in Canadian public life including the moral claims of the Charter as considered here. Iain Benson has shown that despite its scientific and nonreligious rhetoric, usage of the term "secular" is predicated on its own faith claims.[7] At a basic level, human beings must operate with "natural faith" assumptions because they cannot function if they must prove with absolute certainty the nature of everything they do. For instance, we assume the "floor is there in front of my foot" when we step, even though we do not seek to prove it has sufficient weight-bearing strength or that a mouse did not eat through its supports last night. In a broader sense, human action presupposes a natural faith in a stable cosmos in which human beings can plan and make decisions. This faith extends to politics because all societies presuppose what might be termed a cosmic-representative framework for their particular existence and for viewing their particular actions as significant and honorable to themselves and the world. Seen in this light, the difference between preambles to the Code of Hammurabi and the Charter of Rights and Freedoms is slight because both make similar assumptions about their cosmic-representative status, even though they differ in symbols and outlook. Benson observes that political evocations of secularism presuppose a belief in the historical unfolding of the amelioration of the human condition, that is, the ideals of the Enlightenment. Political philosopher Eric Voegelin argued in numerous places that the Enlightenment belief in an ever-perfecting future is an ersatz faith based on unfounded claims about how specific intellectual and civilizational entities are representative of future humanity. The collapse of European colonial powers, whether French, English or Soviet, tends now to make us skeptical of grandiose claims concerning the meaning or even end of history, but the faith in an increasingly progressive, egalitarian and free future is common among democratic societies. It forms the basis of contemporary evocations of dignity, as argued below.

The most recent attempt to evoke civil religion is found in the myth that the Charter of Rights and Freedoms represents the progressive historical unfolding of human potentiality, freedom and equality. This myth is meant to unify a society fractured along regional and cultural lines; it attempts to rectify a legitimation crisis. Instead of drawing its sacred symbols from historical Christianity, it draws its symbols from the "democratic faith" of pluralism, tolerance, cosmopolitanism, autonomy and equality. It is the historical myth political scientist Alan Cairns has in mind when he contrasts the future- and rights-oriented Charter with the more Spartan, organic and quasi-Burkean Constitution Act of 1867, which was oriented toward history and to origins.[8] Political scientist Peter Russell notes the same legitimating myths by contrasting the "evolutionary, piecemeal" Burkean constitution of 1867 with the "great Lockean project of democratically contracting together to adopt a Constitution" of 1982.[9] This change from a dark past to an enlightened secular future can be seen in the statements of Trudeau and others who viewed the Charter as a secular document intended to supersede the age of religion as encapsulated in the Constitution Act of 1867.[10]

Indeed, there might be something about democracy itself that requires a leap of faith in human capacity for self-rule. Since many progressives believe that democratic rule demands a degree of selflessness, tolerance and enlightenment that most people currently lack, they regard democracy as a project for the future. This explains the desired supremacy of the Court over Parliament, which they see as too fraught with common prejudice to serve as an adequate guarantor of human rights. Patrick Deneen summarizes the "democratic faith":

> If faith is a belief in that which is unseen, then it may be that democracy is as justifiably an object of faith as a distant and silent God. This is particularly the case for those who perceive a radical gulf between that system of government that we now call democracy–rife with apathy, cynicism, corruption, inattention, and dominated by massive yet nearly unperceiveable powers that belie claims of popular control–and the vision of democracy as apotheosis of human freedom, self-creation, and even paradisiacal universal political and social equality that coexists seamlessly with individual self-realization and uniqueness. In absence of such a faith, ambitions might wither amid cruel facts and hopes dissipate in the face of relentless reality.[11]

"Individual self-realization and uniqueness," equality, freedom, self-expression, autonomy and other symbols are hallmarks of the progressive myth. Drawing upon Isaiah Berlin for the Canadian context, Janet Ajzenstat refers to the sentiments behind these ideals as Romantic: "the essence of the romantic movement, so far as I can see [is] will and man as an activity, as something which cannot be described because it is perpetually creating; you must not even say that it is creating itself, for there is no self, there is only movement. That is the heart of romanticism."[12] Insofar as this movement is directed toward some form of idealized future, it is a utopian faith. Ironically, the faith in the future in which selves are unencumbered by religion, tradition, or anything it has not chosen, is meant to bind a Canadian society divided among regional, ideological, culture, ethnic, and other lines. It is ironic to postulate a sense of self that is inherently solipsistic as the balm that would bind Canadian society together. As noted above, modern liberal democratic society is based upon an amalgam of principles that counteract one another, and so the strategy of adopting the unencumbered self as a neutral ground upon which Canadians will purportedly meet and agree will necessarily be found wanting, and will inspire some counter-movements, examined below in some domains of Canadian constitutionalism.[13]

Having seen the reasons for the endurance for civil religion despite (and because of) modernity, and why secularization is a problematic category, we are in a better position to assess Cotler's claim about Canada's civil religion.

Civil Religion in Canada's Past

Civil religion was frequently evoked in the nineteenth- and early-twentieth-centuries, though regional and religious differences made it impossible for a pan-Canadian evocation to take hold.[14] As the "great code," to use Northrop Frye's term, of British as well as French North America, it is unsurprising that the Bible formed the canopy of political symbols Canadians used to portray their way of life. For instance, the French Canadians frequently saw themselves as the New Israelites and Loyalists frequently compared their flight from the American revolutionaries to the Israelites' exodus from Egypt.[15] For the latter, the colonial project over Canada West was justified as a means of preparing it for "Commercial enterprise, mental culture, and moral influence" which was done by bringing the "The Fairyland of the Rockies! [and] The Wonderland of the West!" into submission to the sweet dictates of the Bible.[16] Sectarian difference between Protestant Upper Canada (and then Ontario) and Roman Catholic Lower Canada (and now Québec) prevented the emergence of pan-Canadian civil religion. Sectarian differences frequently meant Christianity was at odds with itself, which favored moves, in 1867 and in the second part of the twentieth-century, to establish political life on liberal principles of consent rather than on the basis of scriptural and ecclesiastical authority.[17] The first part of the twentieth-century saw various attempts to evoke a pan-Canadian civil religion, including the Social Gospel movement and Prime Minister Mackenzie King's attempt to wed Christian theology with political economy as a way of overcoming regionalism and of greeting modernity.[18] In the second half of the twentieth-century, the national unity crisis made it risky to evoke pan-Canadian visions, while decreased religiosity in the wake of secularization and Québec's Quiet Revolution made any attempt to ground unity in religious, especially Christian, symbols an especially dubious enterprise. Even so, Québec nationalists frequently draw upon quasi-Hegelian terminology to evoke what they see as the historical inevitably toward independence.[19]

Even so, the national identity crisis, combined with the question of secularization, is the source of more recent evocations of civil religion. While serving as the basis of human rights, the Charter is also a nation-building document meant to transcend the "particularities" of region and language. This is one of the meanings of Trudeau's symbolic "reason over passion," where reason represents cosmopolitan Canada united by law and passions represent the parochial provinces, especially Quebec with its ethnic nationalism. One of the purposes of civil religion is to legitimate a founding act. For this reason, Machiavelli claims Numa Pompilius was more important than Romulus because the former founded the civil religion that legitimated Rome's founding and allowed it to endure.[20] In a similar manner, the Charter has been seen as providing a moral language to form the souls of Canadians. Alan Cairns writes, "A citizenry seized of the constitutional recognition accorded by the Charter would be drawn out of provincialism into a pan-Canadian sense of self…. [T]he Charter was a nationalizing, Canadianizing constitutional instrument intended to shape the psyches and identities of Canadians."[21] Whether a "pan-Canadian sense of self" is something that can be created or discovered, or whether it is a chimera, remains to be seen. Even so, civil religion is the way societies historically have attempted to consolidate themselves. Liberalism usually does not speak of (and often resists) viewing politics as "soulcraft" because such language seems paternalistic and undermines liberal principles of moral autonomy and consent. However, evidence drawn from liberal philosophers, as well as practices of liberal politicians and jurists, suggests it is common to liberal democracies. The question is not *whether* political institutions, including laws, educate us morally, but *how*.[22]

Democratic Faith and the Charter

The democratic myth of a progressively unfolding historical process toward greater freedom and equality most frequently finds its home among those who regard the Supreme Court as the primary guardian of human rights. Former Prime Minister Paul Martin appealed to this constituency when, in the 2006 federal election campaign, he promised to withdraw the federal government's ability to use section 33 of the Charter of Rights and Freedoms to override Supreme Court decisions, a move that would transform the constitutional order from one of supposed balance between Supreme Court and Parliament to one with Court sovereignty. Both critics and defenders of the Supreme Court have noted how it has taken over the role, from churches among others, as the "conscience of the nation," which corresponds to the function of the Charter as a force for secularization in Canadian society.[23] Yet, while Canada can no longer be characterized as a regime of, in John Moir's words, "legally disestablished religiosity," neither can it be understood as a fully "secularized" society, nor even a unitary one.[24]

The Charter myth is meant to overcome a twofold ambiguity that Canada's constitutional order is neither (1) fully secularized (nor fully un-secularized) nor (2) fully pan-Canadian (nor so decentralized to justify dissolving the federation). Pierre Trudeau thought the Charter (with the Supreme Court) could heal both sources of the legitimacy crisis (which he also provoked) and legitimate his founding. The peculiar piety various members of society, including political, legal and academic elites, display toward the Charter and the Supreme Court expresses the attempt to resolve this crisis of legitimacy. Cotler's evocation of human rights as the new secular religion, cited above, is the clearest expression but there are others. Editorialist Jeffrey Simpson stated with some irony, "The Charter of Rights and Freedoms is the closest thing Canadians have to a canon these days with the Supreme Court justices as legal cardinals."[25] One finds more serious references to the "nation's new secular religion" in legal literature. [26] Pollster Allan pinpoints the source of the religiosity of secular liberals when he criticizes them for avoiding moral and political philosophy to discuss major cultural issues. They instead hide behind procedure and sovereign commands by the Supreme Court, in a manner consistent with what Thomas Hobbes refers to the sovereign as a "mortal god."[27] For Gregg, their "secular fundamentalism" of submitting to the court's commands is no less "fundamentalist" than those who resort to divine commands found in Scripture.[28] Among Charter-skeptics and critics of the Court, Robert Ivan Martin refers to the Supreme Court as a theocracy of relativism "in the grip of a secular state religion," with the Supreme Court as its rulers.[29]

Many comparisons of the Supreme Court as a "theocracy" or as "high priests" are polemical, though have a grain of truth insofar as the Charter, the Court, and its decisions are considered sacred and beyond contestation. Even ironic evocations, like that of Simpson, reflect this piety for reasons explained below. Part of this reverence is par for the course in a constitutional democracy in which the Supreme Court has come to be regarded as the final arbiter of rights and freedoms that must be protected from majority power. However, the Charter myth moves discourse beyond merely protecting rights. Chief Justice Beverley McLachlin expresses this added piety when she describes the Charter as the authoritative statement of the "hypergoods" to which Canadian society subscribes, and views the Supreme Court as the primary arbiter between the "total claim" the law makes upon citizens and the "total claim" religion makes on its believers. Following philosopher Charles Taylor, McLachlin regards "hypergoods" as the highest goods to which a society holds. They form the "horizon" of our moral consciousness and they need articulation as a "necessary condition of adhesion."[30] In other words, the Court has the task of making effective the effective truth of human rights, our hypergoods, which, so the argument goes, are higher than others including, perhaps, friendship.

Whether either law or religion makes a total claim upon individuals can be seriously questioned. For instance, Jean Bethke Elshtain, in direct response to Chief Justice McLachlin's argument, observes that because the Supreme Court is a political organ adjudicating both "total claims," the "total claim" made by law ends up a little more "total" than that made by religion. In other words, only law makes a "total claim." But Elshtain argues that neither law nor religion make a "total claim." Referring to the Gospels of Luke and Mark in which Jesus says, "Render unto Caesar what is Caesar's; unto God what is God's," she observes that both law and religion make partial, not total, claims upon the self, and that practical, not legal, judgment is the appropriate manner to negotiate the two claims.[31] For this reason, Elshtain grants greater scope for practical wisdom, negotiation, and compromise exercised through legislatures and civil society to protect rights. The difference between the views of McLachlin and Elshtain reflect widely divergent starting points of political analysis. McLachlin takes it as given that politics and religion make total and ultimately irreconcilable claims upon one another. In this sense her starting point resembles that of Jean-Jacques Rousseau, who advocated a civil religion over and against Christianity because the latter confused people by making them submit both to pope and to sovereign.[32] Elshtain partially follows John Locke, who thought that people are capable of making partial submissions to religion (though not the pope, as long as he commanded divisions) and to sovereign. Elshtain's starting-points enable her to conclude that people in general draw from their partial commitments to look for both legislative ways and nongovernmental ways to protect rights by cultivating citizens' habits of civility and tolerance. McLachlin's starting-points led her to conclude that government, and the Court in particular, is the best if not the exclusive guarantor of rights. If Ajzenstat is correct in her observation that in the past thirty years Canadian liberalism has been transmogrified from its original Lockean form to a Romantic version, then we can expect McLachlin's Rousseauian vision of the place of religion in political society to gain greater prominence.

The Living Tree

The language that various constituencies use to describe the Charter and the Court is weighted with pious imagery that betrays an expectation that they are agents of historical progress toward freedom and equality. This language would be meaningless if it were not accompanied by specific mechanisms and doctrines to guide legal decisions. Two are identified in this section and the next: 1) the Court's "living tree" metaphor and 2) the judges' self-understanding about the nature of judicial decision-making. We begin with the living tree.

A measure of the difference between the nature of the Canadian regime from the American regime, and their corresponding myths and civil religions, can be seen in a recent debate over judicial activism between Canadian Supreme Court judge Ian Binnie and American Supreme Court judge Antonin Scalia, at a conference marking the Charter's 25th Anniversary. Scalia argued that judicial activism can be avoided by maintaining a jurisprudence of original intent, by interpreting the Constitution in light of the intentions of the Founders. Binnie rejected Scalia's originalism in favor of interpreting the constitution in light of contemporary moral standards, the so-called living tree: "I say that if you erect a silo over our court system based on a theory of originalism, it is a very good reason to throw it out."[33] Aristotle wrote of original intent that when in a particular case following the letter of the law would cause an injustice, a judge should decide the case as "the lawmaker himself would say if he were there, and which, if he had known, he would have put in the law."[34] Unfortunately, both Binnie and Scalia failed to see that they were not debating over legal philosophy so much as asserting specific myths about their own regimes. Original intent only makes sense in a regime that has been founded by a lawmaker, and for whom that founding extends moral authority into its present. This is more the case of the United States, whose founding was made explicit by a revolutionary war and by Founders who wrote an extensive prooemium to its laws, namely, the *Federalist Papers*. That Canada was founded is open to question. Peter Russell, the dean of constitutional studies in Canada, reports in the Preface to the first edition to his book, *Constitutional Odyssey*, which is pointedly subtitled with the question, "Can Canadians Become a Sovereign People?," that his broodings were prompted by a remark that American political theorist Walter Berns, and colleague at the University of Toronto, posed to him: "Peter, you Canadians have not yet constituted yourselves as a people." Russell concluded that Berns was right, which caused him to worry that Canada's project of Lockean-style constitutional contracting (which presupposes a founding) was based on a mistake. In the most recent third edition of the book, he is more optimistic that Canadians can be a sovereign people but he is not yet fully convinced.[35] Seen in this light, if the American regime was founded, the Canadian regime is in search of a founding and it has fallen upon its Supreme Court judges to divine the contemporary standards, the "hypergoods," by which to interpret the 1982 document. It is worthwhile pausing to note that if Binnie is correct, then the 1982 document is already out of date except to the extent he can pour contemporary understandings into it.

Because Canada is in search of a founding, a Numa Pompilius as well as a Romulus, Binnie and his colleagues have adopted the "living tree" metaphor of constitutional interpretation. One measure of the extent to which the Supreme Court has taken hold of the progressivist myth is to note the difference between its explanation of the "living tree" metaphor and its original appearance. Lord Stankey originally described the constitution as a "living tree" in the famous Persons case that extended voting rights to Canadian women.[36] In it he defended a purposive reading of the law that would transcend the intention of those who framed it. They could not have anticipated all the possible applications of the law. Stankey wrote:

> The British North America Act planted in Canada a living tree capable of growth and expansion *within its natural limits*. The object of the Act was to grant a Constitution to Canada. Like all written constitutions it has been subject to development through usage and convention. Their Lordships do not conceive it to be the duty of this Board—it is certainly not their desire –to cut down the provisions of the Act by a narrow and technical construction, but rather to give it a large and liberal interpretation so that the Dominion to a great extent, *but within certain fixed limits*, may be mistress in her own house, as the provinces to a great extent, *but within certain fixed limits*, are mistresses in theirs [emphases added].

Three times in his evocation of the "living tree" metaphor, Stankey mentions the "natural" or "fixed" "limits" of the law. This is appropriate for the metaphor because trees are objects that grow but have a nature that gives it form and limit.

Stankey's emphasis on limits contrasts with more recent Supreme Court evocations of the "living tree": "The 'frozen concepts' reasoning runs contrary to one of the most fundamental principles of Canadian constitutional interpretation: that our Constitution is a living tree which, by way of *progressive* interpretation, accommodates and addresses the realities of modern life."[37] When asked by interveners in the Same-Sex Reference case to consider Stankey's reference to "natural limits," the Court cited differences in opinion over the nature of those limits as evidence that no such natural limits exist, as if difference of opinion establishes the impossibility of truth.[38] Besides, the Court asserted it was obliged only to rule on the legislative act before it, which spoke only of same-sex marriage.

The living tree metaphor distills the "progressivist" or historicist jurisprudence of the Court and signals that it reads the Charter as a mechanism to bring about freedom and equality. Its basis is not so much philosophy as a faith that history is unfolding in this manner. As shown in the next section, they might respond that legal interpretation requires reference to unwritten principles that have some relationship to natural law or some moral aspiration that the Charter might embody to restrain Canadians so as to remind them of the necessity of respecting each others' rights. While the Charter, along with judicial review, serves this function, it takes a particular mindset and ideology to assume the principles of natural law or the law's moral aspiration are to be found in "progress." "Progress" implies that time is moving toward an end-point, and end of history. As noted, progress and end of history are the hall-marks of the philosophic Enlightenment, as seen in thinkers including Voltaire, Mill, Comte, Hegel and Marx. Common to these end-of-history ideologies is the assumption that history must be guided by an intellectual vanguard who has divined the end of history in such a manner that makes it inaccessible to the rest of society. While the ideologue frequently acts in the name of democracy, in extreme versions democracy becomes irrelevant, a condition referred to as "Talmon's Fork": "either a democratic vote elects the enlightened power, or it does not. If so, it is unnecessary. If not, it is pernicious."[39] Many have noticed its "religious" and "prophetic" dimension precisely because the end of history is taken as a revelation, given exclusively to the elite, a "democratic faith" that gives hope when the theological virtue of hope has been abandoned in favor of political utopianism.[40]

Even so, when jurists appeal to the living tree metaphor, they engage not in legal interpretation but in a kind of reasoning closer to moral philosophizing. Legal reasoning takes the form of moral deliberation because jurists are liberated from the constraints of text and original intent in favor of "fundamental values."[41] As Roderick MacDonald observes of trends in judicial reasoning and Canadian legal education:

> The broadening of justificatory materials may evidence a democratization of legal reasoning, but it also invites judgments in which reasons for decision sometimes seem more a recitation of *ex post facto* rationales than an engagement with the disciplining *ex ante* constraints of a coherent normative regime. That there is a concurrent professorial tendency to pass directly to questions of high political theory without careful consideration of the specific issue to be decided and the intermediate level questions of political, economic and social policy is hardly surprising. For many law teachers today, the judicial decision serves simply as a pretext for armchair philosophizing.[42]

But these fundamental values are not those of society so much as those to which society aspires. As such, the line between legal reasoning and moral reasoning, and indeed, prophecy, gets blurred. Moreover, if the Court is in the business of legislation, then expertise in judicial, as opposed to moral, reasoning becomes less crucial for eligibility to serve. The courts' evocation of special wisdom undermines its own claims, just as demonstrated in the next section, its evocation of unwritten principles of dignity undermines dignity.

Unwritten Principles

In December 2005, Chief Justice Beverly McLachlin delivered a speech in New Zealand that outlined her vision of how judges have the authority to appeal to unwritten principles in judging laws.[43] These principles include freedom, equality, dignity, federalism, democracy, constitutionalism and respect for minorities. Judges can derive these principles from three principal sources: 1) customary law or "usages" of political actors who "acknowledge and respect the legitimate constraints on their spheres of decision-making"; 2) "inference from the constitutional principles and values that have been set down in writing"; and 3) international law. The second source is of principal concern in this analysis of the Charter as civil religion.

Chief Justice McLachlin claims "the contemporary concept of unwritten constitutional principles can be seen as a modern reincarnation of the ancient doctrines of natural law. Like those conceptions of justice, the identification of these principles seems to presuppose the existence of some kind of natural order. Unlike them, however, it does not fasten on theology as the source of the unwritten principles that transcend the exercise of state power. It is derived from the history, values and culture of that nation, viewed in its constitutional context. Contemporary judges are to work out the implicit principles of the "rich intellectual tradition" that Canada has inherited from the "common law thinking from medieval times, through the English and American revolutionary ages, and into the high Victorian era of empire out of which Canada's written constitution emerged."[44] McLachlin, and Binnie in his debate with Scalia, is animated by a desire to oppose sheer sovereign will, and she accordingly cites the examples of Nuremberg which saw Nazis commit evils because they were simply following orders, and Sir Thomas More's resistance to King Henry VIII. While they display salutary skepticism towards claims of the inherent goodness of democratic decision-making, their invocations of Nazism and Henry VIII suggests the inherent badness of liberal democracy, or at least of legislatures, which is self-serving.

Responding to claims (like those of Scalia) that judges simply resort to private conscience when they resort to unwritten principles, McLachlin claims, referring to More (as portrayed in the film, *A Man For All Seasons*), "it is clear that what he means is the legal conscience of a jurist who has considered the nature of law." A shift of tone marks McLachlin's analysis. She begins the speech by outlining the importance of natural law in Anglo-American law, and expounding upon its instances. She ends by locating the legitimacy of jurists in their knowledge of the "nature of law." This is an astounding claim. First, knowledge of natural law is not the same as knowledge of the "nature of law." One may have knowledge of the contents of natural law (e.g., do not murder) without fully understanding their reasons, in the same way one can know the contents of the Ten Commandments without knowing the mind of God. Indeed, McLachlin offers numerous examples of laws that are by nature but she is vague on what is natural about them. Second, claiming knowledge of the "nature of law" is to claim philosophical wisdom, not simply knowledge of the tradition of common law dating back to medieval times or found in the "usages" of contemporary political actors.

Knowing the "nature of law" differs fundamentally from knowing its contents. As Eric Voegelin observes, "the law" is the substance of order in all realms of being. As a matter of fact, the ancient civilizations usually have in their languages a term that signifies the ordering substance pervading the hierarchy of being, from God, through the world and society, to every single man. Such terms are the Egyptian *maat*, the Chinese *tao*, the Greek *nomos*, and the Latin *lex*."[45] Voegelin observes that the Egyptian notion of *maat* signified order of the gods who create the order of the cosmos. Contemporary society replaces the order of the gods with the progressive myth of humanity's unfolding freedom and equality. In ancient Egypt, the *maat* was preserved by the Pharoah; in China the *tao* was preserved by the king who ruled "all below heaven"; in Greece and in Rome, the *nomos* and *lex* were preserved by the piety instilled by the civil religion of the polis and empire. The *nomos* and *lex* were preserved by the civil religion, though philosophers including Plato and Cicero asserted the authority of philosophical wisdom of the nature of law. Unfortunately, if McLachlin were to follow the Anglo-American understanding of the nature of law more closely, her defense of the legitimacy of judicial interpretation would fall apart. For philosophers like John Locke, all human beings can have access to the natural law.[46] Nature, or nature's God, is their legislator while the sovereign executes the natural laws for them. The Anglo-American tradition of political and legal thinking does not necessarily require a special caste of judges who know the natural law, though contemporary judicial activism appears to exaggerate the central but "cloaked" position in the regime that the Anglo-American legal tradition gave them.[47] Even so, claiming knowledge of the "nature of law" emphasizes moral philosophy, which, as argued above, would make moral philosophers more qualified than (or at least as qualified as) legal practitioners to serve as judges.

McLachlin appears closer to Plato and Cicero because she ostensibly appeals to the rational basis of the unwritten constitutional principles. However, she can only do this because part of Canada's inheritance has been the Enlightenment, with its conflation of philosophical wisdom and political authority. Put another way, Canada has inherited the Enlightenment assumption that political society can be made rational, which, as Canadian political philosopher George Grant pointed out long ago, derives from the Enlightenment transformation of wisdom into technology and politics into administration: not quite rule by philosophers so much as rule by sociologists.[48] As noted above, McLachlin refers to the Court's role in articulating society's "hypergoods," those goods beyond which no goods can be understood, and its role in articulating the "total claims" those "hypergoods" place on citizen-subjects. The judiciary's claim to having a special knowledge corresponds to its role as controlling the language with which people use to shape their moral lives. By claiming to shape language, the Court takes on the role of poets as well. Historically, it is the role of poets to articulate the fundamental principles of a civilization. Examples include Homer for Greece, Dante for Italy, Shakespeare for English-speaking peoples, Goethe for Germany, and Cervantes for Spain. It is also the role of sacred texts, the "great code" of the Bible, to articulate those principles. McLachlin's claims about "hypergoods" push them toward "great code" status.

Despite the grandiose claims of its partisans, Pierre Manent has more recently observed of contemporary manifestations of the working-out of the Enlightenment, that democratic societies, guided by judges, hold out utopian promises of actualizing human dignity, freedom and equality, but at the expense of eliminating the "mediating" activities of self-government, and ultimately, political life. Judicial invocations of dignity constitute the "spiritual" or religious component of contemporary politics, but they are self-defeating because the inherent separation of powers found in Anglo-American constitutionalism, and inherent in modern life in general (i.e., the split between religion and politics, state and society), ensures that each utopian evocation will be resisted or countered in some way.[49] Part of the genius of liberal democracy is that it is composed of multiple and frequently contradictory principles that check one another. For example, exponents of equality usually refrain from seeking the full implications of their desire for equality when they realize they would harm liberty, especially their own liberty.

The same leavening (and at times, undermining) of principles holds for dignity. McLachlin calls "basic human dignity" the notional heart of "today's fundamental norms." It is the basic "hypergood." Dignity is rooted in reason, as with her natural law thinking generally. By taking this route, she seems to reject a major view among legal scholars, such as that of Michael Perry, according to which "every human being is sacred" and that sacredness can be justified along nonsectarian lines.[50] McLachlin also avoids describing dignity as the absolute uniqueness of the individual and the "infinite value" of personhood in the manner of Jacques Maritain, who influenced both Pierre Trudeau and the participants of the 1948 Universal Declaration of Human Rights, a central document from the third source she lists of Canada's unwritten principles, international law.[51] Dignity is the basis of "government by consent, the protection of life and personal security, and freedom from discrimination," and she notes these can be "supported by a democratic argument grounded in conceptions of the state and fundamental human dignity that we have developed since John Stuart Mill."[52]

Her statement requires some clarifications. Dignity as a philosophic concept was fully stated by philosopher Immanuel Kant. So strongly did he assert it that he called dignity not a quality of human beings, but their very definition: "Humanity itself is a dignity, for man can be used by no one (neither by others nor even by himself) merely as a means, but must always be used at the same time as an end."[53] Kant's influence can be seen by observing that dignity is absent from the 1789 Declaration of Rights of Man and Citizen but is in the opening words of the preamble of the 1948 Universal Declaration of Human Rights. Dignity is the respect for the moral law within human beings, which shows them how to act with pure moral motive and not from self-interest, as a Hobbesian doctrine of modern natural rights would assert. Yet modern natural rights, with their grounding in self-interest, form the basis of those aspects of democratic life that McLachlin grounds in dignity: "government by consent, the protection of life and personal security, and freedom from discrimination." While Kant gives us dignity, one can derive government by consent and the other implications from Thomas Hobbes, for whom human beings are naturally more brutish than dignified. As Manent observes, "To put it rather bluntly: human rights concern natural freedoms, including and above all animal and physical nature; human dignity is freedom against physical or in general selfish nature, and it is spiritual liberty."[54]

Unsurprisingly, contemporary jurisprudence ignores this contradiction between the rhetoric of dignity and the actual way it is applied and justified. Instead, jurists think they are able to reconcile them. Kantian dignity is rigorous and rather ascetic while contemporary usurpations of Kantian dignity are meant to protect Hobbesian impulses: "To respect the dignity of other human beings is no longer to respect the respect they hold within themselves for the moral law. Today it is more to respect the choice they have made, whatever that choice may be, in asserting their rights. For Kant, respect for human dignity is respect for humanity itself; for contemporary moralism, respect for human dignity is respect for the 'contents of life,' whatever it may be, of other human beings. The same words are used, but with an altogether moral perspective."[55] Indeed, Manent's assessment is mild compared to that of Kant: "Being persuaded of the magnitude of one's moral worth, but only through want of comparison with the law, can be called moral arrogance."[56] Contemporary morality leads to the politics of recognition, whereby the state is obliged to recognize all other lifestyles. Obviously, not all lifestyles can be recognized. Thus, the Court found itself recently having to weigh the rights of religious believers against the most recent lifestyle demanding recognition, homosexuals. Just as the Court's Kantian rhetoric masks Hobbesian natural rights, so too does its task of "balancing" mask the reality that recognizing some lifestyles undermines others.[57] Indeed, the Court's "living tree" metaphor also reflects its way of invoking Kantian morality for Hobbesian politics. Understanding dignity and human rights in light of "the times" simply obscures the fact that one understands them in terms of the majority's understanding, or what the Court deems its opinion should be when it knows its interests. What else are "the times" but an expression of society's "usages" and customs (the first of McLachlin's sources of unwritten principles)?

This last point, which is a question of public morality, returns us to McLachlin's comment about John Stuart Mill. As a philological point, Mill was not as concerned about dignity as he was of individuality. But the philological point reveals Mill's philosophical point. In *On Liberty*, Mill mentioned dignity only a few times and by it he meant honor and self-worth. Conversely, Chapter Three is titled, "On Individuality, as One of the Elements of Well-Being." For Mill, individuality was about expressing personal genius. While liberty, in the sense of prohibiting the state from interfering with private lives, benefits all, the liberty of geniuses benefits society most of all because it is the spur of progress. Mill considered the leveling effects of modern liberty as serious a threat to the liberty of genius as state coercion. Unlike McLachlin, Mill did not think all lifestyles deserve to be protected. Some are more harmful and shameful than others. Mill thought it should be up to society, not the state, to enforce public morality in the form of shunning, verbal protest or boycott. Mill acknowledged that public morality is in need of a moral system that encourages human beings, in seeking their self-interest, to have humanity as the object of their interest. Borrowing from French sociologist Auguste Comte, Mill up to his last writings defended the notion of the religion of humanity as the moral basis of liberalism.[58] Kant also considered history as progressive and humanity the proper object of moral action. Indeed, history as progressive helps to constitute human rights because it is only at a late stage of human "development" when we see others as "human" and inherently like ourselves rather than as members of a particular class, race or nation, and thereby worthy of the same respect we seek for ourselves.

As many Enlightenment thinkers up to Friedrich Nietzsche show, the very notion of humanity as an object of contemplation and action presupposes a historical understanding of human development. Humanity is built upon the historic individuality of every individual and the increasing consciousness of each generation that its object of action is humanity, not simply family, tribe, polis, sect or religion. While sounding noble, what this sentiment means however is that only the present generation can fully be said to be human: "Thus, just when today's humanity seeks and is proud to exclude nothing of what is currently human, it excludes its whole past, all past generations. At the very moment when it embraces itself wholly, it ceases to comprehend itself."[59] Humanity as the current generation, for whom the "living tree" would be most alive (a form of self-flattery, or "moral arrogance" as Kant would say), might help to explain why the Court seems to favor a form of dignity that emphasizes personal autonomy and respect "more a function of what one can do, than simply the fact that one exists regardless of one's condition or abilities."[60] Dignity as rational agency instead of the irreplacability of the person favors the active and the strong, not the disabled, unborn or dying. It favors the present generation and pushes the new arrivals and those leaving further to the margins. For most Enlightenment thinkers including Comte and Mill, humanity as the end of moral action is ennobling. For Kant it is noble but problematic because the idea of one generation progressively superseding previous generations means they end up treating previous generations as means, which contradicts the categorical imperative of treating human beings as ends. Finally, Nietzsche thought humanity expresses the flattest disposition of the soul, the Last Man, because historical progress revealed only its animality. The laws of humanity have become the "hypergoods" of Canadian constitutionalism. Yet, the more McLachlin and her colleagues side with the religion of humanity in Mill, Comte and to some extent Kant, the less they are able to uphold the "spiritual" unencumbered self propounded in their writings, and the more they must resort to Hobbesian realpolitik.

Conclusion

The increasing frequency with which civil religion has been evoked in Canada betrays a deepening anxiety that the twin legitimation crises the Charter is meant to heal – (1) regionalism and (2) the question of secularization – are in fact festering. The more the Court appeals to a "progressive" reading of the Charter that seeks unwritten principles in a natural order that is said to transcend sovereign will, the more they must rely on sovereign will to enact it and even to legitimate, it. This split-mindedness enables elites to make simultaneous and contradictory claims that are serious (e.g., Irwin Cotler), ironic (e.g., Jeffrey Simpson) or politically calculated (e.g., Paul Martin) proclamations of the Charter's divinity.

The attempt to create a civil religion out of the Charter is also self-defeating because it is based upon the Enlightenment myth of progress, which is less widely adhered to than it was even twenty years ago. A variety of critics, many of whom may be characterized "postmodern," have criticized the myth of progress to the point that faith in it may be regarded as dead. David Walsh, in his mediation upon our "postmodern"

civilizational moment, explains the endurance of this faith in the secular
world and the reasons for its death:

> What has made a secular world possible has been its capacity to draw us
> onward through the mysterious promise of a future that transcends our
> past. Its whole secret has been its ability to persuade us that we are moving
> toward a state that will be qualitatively better and different than that in
> which we are now. That is, a secular ethos trades on the residue of
> transcendent longing and mystery still present within us even if we no
> longer accept the spiritual articulation of that movement. As soon as we
> recognize that there is no great or glorious future awaiting us, that the
> satisfactions we possess now are the best that can be attained in the future,
> that we are literally going nowhere, the whole project is undermined. The
> secular emperor is revealed to have no clothes. That collapse of the modern
> project is the source of the disorientation we now encounter in our
> civilization.[61]

Our postmodern situation is marked by moral fragmentation as well as
renewed openness to spiritual concerns, which makes talk of "hypergoods"
making "total claims" upon us inadequate if not dangerous. Jean Bethke
Elshtain's observation that politics and religion make partial claims is
more attuned to the needs of our society.

Whether the problem of civil religion, which seems to be a permanent
feature of political life in general, will endure in Canada will depend on
whether Canadians can answer in the affirmative to Peter Russell's
question of whether Canadians can be a sovereign people. Because of the
indelible cosmic-representative features of political life, perhaps it would
be more reasonable instead to ask *what kind* of civil religion Canadians
would have if they were to become a sovereign people. If they do become
sovereign, then their constitutional crises might make it less tempting to
articulate an assertive civil religion such as that articulated by Chief
Justice McLachlin, Irwin Cotler and others, which can be done by
avoiding the grand constitutional engineering that characterized the 1980s
but that politicians avoided throughout the 1990s.[62] Assertive evocations
of civil religion are attempts to consolidate power to deal with a crisis of
legitimacy. Once a regime is legitimated, civil religion reinforces its
founding as occurs in the United States. If a regime follows the path of the
living tree, by which the founding process is perpetual, then civil religion
will increase in its assertiveness.

Canadians have gotten used to being told that their society has
successfully separated religion from politics and that it is a secularized
society. This essay has shown that this view is based on a flawed
understanding of what secular means and that Canadian political life is

indeed imbued with religiosity, though not in the form Canadians normally expect. By achieving greater clarity on the nature of political and religious life, it may be possible to negotiate their corresponding claims with greater tolerance and understanding.

Notes

[1] E.g., Irwin Cotler, Speech to Parliament of Canada, *Hansard* (37th Parliament, 2nd session), October 28, 2002 (http://www.parl.gc.ca/37/2/parlbus/chambus/house/debates/016_2002-10-28/han016_1355-E.htm).

[2] As indicated by the subtitle of David Lyon and Marguerite Van Die, eds., *Rethinking Church, State, and Modernity: Canada Between Europe and America* (Toronto: University of Toronto Press, 2000).

[3] From a communitarian perspective, Michael Sandel refers to the vision of self proposed by this kind of ideology as the "unencumbered self" (*Democracy's Discontent: America in Search of a Public Philosophy* (Cambridge, MA: Belknap, 1996), 65). Similarly, Harvey Mansfield, Jr., refers to it as the "expressive self" (Harvey Mansfield, Jr., *America's Constitutional Soul* (Baltimore: The Johns Hopkins University Press, 1991), 198).

[4] This story has been told numerous times., most recently by Michael Burleigh, *Earthly Powers: The Clash of Religion and Politics in Europe from the French Revolution to the Great War* (Toronto: HarperCollins, 2006) and *Sacred Causes: The Clash of Religion and Politics, from the Great War to the War on Terror* (Toronto: HarperCollins, 2007), and most deeply by Eric Voegelin, *Modernity Without Restraint: The Political Religions; The New Science of Politics; and Science, Politics, and Gnosticism*, vol. 5 of *Collected Works of Eric Voegelin*, ed. Manfred Henningsen (Columbia, MO: University of Missouri Press, 2000). See also *History of Political Ideas, Collected Works of Eric Voegelin*, vols. 19-26; *Order and History, Collected Works of Eric Voegelin*, vols. 14-18.

[5] Douglas Farrow, "Of Secularity and Civil Religion," in Douglas Farrow, ed., *Recognizing Religion in a Secular Society: Essays in Pluralism, Religion, and Public Policy* (Montréal-Kingston: McGill-Queens University Press, 2004), 140-82.

[6] See Peter L. Berger, *The Desecularization of the World: Resurgent Religion and World Politics* (Grand Rapids, MI: Eerdmans, 1999), and Pippa Norris and Ronald Inglehart, *Sacred and Secular: Religion and Politics Worldwide* (Cambridge: Cambridge University Press, 2004); John von Heyking, "Secularization: Not Dead, But Never What it Seemed," *International Studies Review*, 7:2 (2005): 279-84.; Alexis de Tocqueville, *Democracy in America*, trans. Harvey Mansfield and Delba Winthrop (Chicago: University of Chicago Press, 2000), II.4.6.

[7] Iain T. Benson, "Notes Toward a (Re)Definition of the 'Secular,'" *University of British Columbia Law Review*, 33 Special Edition (2000): 519-50 and "Considering Secularism," in Farrow, *Recognizing Religion*, 83-98.

[8] Alan Cairns, *Reconfigurations: Canadian Citizenship and Constitutional Change* (Toronto: McClelland & Stewart, 1995), 97-118.

[9] Peter Russell, *Constitutional Odyssey: Can Canadians Become a Sovereign People?*, 3rd ed. (Toronto: University of Toronto Press, 2004), vii. Distinguishing 1867 as Burkean from 1982 as Lockean is questionable. As Leo Strauss argues, Burkean natural right is closer to Locke, and therefore less "organic," than most Burkean conservatives notice (*Natural Right and History*, [Chicago: University of Chicago Press, 252-93]). Moreover, Janet Ajzenstat demonstrates that Locke was indeed present in 1867 (*The Canadian Founding: John Locke and Parliament*, [Montréal-Kingston: McGill-Queens, 2007]). For Ajzenstat, Canadian constitutionalism of the past has been marked by a turn towards political romanticism, which suggests 1982 marks a change from Locke to Rousseau and his romantic heirs.

[10] George Egerton, "Trudeau, God, and the Canadian Constitution," in Lyon and Van Die, *Rethinking Church, State, and Modernity*, 96.

[11] Patrick J. Deneen, *Democratic Faith* (Princeton: Princeton University Press, 2004), xvi. This future-oriented democratic faith is also criticized in Janet Ajzenstat, *The Once and Future Canadian Democracy* (Montréal-Kingston: McGill-Queens University Press, 2003).

[12] Isaiah Berlin, *The Roots of Romanticism*, quoted in Ajzenstat, *The Once and Future Canadian Democracy*, 131.

[13] I have explored others, specifically the Supreme Court's jurisprudence concerning religious organizations, in light of Alexis de Tocqueville's account of democracy in, "Civil Religion and Associational Life Under Canada's Ephemeral Monster," in *Civil Religion Then and Now: The Philosophical Legacy of Civil Religion and Its Enduring Relevance in North America*, eds. Ronald Weed and John von Heyking, unpublished manuscript. This current essay elaborates an assertion made in the previous essay concerning the Court's problematic reliance on "anticipated consensus" to justify rights.

[14] Andrew E. Kim, "The Absence of Pan-Canadian Civil Religion: Plurality, Duality, and Conflict in Symbols of Canadian Culture," *Sociology of Religion* 54, no. 3 (1993): 257-75.

[15] Northrop Frye, *The Great Code: The Bible and Literature,* vol. 19 of *Collected Works of Northrop Frye,* ed. Alvin A. Lee, (Toronto: University of Toronto Press, 2006). See Norman Knowles, *Inventing the Loyalists: The Ontario Loyalist Tradition and the Creation of Usable Pasts* (Toronto: University of Toronto Press, 1997), 97; Louis François Laflèche, *Quelque considérations sur le rapports de la société avec la religion et la famille* (1866), excerpted in Ramsay Cook, ed., *French Canadian Nationalism: An Anthology* (Toronto: Macmillan of Canada, 1969), 102.

[16] R.W. Norman, *Our Duties and Opportunities* (Montreal: 'Gazette' Printing House, 1877), 189 and 210. These references are covered by Preston Jones, "Sacred Words, Fighting Words: The Bible and National Meaning in Canada, 1860-1900," in *Civil Religion Then and Now.*

[17] See Frederick Vaughan, *The Canadian Federalist Experiment: From Defiant Monarchy to Reluctant Republic* (Montréal-Kingston: McGill-Queens University Press, 2003), 134-51; Janet Ajzenstat, *The Political Thought of Lord Durham* (Montréal-Kingston: McGill-Queens University Press, 1988), 35-41.

[18] Ramsay Cook, *The Regenerators* (Toronto: University of Toronto Press, 1985); William Lyon Mackenzie King, *Industry and Humanity* (Toronto: University of Toronto Press, 1973).

[19] Barry Cooper, "Quebec Nationalism and Canadian Politics in Light of Voegelin's *Political Religions,*" in *Politics, Order, and History: Essays on the Work of Eric Voegelin,* eds. Glenn Hughes et al., (Sheffield: Sheffield Academic Press, 2001), 208-232.

[20] Niccolò Machiavelli, *Discourses on Livy,* I.11.

[21] Cairns, *Reconfigurations,* 197.

[22] See the essays in Dwight D. Allman and Michael D. Beaty, eds., *Cultivating Citizens: Soulcraft and Citizenship in Contemporary America* (Lanham, MD: Lexington Books, 2002).

[23] Egerton, "Trudeau, God, and the Canadian Constitution," 108.

[24] John S. Moir, *Church and State in Canada: 1627-1867: Basic Documents* (Toronto: McClelland and Stewart Limited, 1967); xiii; Egerton, "Trudeau, God, and the Canadian Constitution"; Farrow, "Of Secularity and Civil Religion," 140-82; Iain T. Benson, "Considering Secularism," in *Recognizing Religion,* 83-98 and "Notes Toward a (Re)Definition of the 'Secular,'" 519-50; John von Heyking, "Harmonization of Heaven and Earth?: Religion, Politics, and Law in Canada," *University of British Columbia Law Review,* 33 Special Edition (2000): 663-98; Peter Emberley, *Divine Hunger: Canadians on Spiritual Walkabout* (Toronto: HarperCollins Canada, 2002).

[25] Jeffrey Simpson, "Leave the Prayerbook at Home, Stockwell," *Globe and Mail* (Toronto), March 31, 2000, sec. A15.

[26] Bruce Ryder, "State Neutrality and Freedom of Conscience and Religion," *Supreme Court Law Review,* 2005, 29(2d): 175.

[27] As predicted for a political society guided by Hobbesian principles; see Travis D. Smith, "Hobbes on Forgiving Those Who Trespass Against Us," in *Civil Religion Then and Now.* See also Thomas Hobbes, *Leviathan,* XVII.

[28] Allan Gregg, "The Christian Comeback," *Saturday Night Magazine,* November 2005, 22. A scholarly analysis of "secular fundamentalism" can be found in Paul F. Campos, "Secular Fundamentalism," *Columbia Law Review,* 94(1994): 1814-27.

[29] Robert Ivan Martin, *The Most Dangerous Branch: How the Supreme Court of Canada Has Undermined Our Law and Our Democracy* (Montréal-Kingston: McGill-Queens University Press, 2003), 1.

[30] The Right Honorable Beverley McLachlin, P.C., "Freedom of Religion and the Rule of Law: A Canadian Perspective," in *Recognizing Religion in a Secular Society,* 12-34.

[31] Elshtain, "A Response to Chief Justice McLachlin," in *Recognizing Religion in a Secular Society,* 35-40.

---

[32] McLachlin cites Paul Kahn, *The Cultural Study of Law: Reconstructing Legal Scholarship* (Chicago: University of Chicago Press, 1999), 84, 123-4. See also Jean-Jacques Rousseau, *Social Contract*, IV.8. For details, see Ronald Weed, "Jean-Jacques Rousseau on Civil Religion: Freedom of the Individual, Toleration, and the Price of Mass Authenticity," in *Civil Religion Then and Now.*

[33] Kirk Makin, "Senior U.S., Canadian Judges Spar Over Judicial Activism," *Globe and Mail,* February 17, 2007, sec. A.2

[34] Aristotle, *Nicomachean Ethics*, trans. Joe Sachs (Newburyport, MA: Focus Publishing, 2002), 1137b23.

[35] Russell, *Constitutional Odyssey*, ix.

[36] *Edwards v. Canada (Attorney General)* [1930] A.C. 124 (P.C.) at 136 (http://www.chrc-ccdp.ca/en/browseSubjects/edwardspc.asp).

[37] *Reference re Same-Sex Marriage* [2004] 3 S.C.R. 698, 2004 SCC 79. Emphasis added.

[38] *Reference re Same-Sex Marriage* at 27. In fact, it is hard to resist concluding that same-sex marriage, which changes the legal definition of marriage from a man and a woman to two persons, also undermines the Court's ability to restrict marriage to a union of two persons because "two" depends on viewing marriage as needing two to procreate. Both those who wish to preserve the older definition of marriage, and those who wish to move "beyond conjugality," consider same-sex marriage a way-station to abolishing marriage as a meaningful category altogether. Some celebrate this move in the name of freedom and self-realization, while others, who view marriage as uniquely situated to raise the next generation and as an important intermediary civil society institution, see it as dangerous. See John von Heyking, "Why Exclude Oedipus?: On the Incoherent Statism of Same Sex Marriage." *The Interim*, September 2006, XXIV(7): 10-11.

[39] Kenneth Minogue, *Alien Powers: The Pure Theory of Ideology* (New York: St. Martin's Press, 1985), 183.

[40] In addition to Voegelin, see Minogue, *Alien Powers.* The best critique of end-of-history ideology remains Barry Cooper, *The End of History: An Essay on Modern Hegelianism* (Toronto: University of Toronto Press, 1984).

[41] Iain T. Benson, "Considering Secularism," 83-98 and "Notes Toward a (Re)Definition of the 'Secular,'" 519-50. According to Cairns, "'Rights' pushes university law faculties in the direction of legal theory and political philosophy" (*Reconfigurations*, 202).

[42] Roderick A. MacDonald, "Post-Charter Legal Education: Does Anyone Teach Law Anymore?," *Policy Options*, February 2007, 77.

[43] McLachlin, "Lord Cooke Lecture," Wellington, New Zealand, 1 December 2005 (http://www.scc-csc.gc.ca/aboutcourt/judges/speeches/UnwrittenPrinciples_e.asp). Unpaginated.

[44] McLachlin quoting M.D. Walters, "The Common Law Constitution in Canada: Return of *Lex non Scripta* as Fundamental Law," *University of Toronto Law Journal*, 51 (2004): 136.

[45] Voegelin, *The Nature of Law and Related Legal Writings*, eds. Robert Anthony Pascal, James Lee Babin, and John William Corrington (Baton Rouge: Louisiana State University Press, 1991), 24.

[46] John Locke, *Second Treatise of Government*, chap. 2.

[47] Paul Carrese, *The Cloaking of Power: Montesquieu, Blackstone, and the Rise of Judicial Activism*,(Chicago: University of Chicago Press, 2003).

[48] George P. Grant, *Technology and Empire* (Toronto: House of Anansi, 1969). Grant's account of "modernity," and Canada's position in it, is not unproblematic. See John von Heyking and Barry Cooper, "'A Cow is Just a Cow': George Grant and Eric Voegelin on the United States," *Athens and Jerusalem: George Grant's Theology, Philosophy, and Politics*, eds. Ian Angus, Ron Dart, and Randy Peg Peters, (Toronto: University of Toronto Press, 2006), 166-89.

[49] Pierre Manent, *A World Without Politics?: A Defense of the Nation State*, trans. Marc A. LePain (Princeton: Princeton University Press, 2006).

[50] Michael J. Perry, *The Idea of Human Rights: Four Inquiries* (Oxford: Oxford University Press, 1998). See also Jean Bethke Elshtain, "The Dignity of the Human Person and the Idea of Human Rights: Four Inquries," *Journal of Law and Religion* 14, no. 1 (1999-2000): 53-65. Liberal thinkers generally have underestimated dignity's intractable relationship with the divine, which was more explicit in ancient and medieval understandings. See the essays in Robert P. Kraynak and Glenn Tinder, *In Defense of Human Dignity: Essays for Our Times* (Notre Dame, IN: University of Notre Dame Press, 2003). See also David Walsh, *The Growth of the Liberal Soul* (Columbia, MO: University of Missouri Press, 1997).

[51] See Max Nemni, "The Charter's Christian Roots," *National Post*, February 17, 2007, sec. A23.

[52] McLachlin, "Lord Cooke Lecture."

[53] Immanuel Kant, *The Metaphysical Principles of Virtue*, trans. James Ellington (New York: Bobbs-Merrill Company, Inc., 1964), 127.

[54] Manent, *A World Without Politics?*, 193.

[55] Manent, *A World Without Politics?*, 193.

[56] Kant, *The Metaphysical Principles of Virtue*, 98. Susan Shell distinguishes Kantian dignity from its contemporary evocations ("Kant on Human Dignity," in *In Defense of Human Dignity*, 53-80).

[57] Heyking, "Why Exclude Oedipus?"

[58] John Stuart Mill, "Theism," in *Three Essays on Religion* (Amherst, NY: Prometheus Books, 1998), 255-57; Linda Raeder, *John Stuart Mill and the Religion of Humanity*, (Columbia, MO: University of Missouri Press, 2002).

[59] Manent, *A World Without Politics?*, 129.

[60] David M. Brown, "'Human Dignity,' Human Rights and the End of Life: The North Wind Blowing From Canada," Paper presented to Conference on Suffering and Hope, University of St. Thomas, Houston, TX, November 10-13, 2005: 14-15.

[61] David Walsh, *Guarded By Mystery: Meaning in a Postmodern Age* (Washington, DC: Catholic University of America Press, 1999), 101.

[62] Throughout this essay I have written of Canada's twin legitimacy crises as revolving around (1) regionalism (mostly Québec) and (2) the question of

secularization. The constitutional bickering of the 1980s addressed the first of these, and it is tempting to refer to the growth of freedom of religion cases in the late 1990s as a result of the second. On the latter, see my "Harmonization of Heaven and Earth?"

CHAPTER THREE

THE AUTONOMY COMPLEX: FROM CREATIVITY TO ALIENATION AND OPPRESSION

BORIS DEWIEL

Modernity is less thoroughly secular than has often been imagined, not only because overt religious faith remains influential among many but also because unrecognized religious beliefs continue to be held by others who see themselves as secular. This chapter argues that the widespread belief that humans are ultimately creative produces a set of political attitudes named here as the autonomy complex. The chapter briefly traces the history and discusses the meaning of the cognate ideas of creativity and autonomy in order to examine some of the more common manifestations of the autonomy complex in contemporary Canadian politics.

The autonomy complex is caused by the belief in human creativity, the idea that humans have the power to create something out of nothing. Autonomy, understood not just as independence but more literally as the power to create one's own laws, is a political value derived from the idea of creativity. Creativity for the believer is not just an attribute that some people have but is the defining essence that makes one human. In this belief system, the reality in which we live should ultimately be of our own making. However, this belief produces feelings of disillusionment and distrust when believers confront realities they did not create.

The autonomy complex is that set of political attitudes in which the unexamined expectation inherited from religion, that one should have reality-creating powers, produces overt feelings of alienation and oppression. The idea of ultimate creativity is a belief that began from biblical stories that were interpreted to tell of a God whose essence is the power to create the laws of reality *ex nihilo* and who created humans in his own likeness. The long cultural influence of these ideas eventually led modern believers, typically self-identified as secular, to see themselves as ultimately creative in their essence.

Modern believers in human self-creativity have lost knowledge of the origin and the religious character of their belief. For most lay believers, the idea of ontological autonomy operates as an unexamined expectation in the background of thinking producing unarticulated hopes about how life should be. When these are frustrated by heteronomous realities, the result is not conceptual adjustment but emotional reactions of disillusionment and distrust. Because creativity is a belief in an otherworldly power, the real constraints of the perceived world feel alien and oppressive. Although the feelings of alienation and oppression are experienced directly and often forcefully, their cause, the unexamined belief in the magic of creativity, is occluded from the believer's self-understanding. In politics, the positive feelings of hope and negative feelings of disappointment belonging together to the autonomy complex tend to manifest themselves in recurring patterns of attitudes toward political issues, as we will see.

The Origin and Meaning of the Idea of Creativity

In a culture that takes creativity and originality as universal terms of approbation, it may be a surprise to learn that these are not universal human values or ideas. Creativity is the idolization of newness, which is a thoroughly modern value. In an oral society like that of Homeric Greece, the role of story-tellers was to repeat faithfully (which means never to create) the traditional tales that contained a people's knowledge of itself. Creativity, were it conceivable, would have been condemned as an utter failure of the social role of story-teller and a deep violation against the community. Traditional societies do not idolize newness because it is the opposite of tradition. For a traditional society, the creation of newness (if comprehended at all) would be met with suspicion and enmity.

With the coming of literacy to ancient Greece, creativity did not thereby come to be valued as the source of truth and meaning. For the first Greek philosophers, knowledge was to be *discovered,* not created, in the eternal substratum of reality. The pre-Socratic naturalists like Thales, Anaximander and Anaximenes saw this unchanging substratum as a stable element or set of elements. For the Pythagoreans, the eternal reality was to be found in the higher realm of mathematics. Even for Heraclitus, the great philosopher of transformation and flux, beneath the surface of changing appearances there is an underlying *logos,* perhaps (the record is fragmentary) in a structure of natural oppositions. For the paradoxical logicians, Parmenides and Zeno, the permanence of Being is so total that all change must be an unreal illusion, which their paradoxes were meant to expose. For Plato, the world of change or Becoming was inferior and untrustworthy compared to the higher–because eternal–truths of Being that he called the Ideas or Forms. In Plato's *Timaeus,* a creation myth superficially similar to the story of Genesis (which Athens by his time would have heard in its trade with Jerusalem), Plato's demigod is not a creator of anything fundamentally new but is only a shaper of existing materials according to an eternal plan. For Protagoras, the relativistic Sophist, "man is the measure of all things" not because humans create their own truths but because conventions and traditions vary from place to place. The relativism of varying traditions is opposite in principle to the modern relativism of self-invention precisely because the principle of conventional fidelity is contrary to that of creative newness. The relativism of self-creation belongs to the modern but not to the ancient world because they understood neither their gods nor themselves to be creative in any deep or important sense.

The belief in human creativity and the idolization of newness is a specifically modern, western phenomenon that belongs to one era and one of the world's cultures or civilizations. In short, creativity is nothing like a universal value.[1] Therefore, it must have a specifiable source in the history of that particular culture in which it appeared. The culture of European modernity has broadly speaking two cultural parents, Athens and Jerusalem, and the idea of creativity as a positive value comes only from the latter. Creativity is a belief that came from and belongs to the Bible. As a secularized idea, it is a post-biblical belief. Moreover, because the modern belief in human creativity in its most profound and full sense retains the essential premise that reality is created and not merely discovered, it remains a religious belief. Creativity in its full sense is a power over nature, which means literally that it is a supernatural belief in something beyond the given realities we perceive. To give it anything less than this full sense is to trivialize the idea by abandoning its central meaning. Creativity without religiosity, or at least magicality, is an empty platitude. The power to create newness can only be understood properly as the power of existence itself.

The extent to which the Hebrew Bible explicitly contained self-existential ideas as has been disputed. Pope Benedict XVI for example has argued that such passages as Exodus 3:14 in which God identifies himself to Moses as "*Ehyeh Asher Ehyeh*," translated in the King James Version as "I AM that I am," did not for the ancient Hebrews consciously connote the idea of God's self-existence. Rather, the "idea of Being," which is "the central concept of the Platonic philosophy" was not given to the Old

Testament until early Hellenic Christians translated it into Greek.[2] The Hebrew writers of the Bible in this view were simply not concerned with philosophical ideas about existence because philosophical controversies over Being (eternal reality) versus Becoming (the world of impermanence and change) belonged only to Athens and not to Jerusalem.

Perhaps, but if so the early Christians answered the questions of Athens using ideas and images from the stories of Jerusalem. The portentous combination of voluntarism, monotheism and creationism, none of which belonged to Athens, allowed the Athenian question of Being versus Becoming to be resolved in the parallelism of Creator and Creation. The ideas of voluntarism, monotheism and creationism have different sources of emphasis in the Old Testament. The notion of the divine will is emphasized by the covenant story, for example as described by Eichrodt,[3] just as voluntary consent is central to the derivative modern idea of the social contract. Monotheism developed from monolatry (the worship of only one god among others believed to exist), such that a god with power over local gods became the single God of omnipotence. The creation story in the Bible is commonly believed to have been influenced by sources like the Babylonian creation myth,[4] though these were neither voluntaristic nor monotheistic. Combining the three ideas, the theory emerges of the single God who is all-powerful and whose power is entirely voluntary and essentially creative.

The combination has inescapable logical implications. Because this single God is seen as both ultimately powerful and the creator the world, it follows that he can have no source of existence outside of himself, not in any previous divinity nor in any pre-existent heavenly or earthly nature beyond or outside of himself. In short, such a God can only be self-existent or existentially self-sufficient. If this idea was not articulated consciously until Hellenic Christians did so, it resided implicitly in the earlier union of stories. Having answered Greek questions with Hebrew ideas and imagery, Hellenistic Christians explicitly identified the idea of God with that of existential self-sufficiency. Whatever its original connotations in Hebrew, the Greek translation, "Ego sum qui sum," to philosophical Christians naturally meant, "I am that which is" and "I am because I am." The God of Being is a Self-Being.

Moreover, the Jewish and Christian deity is not a mere philosophical abstraction nor an unrelenting force of nature but a personal God, a God conceivable as a person and who has a personal relationship with humans. Hence the self-existence of God is literally the existence of a *self* or person. The creator of time and space is not a creature within time and space but can transcend the godly and earthly realms to appear before humans. But unlike humans who were created with physical bodies, the person of God is defined by his infinite existential power, which is his *creative* power, antecedent to which nothing can have existed. Hence God's creativity came to be seen by many Christians as the power of creation *ex nihilo*.[5] The source of all being can have no other source of being. It exists out of nothing, out of nothing and nowhere. This is the essential meaning of creativity: to make something exist that did not exist before. A being defined by such a power, if understood as a self, must be self-created out of nothing that existed before. Self-creativity is the power of self-existence, the power to exist out of nothing pre-existent and nothing outside of oneself. Creativity requires the power of self-creation *ex nihilo*.

When philosophical Christians read in Genesis that God created man (in Hebrew, *adam)* in his own image and likeness, many understood this to mean that humans had been given the power of free will as their higher essence. However, this freedom was then misused to create evil. Given the ambivalence of this story, it is unsurprising that the power and goodness of the human will has been long contested, as from Augustine vs. Pelagius to Luther vs. Erasmus. For the optimists, the human creation in the likeness of God meant that humans shared a tiny spark of the godly essence of creativity. It is to this optimistic tradition that the modern religious belief in creativity belongs. As a Canadian poet, approvingly describing the views of William Blake, precisely put it,

> [T]he creative imagination links us most to the divine and if God is
> inherently creative then we as beings made in the image of the divine are
> also inherently creative. When we are exercising our creative faculties in
> whatever capacity, we are most in touch with our essential selves.[6]

Creativity is the ability to make something new, which is to bring into existence something that did not exist before. Even if we imagine creativity only as the ability to reshape an existing material into a new form, the newness belongs only to that part of the production that had never previously existed. In the simple meaning of words, if something has existed before, it is not new. Creativity in short can only mean coming into existence of something that previously did not exist, which means that artistic creativity is always a localized form of creation *ex nihilo*, the bringing of something from non-existence into existence. Human creators (unless they are idealistic philosophers) do not normally think of themselves as bringing the entire universe into being but creativity in its simple meaning is always the bringing to being of something out of non-being, which is the making of something out of nothing. Even in its more limited senses, therefore, creativity always means creation *ex nihilo.* It is an existential power, the belief in which, whether Christian or post-Christian, can only be called religious.

Today, we may think of free will only as the ordinary ability to command our own muscular actions but the idea of pure voluntarism in our actions is also related in origin and meaning to that of creativity *ex nihilo.* Free will in one's actions does not mean only that one's actions are uncaused by outside forces but more importantly it means they must be caused only from within oneself. In this understanding, I must be the sole originating source of my actions. To be free, *I must be the creator of my own actions out of nothing,* because my actions cannot be caused by anything pre-existent and external to myself. My actions cannot have a cause outside of myself; hence independence is necessary but not sufficient for this concept of freedom. Instead, my actions must have their first and only cause within myself. In the world of physics, wrote Kant, there is "nothing that could begin ... absolutely and from itself" like a voluntary action, which if it is free must be purely original and without prior physical cause. "An original action [is one] through which something happens that previously was not."[7] My free actions must come into being from non-being, and my will is the power of this creation of something from nothing.

In the purely voluntaristic concept of freedom, everything in the physical world is determined by a great sequence of causality, but not our free actions. We are the exception to the laws of physics and this exception is possible only because we have a higher power over nature, literally a supernatural power. We are the sole originators or creators of our actions, which means they do not come out of nature or anything outside of ourselves. To be free in our ordinary actions, we must be the creators *ex nihilo* of those actions, the bringers into existence of actions out of nowhere that would not otherwise have existed. Hence freedom of will understood in this way, even in the realm of ordinary actions, is a supernatural concept modeled on the idea of creation *ex nihilo.* Anyone who understands his or her freedom on this way is a copier of a religious idea borrowed from the Bible.

This idea came from religious stories and it remains a religious belief, though its believers may think they are secular. Today's semi-secularists for example idolize originality in art and fiction while distaining the artists of the past who sought only to glorify ideas they did not pretend to invent. The modern art lover stands before representations of the abstracted idea of creativity with feelings of profundity but these are borrowed unknowingly from an older culture. The feelings are powerful but they are borrowed, occasionally with awareness (as with our Canadian poet) but much more often not. Creativity remains a godly idea and its worship is religious whether in churches or in the reading rooms and galleries where it is copied.

Among those who consider themselves secular, the belief in creativity has been severed from the originating co-belief in God. Western modernity over time came to hold, as one of its plurality of competing beliefs, that autonomy is the creation by humans of their own laws of being. If creationism may be defined philosophically as the belief that the fundamental laws of being are created rather than merely discovered, the idea of human autonomy in its most powerful and profound sense is the belief that we are the creators of our own laws of being. This belief developed over many centuries and its secularization or humanization had various causes but among them was the Christian story itself, which with the Incarnation took God in human form as its central figure of worship. Other influences, including religious wars, the breakdown of feudal authority, the emergence of empirical science, and the processes of industrialization and urbanization, had their own secularizing influences but for the development of the modern European idea of autonomy, Christianity itself was the cultural *sine qua non.*

Autonomy is only one of the values of modernity and others have their own sources, but autonomy comes only from religion. The autonomy of God is biblical belief while the autonomy of humans is post-biblical, but they share without change the Christian premise that the laws of being are created and not just discovered. The Christian formula God-as-man was merely inverted by post-Christians without disturbing the religious premise of creationism. Unlike the ancient Greeks, for whom the laws of ultimate existence were eternal and had no creation, for Christians and post-Christian alike the ultimate laws of being have their first and only source in a creator. Creationism in its modern political form, as in the idea of autonomy properly understood, remains a religious or supernatural belief in which creativity is the source of the real.

Autonomy Properly Understood: Immanuel Kant

Autonomy in its modern meaning is much more than mere independence. Thus it differs from the Greek *autonomia,* which carried only the more limited meaning. The Greek *nomos* meant custom, "that which is in habitual practice, use or possession," rather than law in the sense of sovereign command, though the latter usage appeared notably in later Greek translations of the Old Testament.[8] Thus the ancient *autonomia*

meant only the freedom to retain traditional laws and local customs with
no allusion to the creation of law. The Greeks did not see political will as
the source of social order because their language and worldview lacked the
notion of will as a creative power.[9] In its full modern meaning, autonomy
is the power to create out of nothing not just one's own regulative laws of
behaviour but one's own constitutive laws of being, but the ancient Greeks
simply did not understand themselves in this way. Neither they nor their
gods were imagined as having the miraculous power of existential
creativity. Athens instead gave to modernity the belief in an eternal
rational order in which creative newness has no place.

The most important theorist of autonomy was Immanuel Kant, who
brought the Christian syncretism of Greek rationalism and biblical
voluntarism into moral philosophy. According to Alfred Weber:

> It is, undoubtedly, not Kant's intention to 'humiliate' reason … but to assign
> to it its proper place among all our faculties, its true role in the complicated
> play of our spiritual life. Now, this place is, according to Kant, a
> subordinate one; this function is *regulative* and modifying, not *constitutive*
> and creative. *The* WILL, *and not reason, forms the basis of our faculties
> and of things*: that is the leading thought of Kantian philosophy.[10]

In the *Critique of Pure Reason*, Kant was concerned with limiting the
hubris of theoretical speculation, a fruit not meant for human consumption,
but in the *Critique of Practical Reason,* he sought a positive conception of
willful reason as active (or "practical") in the sensible world. Relying on
the Aristotelian distinction between form and matter, Kant argued that the
will is undetermined by *material* conditions but the *form* of law, which is
its universality, is permanent and unchangeable. Hence the will is free
from the universal laws of nature but not from the criterion of universality
itself. A command that lacks the form of universality is a mere maxim and
not a true law.

The influence of biblical stories on Kant is evident in his conception of
lawfulness as universality. This understanding follows directly from the
monotheistic creation story: When God created law, he created it as
universal. The Kantian criterion of universality is derived from the belief
that true law is created by a single rational will. Because this creative will
is rational, it will be consistent with itself. But what if there were many
such wills? Why is it irrational to think there could be many creator gods,
each creating its own universe of consistent laws? Or why is it irrational to
think of a single creator of many self-consistent universes? If autonomous
rational gods followed Kant's categorical imperative in creating the laws
of their own worlds, they would produce universal (to their own universe)

and self-consistent sets of moral laws, but these various sets of laws would be non-universal and non-harmonious compared to each other. Each could be consistent with itself but inconsistent and disharmonious compared to the created realms of each other autonomous being. The result is a pluriverse, not a universe.[11]

For Kant, "universal" connoted singularity but this definition belongs not to rationality or logical necessity alone. It is speculative but not irrational to suggest the possibility of multiple or parallel universes. Kant's theory of law is not established by the pure dictates of reason but was a culturally specific inheritance. Kant's reading of universality as singularity belongs to the Hellenic Christian syncretism of reason and will, which he simply accepted without notice: one creator, one universe, one universal law.

From this article of faith follows the categorical imperative. When we give a law to ourselves, it must apply universally to all beings who are its subject. However, there is in Kant's argument a hidden ambiguity of competing notions of equality. On one side is our equality as *subjects* under universal law; on the other side is our equality as *creators* of law. The Kantian criterion of universalizability, if it were accepted, would entail only the former, our equality as subjects of law. Universal laws are those that apply to everyone equally, but this says nothing about the status of the creators of those laws. Hence the universality of law is a criterion relevant only to its application, not to its creation.

The second kind of equality, that of humans as creators of law, is based not on the universalizability of law but on our identity and unity as lawgivers. We are *identical* lawgivers, *united* in our lawgiving, and not just equal-but-separate lawgivers.[12] On this presumption of identity and unity the entire Kantian moral theory depends, but it does not follow from the rationalistic criterion of the universal application of law to all subjects. The sole foundation of the second kind of equality – according to which, as law-givers, we are as one and must therefore rule for all-as-one – is the Christian identification of humans with God as creators, not subjects, of law. Kant's categorical imperative tells us to *identify with* God at the moment of creation of the laws of the universe. This was not a mere analogy but a precise homology. In our autonomy, we are not just *like* God but *of* God. When we give laws to ourselves, we are one with each other and with the Creator of the scientific laws that govern nature, but it is our oneness through and not the universality of our laws that makes equal as law givers.

For Kant, the fundamental meaning of autonomy is unconditioned self-existence, just as heteronomy is dependent existence. Heteronomy is the condition of phenomena which have their source of being outside of themselves. Autonomy belongs only to noumena because they alone are self-existential. For Kant, moral self-legislation is a special subcategory within the broader category of existential self-sufficiency. Moral autonomy is possible only because we have existential autonomy. Freedom, our uncaused or "unconditioned causality," is made possible by the "unconditioned existence" of the noumenal realm, which is "a reality subsisting by itself."[13] The religious thought behind Kantian moral freedom is the idea that we are the creators *ex nihilo*, out of nothing pre-existent, of our willful actions and therefore the bearers of moral responsibility for them. In Kantian moral theory, the source of our actions is not part of our natural selves, as in the Hobbesian, Lockean or Humean theory of human nature. The empiricists' self-understanding led to a morality based on the temporality of one's character developed over time, whereas autonomy requires the supratemporality of creative newness in which free actions are thoroughly unconditioned by any causal past.

Creative freedom is a power not of reason but of will, though Kant often conflated the two. For God, this conflation is perhaps thinkable but only on the presumption that God's reason and his will are extra-temporal. The notion of God as the Eternal Becoming may be seen as an attempt to synthesize rationality (permanence) and creativity (newness) in the notion of divine extra-temporality. Outside of time, God can both be and come to be at once; the ancient tension between Being and Becoming, permanence and newness, is resolved in the extra-temporality of God. But for temporal humans, reason can only be the power of discovery, of understanding things as they exist, while will is the power of creativity, the making of something that does not yet exist. For earthly humans, discovery by reason and creation by will are irreconcilable as ultimate sources of law. Kant tried to solve the problem by arguing that humans share God's supratemporality.[14] Anything less than the belief that we belong to the timelessness of the noumenal realm of things in themselves, the realm of existential self-sufficiency, is inadequate for the syncretism of reason and will.

If the God of the philosophers is the idea of pure unconditioned existence, Kant's noumenon is its heaven. The supernaturalistic theory of the noumenal was not just an awkward complication in the Kantian philosophy but the indispensable foundation for his understanding of higher freedom, which was "freedom in the strictest, that is, the transcendental sense."[15] His attempt was to work out the implications of the idea of autonomy properly understood as the power of self-existence, which he knew requires one to understand oneself as a member of a higher realm of self-being. Moral autonomy is made possible only by one's noumenal self-sufficiency, the power of self-existence. The moral law within us, argued Kant, provides us with practical evidence of the intelligibility of the noumenal realm but autonomy is more than moral self-rule. It is only one manifestation of the higher power of existential self-sufficiency. For Kant, who understood the idea properly but failed to ground his belief in reason alone, autonomy is nothing apart from the larger power of godly creativity.

The Autonomy Complex

It has been said that at the center of every great philosopher's edifice, there is a simple idea.[16] Much of the emerging modern western philosophy, especially in the Continental tradition, is the various and complex retelling of the simple post-Christian story of human self-creativity. Because it is otherworldly and amorphous, the image of self-creativity could be imagined as embodied, realized or naturalized in many ways. Spreading from Germany, self-existentialism came to be associated with a wide variety of higher objects, including the ideal of diversity itself. As Arthur Lovejoy wrote of the "principle of plenitude" in the late eighteenth century:

> Since the strain in Western thought summed up in the doctrine of the Great Chain of Being thus consisted in an increasing emphasis on the conception of God as insatiably creative, it followed that the man who, as moral agent or as artist, would imitate God, must do so by being himself "creative."[17]

Lovejoy's famous work describes the pervasiveness of the principle of plentitude throughout the Christian millennia, yet it too is only one version of the story of self-creationism. Other versions are familiar. For Hegel, history is the process of the self-creation of *Geist*, the human mind or spirit, which knows itself as self-created when it awakes to self-consciousness at the end of history. Marx praised Hegel for recognizing "the self-creation of man" but inverted him so that Hegel's process of mental production became the simple power of physical labour.[18] Hence man is self-creative "not only intellectually, in his consciousness, but actively and actually, and he can therefore contemplate himself in a world he himself has created."[19] The post-Marxist Herbert Marcuse later repeated the idea that "Labor is man's 'act of self-creation,'" which he precisely identified as man's "being and becoming."[20] Schopenhauer's "will to live," Nietzsche's "will to power" and Bergson's *élan vital* are variations on the idea of a primal force of self-existence. Bergson described it as "life, the power of creation which makes and remakes itself at every instant."[21] Freud was obsessed with sexuality because he identified libido with the instinct for self-existence. For existentialists like Sartre, self-existence is prior to self-essence: we are not beings who *have* creativity, we *are* creativity–our subsequent essence comes from our antecedent self-creativity.[22] For European post-structuralists, there are no pre-existing structures of reality other than those of human self-making. For Derridean deconstructionists, *différance* is the coinage combining "difference" and "deference," which are the respective modes by which we create spatiality (we *differ* one point from another) and temporality (we *defer* one moment from the next).[23] Hence we are the creators of the basic parameters of reality, space and time. In the jargon of post-modernism, the "facticity" of life does not mean factuality. "Facticity" instead signals the belief that the facts of reality are of human making. This belief was characterized rightly by Heidegger in the biblical terminology of Exodus 3:14: "[I]n a concretely factical manner, from out of my 'I am' – from out of my spiritual, indeed factical heritage … existence rages."[24] When academics speak of the "social construction" of reality, they convey both skepticism about the givenness of reality and optimism for the possibilities of communal self-invention. The characterization of nations as "imagined communities" has been copied by thousands who have not read the ambivalent work from which the phrase came because it captures the copied idea of creativity as political unity.[25]

The idea of self-creativity has been copied from Christianity in many ways, sometimes differently by a single thinker, but always it is a borrowing and never a creation.[26] Modern adherents have this belief because they are members of a culture of ideas copied from previous thinkers, who similarly were not inventors but retellers with alternative versions in which the part of the self-creative character was played by different actors – history, *Geist,* the poets, the artists, the social rebels, the revolutionaries, the French Citizen, the Soviet Comrade, the laboring class, the *Übermensch,* the Individual, the nationalist leaders, the community, the nation, the youth, the wise, the engaged and so on. The talent of the retellers was in producing competing versions of a central story that their audiences were predisposed by an old culture to find profound. The popularity of the thinkers who articulated these borrowed beliefs is not due to their creativity but is evidence of the ubiquity of creationism in the culture of modernity. What was powerful in their various stories was not the parts that were new or different but the central part, which was old and copied.

Among non-philosophers, the unexamined belief that one is self-creative, which is manifested in lay believers more as a *feeling* of expectation than as an articulated self-concept, has been understandably popular. It is a belief that promises to humans the greatest power imaginable in the idea that the Being-of-Being, the power for existence, is inside oneself. This is the belief that Luther and Calvin taught not just to Rousseau and Kant but to the culture of post-Christian Europe. Look inside yourself, said Luther, not for the puny human will but for the infinitely greater power of godliness. Do not look outward to the church but inside yourself for God. Deny your own will in order to feel the divine will within you. Your redemption can be found only in the residing godliness within yourself, which if you are saved has taken the place of your fallen humanness. This is the central thought of the German philosophy and the spiritual core of the inarticulate self-creationism of the broader lay culture.[27]

Self-existence for ordinary believers is an inherited family story, half-forgotten in the background of self-understanding, which nonetheless provides post-Christians with enchanted hopes and self-expectations. These are expressed as feelings, rather than theories, about how their lives should be. Severed from the knowledge that self-creativity is a supernatural concept that does not belong to the realities of nature, the belief in autonomy produces an inevitable reaction. When expectations of enchantedness fail to be satisfied in modern life, the result is feelings of disappoint and distrust. Trapped in a mundane reality with expectations of something greater, one cannot help feeling commensurately frustrated and disappointed. We were promised the heavenly power of self-creativity but we do not have it on earth. It is as if we were thrown out of our proper home. We are magical beings in our essence but earthly beings in our present reality, self-creators lost in a fallen world. Our power is our sin when it appears as earthly, but when it is absent we yearn for it as our lost essence. Hence autonomy is both our guilt and our loss.

Autonomy and alienation are the obverse faces of a single coin of thought but its manifest effects are more emotional than conceptual. The belief in unearthly power causes feelings of earthly guilt and disappointment. Alienation is the *feeling* of loss when the enthusiasms and ecstasies of autonomy–the *feelings* of godly possibility– have receded and one returns to the prosaic world of constraints and heteronomy. Alienation is the post-Christian feeling that this fallen earth is not our true home, that we are self-creative beings in an other-created world. We are trapped in this *alien* world, this other-made realm into which we have *fallen*. Our true nature is to be self-caused and existentially unconditioned, and so we feel alienated from and oppressed by this objective world of other-causality and conditional existence. Just as autonomy is the religious feeling of our self-creative power, alienation is the feeling of religious disappointment when we look about us at the world as it is. The autonomy complex is this combination of worldly unhappiness produced by unworldly expectations.

Feelings of alienation and oppression are the common political neuroses (and sometimes worse) of post-Christianity.[28] For the alienated self-creationist, science and technology are not tools of human convenience but are the manifestation of a deeply oppressive "machine world." The world of technology lacks the magic of nothing-POOF-something, the power of creativity *ex nihilo*, promised to us by our post-biblical culture. I have the power of creation within myself, said the Bible and two-thousand years of Christianity, but here I am, trapped in the world of scientific reality that I did not create and over which I have no power. Having been over-promised the power of autonomy, modern believers feel abandoned as magical beings in an unmagical world.

For articulations of the discontents of autonomy, we must turn again to the philosophers. The post-Christian story of loss and disappointment has been variously retold, sometimes with self-awareness.[29] When Romantics rebel against rationalism and technology, they are expressing both their alienation from reality and their longing for the lost innocence of the origin. Romantics look inward for the pureness of natural sentiment, just as Luther had looked inward for God. When Rousseau had his famous epiphany on the road to Vincennes, he saw the possibilities of primal autonomy lost to the oppressions of civilized life. For Marx, labour under capitalism is our self-creativity in its fallen, earthly form. "Labour is *man's coming to be for himself*," but capitalism reduces our higher power to that of mere individualized self-sustenance.[30] Under capitalism, the divine-human life force is rendered into a mere object of exchange. "Money is the estranged essence of man's work and existence…. The god of the Jews has been secularized and become the god of the world."[31] For Heidegger, *Dasein* is not merely *Sein* or "Being" but "Being *There*," which is the situatedness of *pure* being in a constrained world of *thereness*.[32] For existentialists, we are thrown into the world – thrown out of heaven! – condemned to be responsible for the realm of our entrapment. Existentialism is the religious philosophy of god-men abandoned to earth. When Freudians say that mental illness is caused by repression, they mean that the instinctive life force within us, the creative power of self-existence which we cannot see but which is our higher essence, has been oppressed and estranged from us.

In European nihilism, as described by Karl Löwith, *nihil* is the prerequisite to creativity:

> At the same time as Marx and Kierkegaard, all the other radical followers of Hegel made the negation of what exists into the principle of their thinking. Marx destroys the capitalist world; Kierkegaard intensifies the "absolute negativity" of romantic irony up to the point of leaping into faith; Stirner placed himself upon "Nothing"; Feuerbach says that we must be "absolutely negative" in order to create something new; and Bauer demands "heroic deeds from out of Nothing" as the presupposition of new worlds.[33]

A better name for this nihilism is creationism *ex nihilo*. In Nietzsche's version of the post-Christian story, the will to annihilation is preliminary to the will to self-creation. When Nietzsche wrote of "the will to nothingness, nihilism," and again of "the 'last will' of man, his will to nothingness, nihilism" in which "man would rather will *nothingness* than *not* will,"[34] his diagnosis of modernity was not dark but hopeful. He did not see the nihilism of his age necessarily as weakness and passivity; he thought it could be the precursor to creativity, "a sign of increased power of the spirit: as *active* nihilism."[35] This kind of nihilism for Nietzsche was the empowering belief that comes when one realizes that "becoming has no goal and that underneath all becoming there is no grand unity," from which it follows that "one grants the reality of becoming as the only reality."[36] Nihilism therefore is only the beginning of the formula, the preliminary stage for the creationism of the *Übermensch* to follow.

But in reality the *Übermensch*, like Godot, never comes. Nietzsche never found the will to power over nature but died mad of physical causes. For living believers, creationism *ex nihilo* can only lead to disappointment as the expected two-part drama stalls forever in the first act. The promise of magic is always elsewhere and never comes to earth. Nihilism for its believers is the endless wait for creativity. Among those for whom the wait becomes tedious or unbearable, nihilism inevitably turns to the weakness of defeat that Nietzsche abhorred.

The religious idea of self-creativity, transformed into the semi-secular belief in autonomy, inevitably produces feelings of alienation and oppression. The culture of modernity idolizes creativity and newness but these ideas are borrowed and old. As secular beliefs, they are inauthentic to themselves. For those who are authentically religious, creativity belongs ultimately only to God, while for those who are authentically secular, such creativity is unreal. In the real world in which truth is discovered rather than created, the belief in autonomy can only lead to disillusionment and distrust.

Alienated post-Christians do not know the source of their unhappiness because they have forgotten the genesis and proper meaning of their belief. Marx at least knew, as he followed thinkers like Hegel and Feuerbach in transposing the idea of creativity from the divine to the human, that he was writing of the ontological power of self-creation. He knew that he was redescribing the supernatural power of self-existence as the ordinary power of labour. He also knew that he was retelling an older story of alienation as the spiritual loss by humans of their self-creative essence. Marx knew that these were religious stories, which he consciously reframed as secular because he believed them without believing in God. Before him, Kant knew noumenal freedom was a godlike power and Hegel knew the supernaturalism of his idea of the human *Geist*, while more recently Heidegger understood the religiosity of his Nazi period. "Do we know of this spiritual mission? ... Does this essence truly have the power to shape our existence? It does, but only if we *will* this essence fully."[37] For self-aware believers, like the Protestant existentialist Paul Tillich, alienation is an explicitly religious phenomenon in which humans feel the loss of godliness as estrangement from their true and higher being.[38] In any form, alienation is the feeling that in one's present concrete reality, one has been separated from one's true and higher being. This story comes from and belongs to religion. As secular, it is a false belief that causes real but misunderstood feelings.

This loss of understanding is a self-reinforcing error. Those who idolize creativity and newness must deny the influence of old ideas, which leads them to oppose the obvious truth that creativity and newness are old and borrowed. This is not a "paradox" or an "irony" but a simple mistake, a failure of recognition caused by a self-perpetuating falsehood. The denial that one has merely borrowed the idea of creativity is caused by the desire to see oneself as the creator of one's own ideas. This leads believers in autonomy to misunderstand the source and meaning of their unhappiness. Instead of recognizing that life on earth is constrained and heteronomous and that the expectations of higher autonomy are unreal, modern semi-secularists tend to feel oppressed by ordinary social processes and structures. Society is an "iron cage" of oppression, lamented the depressive Max Weber.[39] But Weber still knew that disenchantment was the loss of *religious* enchantment. For today's semi-secularists, feelings of oppression remain palpable as the loss of higher freedom but the knowledge that this belief is supernatural has been lost. Hence the semi-secular believer in autonomy easily sees oppression where in reality there are only the natural constraints of society in which no one has supernatural power.

Words like reality are not popular among self-creationists, who would put it in scare-quotes, and yet they must live in a reality that resists their power. Rather than facing the reality that the world is not of their own making, post-Christians look for the dark sources of villainy that "keep the people down." Even their clichés express the metaphor of fallenness, the hopeful obverse of which is "the political will" to create a new reality on earth. When these expectations fail, it is not because they were unreal but because some oppressive force has appropriated this godly power. The absence of our higher power for the believer cannot be caused by false expectations but must be caused by some earthly others who have autonomous power over us. There must be oppressors at large in the world because we do not have the kind of freedom we believe in. For the believer, one's lack of power is sufficient to prove that someone else has taken it. It cannot be that this theory of freedom is false. If we are alienated from our promised freedom, we must be oppressed by someone. The only legitimate question is whom or what social structure to blame. Fortunately, because the idea is amorphous, it can be imagined in many forms.

Because it arises from an occluded self-understanding, the autonomy complex is manifested more often in feelings than in articulated ideas. It is the *feeling* that in one's higher self one is defined by the ontological autonomy of self-existence, which produces *feelings* of alienation from and oppression by the social and political structures of modernity. The autonomy complex causes its sufferers to look for sources of their unhappiness in social structures and entities that for non-believers represent merely the given order and ordinary constraints of modern life. Believers in autonomy often imagine new forms of self-being – nature, artistic expression, social activism, political solidarity, self-actualization movements, spiritualism, communalism, and so on – to which they can attach themselves to recapture their lost existential power. But the constraints of earthly life always intrude and the promised power inevitably fails to appear. Earthly disappointments, the emotions of alienation and oppression, are unavoidably produced by the unreal hope for magic on earth.

As obverse faces of a single affective complex, feelings of oppression, or feelings of solidarity with those one thinks are oppressed, represent the emotional longing for autonomous power. The political conception of oneself as alienated and oppressed is driven by the same emotional need as the desire to project the image of victimhood onto some chosen group.

Thus the autonomy complex fosters the politics of victimhood even when the ascribed victim groups are not themselves post-Christian. Moreover, the ideology of lost power may also be copied by non-Christians but their grievances are likely to have special resonance among post-Christians.

The Autonomy Complex in Canadian Politics

The Christian self-image resides in the background of modern thought as a half-forgotten family story that tells believers who they are.[40] They are creative, spontaneous, original and unique. They are self-actualizing, self-creative, self-realizing – they are Self-Beings. None of these ideals belonged to Athens; all of them came from Jerusalem by way of Rome and Wittenberg. Post-Christians believe all the world's billions are original and unique but in fact such beliefs belong to one part of one culture. Creationism is easily reduced to a feckless romanticism, as for example in the general retreat of academic postmodernism from politics to the literary arts. Among many citizens, however, it remains a popular belief system residing in the safely unexamined background of thought.

"You're not the boss of me!" cries the post-Christian child, the unknowing ideologue of autonomy. The reaction *by children* when they discover their lack of power against the constraints of social reality reveals the pervasiveness of the autonomy complex in the culture of modernity. We were promised that we were the children of freedom, the godly bosses of ourselves, and yet we are trapped in an other-world of constraints and unfreedom. We were born free but everywhere we are in chains. We are autonomous in our true selves but ruled falsely by earthly powers. We were once innocent, born into purity, and yet we are surrounded by decline and contamination. Our birthright is the garden of self-creativity and yet we live in a world of causal forces. "You're not the boss of me!" is the iconic wail, copied early by children from the soft culture, against the bonds and rules of society.

In Canada, the alien earthly power that most threatens our national autonomy is the dark force to the south. Our nation, our communal origin, has throughout our history been threatened by the dreaded Americans. Canadian nationalism is a protest against earthly oppression, a cry for the loss of communal self-creativity. Unlike patriotism, which is a positive attachment to communal achievements, nationalism is a negative lament for the creative power denied to us by an alien oppressor. This form of anti-Americanism in Canada is part of its collective child's cry for the power of self-being. Such Canadians may claim they dislike only certain politicians or policies but the feelings are too reactive and visceral to be explained in this way. Rather, it is the imagined American power of communal self-making that they fear and hate because they want it for themselves.

Nationalism is the creationism of people and state. It is an imagined script, borrowed from buried memory, in which the part of the creator is now played by the united people and in which creativity is primarily political. Thus nationalism requires not just social or cultural independence but the powers of a state. However, the belief in nationalism as communal autonomy produces the obverse emotions of alienation and oppression. This emotional circle, feelings of empowerment followed by feelings of disempowerment, results in cycles of grievance and inaction. The leading Canadian example is in Quebec. Whenever feelings of imagined power arise among *independiste* Quebecers, the corresponding feelings of weakness emerge in equal measure. Nationalism in Quebec will always lack the confidence of finality because its expectations are heavenly while its reality is mundane. In a natural universe in which enchantment is false, the wait for its promise is endless.

If a realistic threat to Canadian unity appears in the future, it will be based not on creative nationalism but on traditionalistic patriotism. The latter is a concept of inheritance, not creation, whereas nationalism is a creative notion and therefore anti-traditional. Nationalistic Quebecers cannot be proud of their surviving traditions because autonomy is an idealization of future possibilities, not of past achievements. Creativity means overcoming what was, which is the opposite of upholding it. For such Quebecers, "*je me souviens*" is a lament for the loss of power, a declaration of oppression and alienation, rather than celebration of enduring traditions. I remember the loss of what should be. For nationalists, the past may be romanticized in the name of creativity but it cannot be a constraint on future self-making. Creationists must distrust the past because traditions, when they are active and regulative, *feel* oppressive and never *feel* liberating. Traditions are recalled with fondness only in their absence. Regulative traditions must be revolted against, even if the revolution undermines the foundations of patriotic community. The result in Quebec was the quietist revolution in which patriotic traditions were left behind for the infinitely distant promise of post-Christian newness.

Canadian economic nationalism overlaps with both socialism and nationalism. Socialism is communal self-creativity by economic means. Socialists see economic production not just as a means of sustenance and material comfort but more importantly as the primary mode of social self-being. By controlling the economy, socialists believe we will own the machinery of political self-production. Like socialists, economic nationalists vary in the degree to which they would limit private property but they share the fear of alienation and the desire for communal power via economics. The old biblical story in its half-forgotten form sometimes attracts those who have succeeded in business or management but who want greater powers or who want to see their worldly success as something more, so economic nationalism sometimes attracts followers who are neither socialists nor highly egalitarian. The spectre of alienation and the ghosts of creativity may haunt even those who otherwise live in the real world of work.

Canadian multiculturalism is the combination of the belief in the all-importance of culture together with the denial that Canada has its own. This attitude is satisfying to post-Christians because it combines the desire to eliminate the constraints of one's own traditions while romanticizing the traditions of others. Multiculturalism is the yearning for culture while retaining one's freedom from it. When cultural traditions can be seen as exotic and safely external to oneself, they may be revered. But if they have been institutionalized as regulative within one's own society, traditions are constraints that must be eliminated in favor of newness. For autonomists, culture is always about the possibility of one's own creativity and never about the inheritance of one's ancestors' creativity. The past is respected only in empty symbols like the buckskinned urban *poseur* in a canoe. The traditions that multiculturalists respect are of two sorts: (1) those that are merely romantic and lacking in regulative effect, and (2) those that belong to others and regulate only them. Canadian multiculturalists love the idea of tradition but only from afar. Seen from the inside, cultural traditions appear as a cage; seen from the outside, they are a delightful bazaar of self-possibilities. Hence multiculturalists want to deny that the existence of an assimilated Canadian culture, or a regional variety of Canadian assimilations, because assimilation implies that one accepts, rather than creates, one's traditions. The idea of assimilation is a sin not against anyone's traditions but against everyone's creativity. Immigrants should not assimilate because their purpose for multiculturalists is to represent the exotic possibilities, not the inherited realities, of culture. Come to the multicultural bazaar! See how creatively they sing and dance for us!

Aboriginal peoples for post-Christians represent natural innocence and closeness to nature. These two ideas, innocence and nature, have no implicit or necessary connection and in realistic connotations do not belong together, but they are combined easily in the imagination of a biblical culture because innocence represents proximity to the moment of creation. In the post-Christian understanding, Europeans with corrupt *earthly* power dispossessed aboriginals who, as first-born on this continent, were closer to the garden of origin. It is this background story that allows aboriginals to be easily romanticized as innocent and free from the tainted machine-world of industrial development. As Nietzsche knew, the Christian morality identifies earthly power with evil and victimhood with goodness. Hence feelings of guilt arise from feelings of power. The result is a self-conception among post-Christians that combines feelings of guilt with those of superiority. Hence "white guilt" may be felt by those who still feel superior. While some may feel guilty because white people, in common parlance, stole the land from aboriginals, few of those who express such feelings have thought of returning to their ancestral home. "White guilt" appears more often as an affective rather than as an action-producing belief. Moreover, the attribution of guilt for stealing land is not extended historically to aboriginal groups who dispossessed other aboriginals. Therefore, because (1) it appears almost exclusively as an expressive or affective belief, and since (2) it is an attribution specific to one race or culture, perhaps with some residue of feelings of superiority, the phenomenon of "white guilt" appears not to be fully explicable in terms of the actual blameworthiness for the true villainies of history. The latter were real and deserve blame, but as an explanatory factor for the phenomenon of "white guilt," they do not explain its primarily affective character and its cultural specificity. As a political attitude, the source of this feeling is cultural.

The identifier, "first nations," could not have been better chosen to appeal to the post-Christian consciousness, for which it has double connotations. Before the nineteenth-century modernization of the term, nation meant only common birth, from the Latin *nātus,* derived from *nascor,* to be born. In the eighteenth century, nation meant extended family or tribe, as in "the several Nations or Tribes of Indians" in the Royal Proclamation of 1763. Afterward, the meaning of nation, a word common to English and German, was transformed to take on further connotations of common territory in addition to common bloodlines. It is no cultural accident that the romanticization of aboriginals is especially prevalent in Germany in such phenomena as "Indian clubs" and the popular novels of Karl May. First in Germany, inspired by writers such as Herder and Goethe, the story of birth from God was secularized as the story of birth from the land: God the Father became the Fatherland. Hence nation came to have modern connotations, among others, of communal self-birth from a given soil. *Blut und Boden,* blood and soil, said later Germans more aggressively. In Canada, the Germanic concept of nation as territorial self-birth has been joined to the Christian notion of primogeniture, which in European history produced such political theories as the divine right of kings. In the Canadian coinage, "first nation," the noun connotes communal self-birth from the land while the adjective conveys the notion of first birth, closest to the creation. Hence the combined term suggests not just the legalism of first possession but for post-Christians resonates with the romantic subtext of communal autonomy together with moral innocence.

In the ideology if not the science of environmentalism, the autonomy complex produces a strong and consistent bias on the side of apocalyptic dread. This does not mean that environmental problems are not real but it does suggest they may be likely to be far less dreadful than feared by post-Christians. The historical record of problems that were once thought to be broadly catastrophic is long, with highlights including famine caused by overpopulation, ozone depletion, toxic waste, acid rain, DDT, mineral depletion, energy depletion, the loss of biodiversity, the loss of the rain forest, desertification, soil depletion and agricultural collapse, medicine-resistant plagues, pesticide-resistant insects, global cooling and now global warming. However, from Thomas Malthus to Rachel Carson to Paul Ehrlich and probably to Al Gore, the predictions of our environmental demise have always been exaggerations. When we observe a long historical pattern of failed predictions in which the error is consistently in the same direction, we have evidence of a systematic bias, which therefore must have a cause. The common factor is the dread, not the reality, of our demise. Hence the dread would appear to be caused not by the findings of environmental science but by something independent and prior.

Real environmental problems have a life cycle from growing awareness to improved management. The quality of air and water in most modern cities for example is dramatically better than in the past. Waste water treatment is a relatively recent industrial innovation. In the Great Smog of 1952, thousands of Londoners were killed. Today, the air of western industrialized cities is on average incomparably better than a half-century ago. Anyone old enough to have flooded a carburetor knows the improvements in automotive emissions. But ideological environmentalists resist acknowledging such improvements because for them, the need to solve particular problems is secondary to the emotional resonance of the larger story of environmental decline.

The emotional force of environmentalism is in the feelings of guilt and dread that belong to the autonomy complex. Environmentalists see nature not with the realism of scientists but with the enthusiasm of believers. "The planet" for environmentalists is not a warm rock in space but the primal force of life that we are "killing." For believers, "killing the planet" is not a hyperbolic metaphor but an actual, literal truth-claim. They recognize neither the exaggeration nor that it is a metaphor. "We are Killing the Planet. That is Not an Exaggeration," announced a major newspaper in the UK recently.[41] Canadian school children are taught such things as literal truths; a large majority of British Columbians think the world may end in a few decades because of global warming; and one of their most famous writers told Canadians they may soon "all choke and boil to death."[42] Since the belief that we are literally "killing" a living thing called "the planet" cannot be taken seriously as a scientific idea, neither in its terms of meaning nor in its scale of prediction, the source of the belief must be elsewhere than in science. People mistake the metaphor for literal truth because they believe in the godliness of self-existence, an idea that has been transposed metaphorically from the biblical God to "the planet." Humans are killing God in earthly form once again, though this time they blame not the Jews but the industrialists. The pattern repeats its central themes. We believe this story easily and thoughtlessly in our post-biblical culture because it is so familiar to us. We copy the trope of creativity without awareness because it is one of our oldest cultural codes.[43]

The beliefs of the past survive in the unrecognized metaphors of today. The forgotten metaphor of "the planet" is biblical. Unlike paganism, environmentalism is monotheistic and creationistic. Nature has been supernaturalized. "The planet" is not a mere physical thing or system; it is the highest power of creation that humans have defiled. We are alienated from nature, the self-existential life-force from which we came. To recover our natural innocence, we must again become "one" with nature, our godly Creator. Such ideas are not just rhetorical expressions but are the spiritual core of the post-Christian faith in "the planet." In a culture deeply shaped by the half-forgotten stories of the Bible, environmentalism resonates with the imagery of ideas selected and transposed from the older culture. The ideology of environmentalism, if not the science, is driven most powerfully by the cultural undercurrents of biblical ideas that structure many of today's popular understandings. For scientific environmentalists, the temptation may be to influence public policy by exploiting these beliefs but the danger is that their own thinking may be similarly affected. The background beliefs and hidden metaphors of post-Christian culture can be especially powerful among those best educated into its worldview.

In Canada, environmentalism of this ideological sort is likely to play an important role in exacerbating regional tensions. As the West rises in economic influence, many in the East will be attracted to the story of their alienation from their original power as the true and founding nation. The nationalist ideology produced by the autonomy complex can be easily joined to environmentalism, producing a story in which the alienated East is oppressed by the energy-rich West. In the oldest Canadian provinces, feelings of primogeniture and colonial ownership remain among those who believe they are the first-and-true nation. These emotions can easily be mobilized to support a program of energy policies with nationalist *cum* environmentalist goals, which would intensify regional conflict beyond anything that has been seen before.

Conclusion

The belief in autonomy and its cognates (self-creativity, self-actualization, self-realization and so on) is the product neither of reason nor of empirical observation but is entirely an inherited article of faith. The ideas of creativity and newness come neither from nature nor reason but only from culture and religion. Creativity is not the natural essence of all humans as such. It is only a cultural artifact with a parochial history. In its original form as an authentic religious belief, the idea of God's self-creativity is true to its own premises as founded in faith, but the belief that humans alone have this power does not belong to an authentic secularism. It is the belief in human magic.

The belief in creativity is a copy and thereby false to itself, and therefore any self-conception centered on human creativity is false. The false promise of autonomy as a secular expectation is the cause of the feelings of political alienation and oppression that characterize much of modernity. It is the empty promise of something that was never ours, producing an illusion of deprivation in its believers. The cause of such feelings is not the oppressions of reality but the magical belief in autonomy.

The question of religion in politics today is less a contest of secularists against religionists than it is a conflict of semi-secular or occluded religionists against those who are aware of themselves as religious. Authentic secularists remain comparatively rare. In Canada, church and state are thought to be separate but religious ideas have an influence far beyond what those who support this separation have recognized. The process of secularization may continue or perhaps we will return to a self-consciously religious age, but at present we are in an era of semi-secularism in which religious ideas are ubiquitous but often unseen.

Notes

[1] Those who project this idea onto others are conceptual imperialists in the tradition of the Christian missionaries, except that they knew what they were doing. For example, the popular guru of the "creative economy," Richard Florida: "The most overlooked – but most important – element of my theory and of the creative economy itself is that *every human being is creative*." Florida, "A Source of Creative Energy We're Fools Not to Tap," *Globe and Mail*, November 24, 2007, F1. Emphasis in original.

[2] Pope Benedict XVI (as Joseph Cardinal Ratzinger), *Introduction to Christianity*, trans. J.R. Foster (San Francisco: Communio Ignatio Press, 2004), 118.

[3] Walther Eichrodt, *Theology of the Old Testament*, trans. J.A. Baker (Philadelphia: Westminster Press, 1961), 1:39 ff.

[4] The Hebrew tradition in turn was influenced by earlier stories like the Babylonian creation myth. See for example Hermann Gunkel, "The Influence of Babylonian Mythology Upon the Biblical Creation Story," in *Creation in the Old Testament*, ed. Bernhard W. Anderson (Philadelphia: Fortress Press, 1984), 25-52.

[5] Walther Eichrodt suggested that ancient Near Eastern ideas about magic contributed to the Old Testament concept of creation *ex nihilo*. Eichrodt, *Theology of the Old Testament*, 2:101, fn. 1, and 2:103.

[6] Susan McCaslin, on CBC Radio, "The Divine Mr. Blake," *Sunday Edition*, November 18, 2007. The Blake scholar, Kevin Hutchings, has confirmed to me that this was Blake's view. Personal communication, November 24, 2007.

[7] Immanuel Kant, *Critique of Pure Reason*, trans. Paul Guyer and Allen W. Wood (Cambridge, UK: Cambridge U. Press, [1781/1787] 1997),   538 (AK A543-44/B571-72).

[8] Henry George Liddell and Robert Scott, *A Greek-English Lexicon*, rev. by Sir Henry Stuart Jones (Oxford: Clarendon Press, 1940), s.v. "νόμος." The word "nomia" (s.v. "νομία"), meaning lawfulness, appears in Liddell and Scott only as a "nonce-word" (a coinage used in one instance) to express the opposite of unlawfulness.

[9] Albrecht Dihle, *The Theory of Will in Classical Antiquity* (Berkeley: University of California Press, 1982), 18 ff.

[10] Alfred Weber, *History of Philosophy*, trans. Frank Thilly (New York: Charles Scribner's Sons, 1908), 376. Emphases in the original. See also, Richard Kroner, *Kant's Weltanschauung*, trans. John E. Smith (Chicago: University of Chicago Press, 1956), 6 ff.

[11] This terminology is taken from Carl Schmitt, *The Concept of the Political*, trans. G. Schwab (Chicago: University of Chicago Press, [1932] 1996), p. 53. Schmitt's legal-constitutional decisionism, based on the homology of human and divine sovereignty, led to his famous friend-enemy distinction as the essence of politics. Hence the theory of constitutive autonomy, secularized and pluralized, results in a pluriverse of self-created communities that are always at risk of existential conflict with each other. In recognizing this, Schmitt, perhaps more than Nietzsche, is the great anti-Kant.

---

[12] For example, it is only "the contingent, subjective conditions that distinguish one rational being from another," conditions having nothing to do with the power of lawgiving. Immanuel Kant, *Critique of Practical Reason,* trans. Mary Gregor (Cambridge, UK: Cambridge U. Press, [1788] 1997), 18 (AK 5:21).

[13] Kant, *Critique of Pure Reason,* 546 (AK A559/B587) and 550 (AK A566/B594).

[14] Kant, *Critique of Practical Reason,* 79 (AK 5:94) ff. See also Kant, *Critique of Pure Reason,* 536 (AK A539/B567).

[15] Kant, *Critique of Practical Reason,* 26 (AK 5:29). See also his discussion of "transcendental freedom" as supratemporal, 81 (AK 5:97).

[16] Bertrand Russell as recounted by Isaiah Berlin, *Political Ideas in the Romantic Age* (Princeton: Princeton University Press, 2006), 13.

[17] Arthur Lovejoy, *The Great Chain of Being: A Study of the History of an Idea* (New York: Harper and Row, 1960), 296.

[18] Karl Marx, "Economic and Philosophical Manuscripts," in *Early Writings,* trans. Rodney Livingstone and Gregor Benton (London: Penguin, 1974), 386.

[19] Marx, "Economic and Philosophical Manuscripts," 329.

[20] Quoted in Richard Wolin, *Heidegger's Children* (Princeton: Princeton University Press, 2001), 64.

[21] Henri Bergson, *The Meaning Of The War: Life and Matter In Conflict,* trans. H.W. Carr (London: T. Fisher Unwin, 1915), 38.

[22] For a summary of the post-Christian nature of existentialism and alienation, see Paul Tillich *Theology of Culture* (London: Oxford University Press, 1959), especially "Aspects of a Religious Analysis of Culture," 40-51; "Existentialist Philosophy: Its History and Meaning," 76-111; and "The Theological Significance of Existentialism and Psychoanalysis," 112-26.

[23] Jacques Derrida, "Différance," in *Margins of Philosophy,* trans. Alan Bass (Chicago: University of Chicago Press, 1982), pp 3-27.

[24] Martin Heidegger, letter to Karl Löwith, August 19, 1921, reproduced in Karl Löwith, *Martin Heidegger and European Nihilism,* trans. Gary Steiner (New York: Columbia University Press, 1995), 236.

[25] Benedict Anderson, *Imagined Communities: Reflections on the Origins and Spread of Nationalism,* rev. edn. (London: Verso, 2006).

[26] "In the early 1930s, Heidegger effortlessly transposed the essential concepts of *Being and Time* [1927] ... from the individual "Self" to the Dasein of the German Volk." Richard Wolin, summarizing Löwith's observation, in *Heidegger's Children* (Princeton: Princeton University Press, 2001), 86-87.

[27] For the role of the desire for redemption in the emergence of a range of modern political ideologies, see Mark Lilla, *The Stillborn God: Religion, Politics, and the Modern West* (New York: Alfred. A. Knopf, 2007).

[28] As an example of self-existentialism in more pathological form, Heidegger in a referendum campaign speech in 1933 told German voters that "the Führer ... is giving the people the most immediate possibility of the highest free decision: whether it – the whole people – wills its own Dasein.... There is only one will to the full Dasein of the state. The Führer has brought this will into full awakening." Quoted in Löwith, *Martin Heidegger and European Nihilism,* 162.

[29] For the premodern and early modern history of the concept of alienation, see Ernest Tuveson, "Alienation in Christian Theology," and David McLellan, "Alienation in Hegel And Marx," in *Dictionary of the History of Ideas,* ed. Philip P. Wiener (New York: Charles Scribner's Sons, 1973), 1: 34-37 and 1:37-41.

[30] Marx, "Economic and Philosophical Manuscripts," 386.

[31] Karl Marx, "On the Jewish Question," in *Early Writings*, 239.

[32] In the 1979 film, "Being There," the main character is named "Chance," meaning the uncaused one, who in the end walks on water.

[33] Löwith, *Martin Heidegger and European Nihilism*, 203.

[34] Friedrich Nietzsche, *On The Genealogy of Morals*, in *Basic Writings of Nietzsche,* ed. and trans. Walter Kaufmann (New York: Modern Library, 1992), 532, 558, 599. Emphasis in original.

[35] Friedrich Nietzsche, *The Will to Power,* trans. by Walter Kaufmann and R. J. Hollingdale (New York: Vintage Books, 1968), 17. Emphases in original.

[36] Nietzsche, *Will to Power*, 13.

[37] Martin Heidegger, "The Self-Assertion of the German University," in *The Heidegger Controversy,* ed. Richard Wolin (Cambridge, MA: MIT Press, 1993), 29. Emphasis in original.

[38] See for example Paul Tillich, "Estrangement and Sin," in *The Essential Tillich*, ed. Forrester Church (Chicago: University of Chicago Press, 1999), 165-67.

[39] The accuracy of this translation of Weber's "*ein stahlhartes Gehäuse*" has been disputed but the point remains. The popularity of the metaphor is evidence of the pandemic belief. Stephen A. Kent, "Weber, Goethe, and the Nietzschean Allusion: Capturing the Source of the "Iron Cage" Metaphor," *Sociological Analysis*, 44 (1983), 297.

[40] An alternative story of human nature came from Anglo-empiricism in thinkers like Hobbes, Locke and Hume. Islam has another, in which humans are not self-creative but are to be submissive.

[41] *The Independent,* June 23, 2005.

[42] In the *Globe and Mail*, a story entitled, "Mommy, Why are You Killing the Planet?" reported on "pint-sized eco-warriors" (October 5, 2007). In British Columbia, 72% of poll respondents agreed that "the world may not last much longer than another couple of generations" due to global warming (*Vancouver Sun*, November 18, 2006). According to a column by Margaret Atwood, "the Earth is hotter now than it's been for millenniums ... how long will it take before we all choke and boil to death?" (*Globe and Mail*, November 10, 2006).

[43] See the contribution in this volume by John von Heyking for the effect of this code in the Canadian legal system.

CHAPTER FOUR

STAKING OUT SACRED SPACE:
MUSLIMS IN CANADIAN POLITICS

PAUL S. ROWE

A widening trend in Western societies has been the growth of Muslim populations and the polarization of socio-cultural relations between East and West. The theme has been picked up by an explosion of scholarship detailing the impact of social differences at the international and domestic levels, dealing with the sociological, political, and security implications of the phenomenon.[1] In Canada, the increasing diversity of sources of immigration has encouraged the growth of the Muslim population, although the social impact has not been either as destabilizing or as radicalizing as in Western Europe. Until recently there was some feeling that Canada's Muslim population was immune from radicalized Islam. While the arrest of seventeen young Muslim men on charges of planning terrorist incidents in June 2006 has challenged this assumption, the participation of Muslims in Canadian politics remains remarkably peaceful and democratically sophisticated. By and large, Muslims have adapted remarkably well to the pluralist[2] model of interest representation and the representative model of democracy in Canadian politics.

On a surface level, Canada pursues a pluralist model of interest representation in the matter of religion. The state is secular and does not claim a particular sectarian viewpoint, nor does the state work to organize religious groups in civil society along the lines common under the European model. In public policy discussions, the state consults with a wide variety of interested groups, each of which maintains autonomy in its organization. There are anomalies in this pattern. For example, Canada's constitution recognizes the special rights of Roman Catholic separate schools. Religious organizations are provided special status in the practice of solemnizing marriages under the common law tradition of banns. However, the practice of funding religious institutions through tax credits for charitable donations and the general tendency to avoid government

involvement in religious affairs or in advocating particular religious viewpoints frames the secular pluralist approach.

The relative level of success of Muslim groups in participating in Canadian politics comes as a result of the complex relationship between the diversity of the Muslim population in terms of ideology, class, sect, and ethnic background and the pluralist form of interest representation common in Canada. Jelen and Wilcox have described the American religious arena in terms of religious competition in the marketplace of ideas.[3] A general overview of Canadian religious life displays a similar level of diversity and innovation. Whereas individual Muslims and groups tend to eschew the forms of voluntarism that create an open marketplace of religion among Christians in North America, this has not limited their involvement in a wide variety of advocacy organizations, community networks, and devotional communities. Despite a relative unity of religious identity among Muslims (albeit divided among Sunni, Shi'i and minority sects), the Muslim community in Canada is characterized by a plethora of self-constituted groups that is a quintessential hallmark of the pluralist model.

Elsewhere, Eickelman and Piscatori have described the adaptive ability of Muslim communities among immigrant populations in Western states to address what have become global Muslim concerns.[4] They identify three ways in which a transnational religious consciousness in these communities has had political effects in Western societies. First, they form a wide range of organizations around the Islamic call (known as *dawa*) to revivalism, the spread of the faith, and dissemination of information about Islam. Second, they consolidate ties with coreligionists abroad, strengthening the global solidarity of the worldwide community of Muslims (the *umma*) against the challenge of Western secularism, tethering the development of minority communities to overseas majority communities, and challenging attempts to integrate Muslim minorities into their host societies. Finally, they identify with a range of Muslim interests, defined by the peculiar distinctives of the Muslim faith and the foreign policies of various societies toward the issue of Palestine and the plight of Muslims in war-torn nations.[5] In the years since Eickelman and Piscatori first made their observations, these political effects have only intensified, sometimes threatening to erupt in violent incidents inspired by radicals, always threatening to alienate individual Muslims from the foreign policies of their new homes.

This paper explores the participation of Muslim-Canadians in political life, arguing that the events of 9/11 created a crisis that Muslims were forced to confront in order to reshape the image and place of Islam in

Western societies including Canada. Even though individual Muslims perceived that 9/11 unfairly increased the fear and suspicion of Islamic social movements in Canadian society, Muslim groups have actually made great strides toward gaining prominence and significance. What is more, the challenges have opened up new opportunities for individual Muslims to be involved in public affairs. There remain challenges to Muslim participation, but by and large these are related to the very pluralism that simultaneously boosts innovation and initiative among Canadian Muslims.

Muslims in Canadian Public Life to 2000

Up to the close of the 1990s, Muslims in Canada were perceived in many ways as a marginalized ethnic and immigrant group with few resources for public activism and only localized and sporadic responses to the majority community.[6] This comes in spite of a long-established Muslim community existing since the mid-1930s.[7] Their political clout was equally marginal, with minimal representation in the political elite and weak organization of interests. Into the late 1990s, Muslims remained a curiosity concentrated in enclaves in major Canadian cities. In 1983, Baha Abu-Laban noted that although the Muslim population had grown significantly larger over the period from 1951 to 1980, this group consisted largely of single young men of a diversity of backgrounds, displaying little in the way of institutional organization.[8] Into the 1990s, assessments of the Canadian Muslim community remained focused upon sociological, anthropological, and ethnic studies that reflected the various ways in which non-native Muslims interacted with Canadian society and service provision.

Scholars explored various coping mechanisms for Muslims seeking to live and work within the multicultural and nominally Christian society to which they had come. For example, by the 1990s a wide variety of particular institutions had arisen to serve the Muslim community, such as *halal* butcher shops, provision for loans without interest (proscribed by some readings of Islamic law), and informal community networks.[9] Nevertheless, Muslim political participation was primarily attached to the universal franchise provided under the constitution and on the basis of "accommodation" to Canadian norms.[10] Aside from questions of community integration, internal struggles over identity, and other primarily sociological questions, there was little feeling that the Muslim population had an important role to play in Canadian politics. This was true in spite of a widening interest in the growth of Muslim communities in diaspora among European states and through immigration and conversion in the United States, remarked by a variety of scholars over the years from the mid-1980s to the mid-1990s.[11] In the Canadian case, Muslims were little different from other small religious groups of exotic or sectarian origin: indeed, smaller or more concentrated groups were more likely to be considered relevant to particular areas of the country. Muslims remained relatively unorganized as a political force beyond the various cultural communities in which they were represented at local and national levels.

Various influences contributed to their marginalization as a political force. Marginalization did not arise due to poor levels of education nor from lack of concentration, for Muslims were better educated than the average in Canada and were also concentrated in particular constituencies and urban areas.[12] Their numbers remained relatively small, but were growing substantially in the 1990s from just over 200 000 in 1990 to an estimated 500 000 by the year 2000, a number which has likely already grown past 700 000.[13] However, there was very little thought given to the distinctions in Muslim voting patterns given the size of the community and its division among several provinces. Ethnic divisions were generally more significant, given that Muslims speak many languages and come from a variety of ethnic backgrounds, including south Asian groups with divergent languages, Arabs, Turks, Somalis, and other Africans. It was also significant that Muslims in Canada were not proportionally represented along the lines of the worldwide Muslim community (*umma*), making the Canadian Muslim community somewhat more heterodox than most Muslim communities elsewhere. For example, Nizari Ismailis (a minority Shi'i sect led by the Agha Khan) became a large and established Canadian Muslim community, particularly in the wake of the expulsion of south Asians from Uganda by Idi Amin. This is a group that shares little in common with either the mainstream Sunni or Shi'i traditions but nonetheless has had a dominant role in defining the Muslim minority in the country. Finally, there was the natural inclination for many Muslim émigrés to avoid political identification as Muslims, since many had deliberately fled the impact of political Islam in countries such as Iran (following the 1979 Islamic Revolution) and Lebanon (throughout the Civil War of the late 1970s and 1980s).

Muslims did actively pursue the institutionalization of community-based organizations and occasionally united in national initiatives such as the Council of Muslim Communities of Canada, but inherent divisions, local dispersion, and other natural institutional challenges meant that Muslims were not a politically significant force. They continued to face up to a lack of interest and consideration of Muslim customs and perspectives.

According to Shaheen Azmi, "Gross ignorance o[f] and insensitivity to Islamic mores and norms was universally agreed to be a problem which still persists despite efforts to sensitive mainstream agencies to 'ethnicity'."[14] Absent a recognized institutional interlocutor under Canadian pluralism, arriving Muslims had not yet created self-constituting representation to the larger society.

However, by the late 1990s, the growth of the Muslim community in relative numbers, particularly in clustered diaspora communities in urban and suburban areas of cities such as Montreal, Toronto, Mississauga, Brampton, and London, was beginning to have an impact on local politics. In some urban areas, Muslim communities reached a critical mass and Muslim congregations were able to form functional and suitably financed institutions surrounding mosques and community centres. Traditional Muslims began to find common cause with Christian and Jewish school networks in pressing for choice in education and the provision of full funding to Muslim community schools in the province of Ontario under the aegis of the Ontario Multi-Faith Coalition for Equity in Education in the mid-1990s. This initiative was defeated in a decision of the Supreme Court of Canada to uphold the constitutionality of solely funding public and separate schools in that province under *Adler v. Ontario* in 1996.[15] Nevertheless, the initiative was a watershed, demonstrating a more assertive community organizing as Muslims rather than in reference to varied ethnic backgrounds and one that was not averse to forming partnerships with likeminded activists from other religious communities. It matched observations made by scholars at the time that Muslims were increasingly organized around religious difference as a mode of organization. Studying the communal habits of Somali immigrants in the city of Toronto, one scholar observed that such ethnic communities were more strongly identifying with a Muslim identity than an African one, raising the profile of the religious cleavage as a foundational notion of identity.[16]

One episode revealed the increasing strength of Muslim political activation in the area of London, Ontario in mid-1996. The matter arose in the wake of a rally of conservative Christians known as the "March for Jesus", after which a local minister made reference in a public prayer to the "darkness and deception of the Spirit of Islam."[17] What was remarkable was not the affront that the remarks made to area Muslims so much as the strength and effect of the reaction. In the week that followed, the incident filled the headlines of the local newspaper. A local education board trustee who was also a Muslim brought the issue to light through contacting reporters. Four days after the march, a group of Muslim activists announced a march of their own in order to prove that Muslims were a positive and constructive community which contributed vibrantly to the culture of the city.[18] The ensuing "march for tolerance" drew a large crowd of over 1000 people, mostly Muslims, many of them veiled women.[19] At the end of the day, Muslims claimed a moral victory and reported that inquiries from the general public about Islam and Muslim social activities increased markedly. In addition, the profile of the education trustee at the heart of the incident increased and arguably contributed to his later election to city council.

By the late 1990s, seeing an increase in immigration flows in the form of refugees from countries such as Somalia, Afghanistan, and (in the wake of the NATO intervention of 1998-1999) Kosovo, Muslims continued to increase in number and organization. Observing the increasing assertiveness of Muslim populations in Western societies in seeking accommodation for their own religious institutions and practices, Yvonne Yazbeck Haddad noted "the experience of a general movement from being unnoticed in their overall populations to moving into positions of greater visibility and more obvious public participation."[20] Muslims were beginning to transcend their status primarily as immigrants in a foreign community and taking ownership of their Canadian citizenship as participants in defense of their own concerns and interests.

9/11 and After: A New Urgency

The attacks launched against the New York World Trade Center and the Pentagon on September 11, 2001 had an immediate impact in creating a feeling of siege among Canadian Muslims, as it did for Muslims throughout Western societies. It created a new urgency for Muslims to find interlocutors in the Canadian milieu, and as such underscored the extent to which Muslims were still strongly divided and leaderless as a political force. At the same time, many shared the feeling that the events of 9/11 polarized the public and emboldened press attacks on Muslims, even as it granted freedom to authorities and individual citizens to target identifiable Muslims as potential enemies of the state. Reports of harassment of Muslims and vandalism against mosques added to the level of fear felt in the community.[21] The suspicion of Muslims flowed out of established skepticism of a faith that had been used to justify violent actions throughout the world over the last decade, even as Canada boasted a multicultural ideal.[22]

There was certainly reason for the government to show concern over potential security risks, given that radical Islamists had been active in

Canada in the past. The arrest of Ahmed Ressam, an Algerian who had been evading extradition from Canada, at the US border in December 1999 and his subsequent conviction for planning a terrorist strike at the Los Angeles Airport on New Year's Eve underlined the potential activity of Islamist radicals in the country. In the wake of the 9/11 attacks and the invasion of Afghanistan in 2001, news reports also highlighted the case of the Khadr family. Egyptian-Canadian Ahmed Khadr (killed in Pakistan in early October that year) in addition to his four sons were found to be involved in various ways among the al Qaeda and Taliban movements in Afghanistan. Later it arose that at least two were being held by American forces in detention at the American base in Guantanamo Bay, Cuba. One of these, Abdurahman, was released and eventually returned to Canada in November 2003, to tell a sensational story of the way the CIA attempted to recruit him to spy on al Qaeda.[23] Stories such as these, and the later arrest of alleged terrorist plotters in June 2006, focused Canadian citizens on the potential threats coming from radical movements.

Although Muslims were never explicitly targeted by government agencies as an identifiable group, in practice restrictive measures that arose in the wake of the terrorist incidents gave greater discretion to security services to engage in investigations and interventions. Individual Muslims came to believe that these discretionary procedures would be used to target them *en masse*. In particular, the introduction of the October 2001 *Anti-terrorism Act* and the June 2002 *Immigration and Refugee Protection Act* introduced new policies designed to restrict access. Most of these policies involve interdiction, pre-entry screening, and the use of new technologies to collect information about individuals entering and leaving the country. However, division 6 of the *Immigration and Refugee Protection Act* enshrined the decade-long practice of detaining foreign nationals held to be a danger to Canadian security under the administration of "security certificates."[24] Since 2001, this practice has invariably targeted suspected Islamist militants, and therefore tends almost entirely to target foreign Muslims on Canadian soil.

What was more, the increased profile of security cases in the years following 9/11 appeared disproportionately aimed at Muslims. In September 2002, the detention and rendition of Maher Arar, a Muslim Canadian born in Syria, became a rallying point for protests against new security measures at home and abroad. Arar was rendered back to his country of origin to face interrogation and torture, to be released a year later, able to tell his own story and raise public questions about the complicity of the Canadian security services in providing the intelligence that caused American officials to act. Arar's case proceeded to shine a light on the similar case of Abdullah Almalki and the continued practice of detention under security certificates. Muslims also fell victim to the increasingly strident restrictions placed on foreign-born Canadians and sought to bring attention to the issue.[25] This growing list of complaints against security controls pushed the Muslim public toward activism.

The 9/11 attacks and the increasing attention to Muslims as security risks paradoxically created feelings of insecurity for Muslims even as it opened up new spaces for increased understanding given sudden increase in popular and media interest in the topic of Islam. Reflecting upon the situation of American Muslims after 9/11, Agha Saeed noted that the paradox for Muslims was "characterized by extreme vilification on the one hand, and by a considerable degree of acceptance, even popularity, on the other," and that increasing awareness of Islam "accounts for a complex transition of Muslims from outsiders to insiders."[26] The observation is no less true of the Canadian case, although perhaps the prominence of the Muslim voice in response to global and domestic challenges arose somewhat more gradually. The continued relevance of the international "war on terror," related concerns over the American invasion of Iraq, the periodic eruption of terrorist violence in places such as Bali, Istanbul, Madrid, and London, and a worldwide controversy over the publication of cartoons said to denigrate the Prophet of Islam kept Muslims in the middle of the headlines. Muslims have been pressed to provide political and other representation so as to redirect and steer interest in the topic so as to evade the stereotyping of an entire community by the actions of radicals.

New Sacred Space

In the wake of the 9/11 attacks, Muslims have been increasingly significant as political actors, both in the context of civil society—as plaintiffs before human rights tribunals, as interveners before government committees—and as members of elected legislatures. This contributes to a higher profile for the community and a heightened sense of understanding and interest in Islam in the Canadian population, even if this occasionally stems from fears of Islamist-inspired terrorism or apparent intolerance among Muslims.

The past decade has seen an explosion of local and national groups coalescing around the public representation of Islam and Muslim religious traditions. This includes Islamic Centres focused upon religious practice and instruction, community activist networks, cultural centres, and political activist groups. Perhaps the highest-profile organization is the Canadian Islamic Congress, professed to be "Canada's largest non-profit

and wholly independent Islamic organization," seeking to represent
Muslims of all backgrounds, both Sunni and Shi'i.[27] The organization
remains well-financed and influential even amid controversial statements
and positions that have occasionally met with strident condemnation from
various human rights organizations and observers.[28] However, a plethora
of other organizations have arisen both as rivals and complements to the
work of the Congress, including the Council on American-Islamic
Relations – Canada (CAIR-Can), a chapter of the influential American
lobby group; the Muslim Canadian Congress, a secularist alternative to the
more traditionally-minded groups; as well as more particular religiously-
and ethnically-based groups such as the Ismaili Aga Khan Foundation of
Canada; the Canadian Arab Federation; the Canadian Society of Muslims;
and the National Council on Canada Arab Relations. Dozens of smaller-
scale organizations have also assumed tremendous local profile at times:
these would include provincial and regional groups such as the British
Columbia Muslim Association, the Salahuddin Islamic Centre of Toronto,
Masjid Toronto, the Islamic Centre of Southwestern Ontario and the
Canadian Council of Ahl Sunnah wal Jamaah. These reflect a mixture of
publicly-oriented revivalist groups, community organizations, and more
traditional religious congregations. One must also add to this list active
and increasingly influential organizations of university students in groups
gathered around both Islam and the political aspects of Arab identity such
as the Palestinian cause.

    Prominent individuals have also stepped up to become media experts
on the Islamic community. Media pundits and critics of the Muslim
community both began to create a niche for themselves in publicizing and
discussing the place of Muslims in Canadian and global affairs. Among
the more prominent spokespeople are Toronto Star columnist and editor
Haroon Siddiqui, Muslim Canadian Congress communications director
Tarek Fatah, Canadian Islamic Congress president Mohamed El-Masry,
and self-described Muslim refusenik Irshad Manji, whose 2002 book *The
Trouble with Islam Today* brought her worldwide renown as a progressive
Muslim critic. While the most celebrated media personalities come from
the liberal Muslim camp, they do not fully represent the diversity of
traditional networks that work more closely with the mainstream mosques
and Islamic societies in the urban areas of Canada. Nonetheless, they
underline the extent to which the wide variety of belief in Muslim society
is reflected in the pluralist system.

Having an Impact: Policy Change and Electoral Politics

By February 2003, complaints from the Muslim community and the gathering feeling that global affairs were falling into the pitfall of a division between Western and Islamic civilizations were recognized by Parliament. The interaction of global and domestic affairs on this issue was obvious: Canadian foreign policy toward the Middle East and American primacy would inevitably threaten to alienate Canadian Muslims even as the growth of radicalized Islam could become a threat to the state. The result was a year-long study undertaken by the standing committee on foreign affairs, at the time chaired by Liberal MP Bernard Patry. The committee came to a wide variety of recommendations about Canadian policy toward the Muslim world, including support for civil society and democratization, an emphasis on gender equality, minority rights, and enhancing intercultural and interfaith dialogue as well as the domestic capacity in linguistic and cultural sensitivity.[29] However, it also recognized the extent to which individual Muslims did not feel that they were adequately or sympathetically heard by the government in the formulation of that foreign policy:

> ...it is obviously necessary to take action to address the perception that Canadian Muslim voices are not adequately listened to, by ensuring that they and others are fully consulted in the development of the country's foreign policy. Beyond simple transparency, proper and ongoing consultations will also ensure that Canada's foreign policy benefits from the unique knowledge and experiences of Muslim Canadians.[30]

In this spirit of consultation, the Committee itself heard from a wide swathe of the Muslim community and explored issues with Muslims abroad.

With the dispatch of Canadian forces to join the International Security Assistance Force (ISAF) in Afghanistan beginning in August 2003, the relevance of Muslim positions became even more marked. The government's acceptance of a more robust operation providing security for the area around Kandahar from early 2006 and the increasing number of casualties underscored the importance of this mission to Canadian foreign policy overall. The challenge of ensuring that Canadian foreign and defence policy reflects the diverse notions of Muslim groups, especially in the Afghan theatre, has been noted by other officials in the government. Canada's Chief of Defence Staff, Rick Hillier made public comments to a somewhat skeptical Muslim audience in April 2006 that he would like to increase Muslim participation in the military.[31] It might be surmised that

the lower level of Muslim participation relates both to a lack of more
general political participation but also to some distaste for the potential
involvement in a foreign policy that is often questioned by individual
Muslims. Nonetheless, active recruitment from the Muslim community
demonstrated the growing centrality of the issue to government decisions.

Somewhat more significantly, the events of the years following 9/11
galvanized the Muslim community as an electoral force as well. There is
no strong evidence to indicate that Muslims vote as a bloc for any
particular party, but Muslims have become more engaged as candidates
and party members. There have been an increasing number of Muslims
elected to office in provincial legislatures over the years: presently there
are at least two in the legislatures of both Alberta and Ontario and one in
the Quebec National Assembly. At the federal level, this has also been the
case. The Canadian Islamic Congress made a point of publishing analysis
of candidates' positions on issues of concern to Muslims, and asserted that
in an unprecedented show of new interest in politics, Muslim Canadians
increased their voter turnout from a typical 49% to 80%, surpassing
general voter participation by approximately 20%.[32] A record ten Muslims
stood for public office and three were elected in 2004, including
Conservative Rahim Jaffer, Liberal Wajid Khan, and the first Muslim-
Canadian woman elected to office, Liberal MP Yasmin Ratansi. These
Parliamentarians joined Mobina Jaffer, the first Muslim appointed to the
Senate in 2001. Muslim voters were clearly important in the re-election of
controversial Liberal MP Carolyn Parrish, who had been targeted by a
rival Liberal for her own nomination. Despite the electoral defeat of the
Liberal party nation-wide, Muslim Liberals retained their seats, and a new
Muslim MP, Omar el-Ghabra, was elected in Mississauga-Erindale, to
replace Parrish. As a result, there were four Muslims elected to the
Parliament in January 2006.

The assertion of Muslim groups for more equitable treatment also
reached to the province of Quebec, itself possessed of a different legal
code and tradition of secularity influenced under the French model.
Mainstream acceptance of Muslim practices was bolstered by the
conclusion of an inquiry undertaken by the Commission des droits de la
personne et des droit de la jeunesse (Human and Youth Rights
Commission) in Quebec in March 2006. Complainants to the Commission
were Muslim students of the Ecole de technologie superieure of the
Universite de Quebec a Montreal (UQAM) who had requested a prayer
space and been denied on the grounds that UQAM was a "lay, non-
denominational institution." What was more, the group was denied official
club status on the basis of the same policy. When students began to pray in

the stairwells of the institution, security guards had confiscated the student's prayer mats when they were left behind between prayers and had scolded students who sought to engage in ablutions in the area. The final decision handed down by the Commission did not significantly challenge the institution's claim to laic immunity from religious claims, but it did demand that the school seek to provide space for the students to pray "on a regular basis, in conditions that respect their right to the safeguard of their dignity."[33]

The finding was widely heralded as a victory for the students.[34] While the decision did not create a new framework for the institution in regard to religious student groups, it did require an accommodation. Given the later backlash against accommodations for religious groups, it is unclear that the finding will have lasting effects beyond mediating an internal dispute at a specific institution. However it provided Muslims with strong backing for their practices to be accepted even within the secular system defined by French *laicisme*.

Internal Challenges

The appearance of newly emergent groups and the movement of Muslims into the mainstream of electoral politics demonstrate that Muslims have presented effective challenges to their perceived marginalization in the past few years, but there remain internal and external divisions over the identification of Muslim interests. Muslims are as diverse a population as are any other religious group, divided by class, region, ethnic background, interpretation and sect. It should therefore come as little surprise that attempts to unite or monopolize Muslims are not always particularly fruitful. In addition, the divisions in the Muslim community reflected prior to the turn of the century remain in place and arise in stark relief even as Muslims become more effectively involved as political actors in the Canadian context. Ethnic and sectarian differences tend to be subsumed in a broader philosophic divide between modernist and secularist perspectives taken by groups such as Ismailis and the Canadian Muslim Congress as against a more traditional and parochial approach, represented by groups such as the Canadian Islamic Congress and the plethora of local Islamic centres and mosques. However, the debates among these groups have only served to increase the profile of Muslims as actors in spite of their inherent divisions and the wider suspicion of Islam fostered by presumed and actual radicals in their midst.

In spite of the great strides taken toward Muslim representation in the Canadian milieu, it must be noted that there is uneven participation among

Muslim groups. Of the five Muslims currently holding seats in the Commons and Senate, three are Ismailis, coming from a small minority group within the larger body of Islam. Various reasons might be proffered to explain this. One is the length of time that Ismailis have resided in Canada, many having arrived in the late 1970s. Another is the relative wealth and Westernization of the Ismaili community. Educated in English, enjoying success in a broad array of careers, and comfortable with minority status in a liberal society, Ismailis have integrated well into the mainstream of Canadian politics. However, the extent to which the more traditional and religious Sunni and Shi'i groups that have come to Canada in the last few decades have achieved the same level of mainstream acceptance is not as clear, reflected in their lower relative success in electoral politics as well as anecdotally in a lower socio-economic profile.

In interest group circles, this divide can be seen in the sheer number of self-constituted groups boasting "Muslim" or "Islamic" in their name. More fundamentally, it manifests itself in the distinction between the modernist and liberal perspective of many secularized Muslims and the more traditional and parochial perspective held by devout and religious Muslims. On the modernist side, are many in the community that have disavowed support for *shari'a* courts, separate Muslim institutions, and traditional interpretations of Western behaviour such as the mixing of the sexes and homosexuality. On the traditionalist side are the established Islamic centres and mosque networks as well as most imams.

The debate that arose over *shari'a* courts in Ontario brought out divisions in the Muslim community in stark contrast. The legal dimensions of this debate are explored in greater detail in the following chapter of this volume by John Soroski. The debate also illuminates internal dynamics of the Islamic community in Canada. The controversy arose in 2003 when the Islamic Institute for Civil Justice, an organization led by lawyer Syed Mumtaz Ali, requested recognition of Muslim *shari'a* courts as a method of faith-based arbitration under the 1991 *Arbitration Act*. The *Act* had long allowed religious organizations to participate in helping to arbitrate family disputes in particular subject to the supervision of the courts should appeal be made beyond the initial level of arbitration. Organizations representing both Jewish and Christian communities had enjoyed official recognition under the act. State recognition of religious arbitration was one of the few corporatist-style anomalies to the pluralist form of interest representation among religious groups. In the following months, the request came to be supported by several traditionalist groups and leaders, most notably the Canadian Islamic Congress, which emphasized the ability of courts to overturn verdicts, concluding that "[t]here is no reason to expect that the

Islamic institute will be run as if the Taliban had set up shop in Ontario."[35] In June 2004, the Ontario government appointed former NDP MPP Marion Boyd to oversee a commission of inquiry into the continued allowance of faith-based arbitration under the *Arbitration Act*, with a view to questioning the role that Muslim arbitration courts might play.

The proposal immediately registered opposition among secular human rights activists and Muslims alike, who feared that the adoption of faith-based arbitration under a *shari'a* court might create an alternative law for Muslims. The Canadian Muslim Congress registered its opposition to the move, arguing that "[t]he weakest within the Muslim community, namely the women, will be coerced (into participating) by their community." Such a communalist approach to settling personal status laws, common in many Eastern societies, was held to be "racist and unconstitutional" according to Canadian Muslim Congress lawyer Rocco Galati.[36] Likewise, the Canadian Council of Muslim Women argued that the provision of space for *shari'a* courts to engage in faith-based arbitration might harm Muslim women who "will opt for their communities rather than open criticism, even if it involves their own mistreatment."[37] Many critics of the proposed *shari'a* court took great pains to argue that they were no less Muslim than its proponents, merely that they were concerned with the possible misuse of faith-based arbitration by unscrupulous elements.[38] The secularist grouping represented by these groups eschewed the corporatist approach as a means of creating two classes of people under the law, thereby threatening legal equality and the protection of women as individuals under the law.

The final decision taken by the Ontario government reflected the inherent divisions of Canadian society over the corporatist-pluralist dimension but eventually came down on the side of the pluralist form, reinforcing the position of the Muslim Canadian Congress and Canadian Council of Muslim Women. The Boyd report recommended keeping faith-based arbitration amid a variety of new safeguards when published in December 2004.[39] Nonetheless, the government of Ontario premier Dalton McGuinty decided several months later not to follow through on the report's recommendations, pointedly arguing with the secular-pluralist perspective that there would be "one law for all Ontarians."[40]

Traditionalists and modernists converge and divide on a wide set of issues, but it is likely the status of women and the importance of Islamic family law that polarizes the debate most significantly. To be taken seriously among the establishment of the Islamic community, women in particular often feel compelled to veil. This is reinforced by the external optics of Islamic identity. One Muslim woman was recently quoted in the *National Post* arguing that

> From the non-Muslim perspective, media and people have perpetuated this myth that authentic Muslim women cover their heads. There have been times when I have not been considered an authentic enough Muslim woman because I don't cover my head. [41]

Paradoxically, this suggests that far from representing a submissive approach to a male-dominated community, veiling among Canadian Muslim women can be used as a means of amplifying their public visibility and voice. At the same time, it runs the risk of overly politicizing Muslim women as a token of Muslim integration and concern. A Canadian Congress of Muslim Women report suggested that while Muslim women are less engaged than Muslim men or the public at large in political activity, bridging this gap was not so difficult as it might at first appear but required "national organization" that extended beyond the power of local groups. [42] Increasingly, it would appear that the national organizations based in Ottawa will be characterized by the split between progressive groups and established organizations led by more conservative elements.

The traditionalist-modernist divide seemed to yawn wider with the Canadian reaction to worldwide demonstrations in February 2006 over cartoons that had been published in a Danish newspaper a few months previously. In the wake of international demonstrations, often turning violent, Canadian Muslims largely sought to defuse the controversy. Likely the most visible critic of the reaction was Tarek Fatah of the Muslim Canadian Congress, whose persona grew daily through his involvement in media interviews where he castigated what he identified to be an uncritical and censorious streak in Muslim culture. The consistency of his critique would later cause waves within the larger Muslim community.

External Challenges

Later, on 3 June 2006, renewed media commentary surrounding Muslim radicalism in the wake of the detention of a group of 17 men on charges of planning a terrorist incident again raised the level of concern among the general population. Among Canadian Muslims it created anxiety about the potential for retaliatory taunts and targeted attacks. The arrests sparked worldwide interest about the Canadian Muslim community and sparked a firestorm of discussion in the Canadian media about the trustworthiness of Canada's official policy of multiculturalism. *The Globe and Mail* reported one Toronto-area imam complaining "People are suspicious and there's anger…We are being targeted not because of what we've done, but because of who we are and what we believe in." Reports of vandalism against an Etobicoke mosque reinforced this fear.[43] A knife attack on an imam in Montreal a few days later increased the level of anxiety.[44] The flurry of media attention did little to assuage the fear.[45] The feeling that a rush to judgment impaired the case against the accused was registered by visiting British critical journalist Robert Fisk, who argued that the Canadian media engaged in "an orgy of finger-pointing that must reduce the chances of a fair trial and, at the same time, sow fear in the hearts of the country's more than 700 000 Muslims."[46] Later reports that several area Muslims willingly provided information leading to the arrests, coupled with universal condemnation of the alleged plot, seemed likely to defuse the issue. In addition, the government responded to the controversy by inviting an "open dialogue" with Muslim leaders on 10 June.

The incident initially appeared to strengthen the case of secularists in the Muslim community. The profile of Liberal MP Wajid Khan increased in light of his knowledge of local aspects of the case, who challenged Muslim groups and mosques "to stop making excuses and trying to defend Islam." He added that "It's not an Islamic issue. I think they should be talking and preaching life, and what is really Islamic, and that the Canadian way of life is very much Islamic."[47] Others expressed the more radical view that Muslim leaders were actually fomenting radicalism. Tarek Fatah of the liberally-oriented Canadian Muslim Congress wrote in an op-ed published in the *Toronto Star* that "There is not a single mosque in Canada where Muslims with opposing views can debate anything political, social, or theological. The doors of debate are shut by the cement of orthodoxy."[48] Yet equally clear in media events and reports was the diversity of opinion surrounding the relevance and cause of the alleged arrests. One reporter for the *Toronto Star* went on to bemoan the absence of a single unified voice among Muslims, cynically contending, "So who becomes the public voice of Muslims in a crisis? In the absence of an umbrella group or even a unified vision to create one, the answer seems to be: Whoever is accessible and delivers a great sound bite."[49]

The very contentiousness of speaking for Islam has thus underlined the strengths and pitfalls of the pluralist mode of interest representation. The Canadian setting has provided opportunities for a vast array of groups to present various versions of Islamic social philosophy in the Canadian context, enriching the diversity of Canadian public life and arguably contributing to Islam's own embrace of *ijtihad*, or independent interpretation. At the same time, it occasionally gives way to embittered

debates over the extent to which one Muslim reflects the wider notions of
the *umma*, the Muslim community.

One such debate emerged over the notoriety of Muslim Canadian
Congress spokesman Tarek Fatah, who ran afoul of the more conservative
leadership of the Canadian Islamic Congress with his socially liberal
positions and diatribes on traditional Islamic movements.[50] In August
2006, Fatah officially stepped down from his position as communications
director of the Muslim Canadian Congress, citing high levels of stress and
fear stemming from a series of threats.[51] A few weeks later, the
confrontational tactics of the Congress became the motivation for a split
within the movement. One former leader reflected the division over a
philosophy of tactics when he noted, "Instead of engaging the Muslim
community, [the MCC] was provoking it…Provocation is also acceptable
as long as it is done without alienating."[52] The obvious challenge that
internal divisions create for finding credible leadership in the Muslim
community have not necessarily dimmed the government's enthusiasm in
the vital process of consultation with Muslim groups, though they do
problematize the initiative.

The eruption of warfare over Lebanon sparked by the capture of two
Israeli soldiers in July 2006 and the ensuing need for the new Conservative
government to present a foreign policy front on the issue further
underscored the need for consultation with Muslim groups. Beyond the
original reaction to the crisis in which the prime minister made reference
to the "measured" response of Israeli forces, the government appeared
neither able nor willing to deal with Muslim concerns over the nature of
the conflict and efforts toward a ceasefire. In light of the perceived
disconnect, Prime Minister Harper appointed Liberal Wajid Khan as a
special advisor on the Middle East and South Asia. The development at
once raised the profile of the liberal backbencher and created controversy
among opposition caucus members who were nonplussed by Khan's
agreement to work with the government.[53] This led in time to the MP's
defection from the Liberal Party to the Conservatives in January 2007.
Nevertheless, the attempt to cut through a diversity of voices with the
appointment of a special adviser suggested that the government was taking
the need for consultation seriously, even if it was, as many critics
suggested, only a public relations gesture. However, the move did not
signify a lasting or consistent move toward corporatist consultation with
the Muslim population. A plural set of voices remained engaged from the
Muslim side.

The increased interest in the role of Canadian Muslims and the ongoing
conflict in Afghanistan kept the topic in the media throughout late 2006

and early 2007. Various attempts to accommodate religious and immigrant communities in Quebec such as the UQAM prayer space decision and a similar decision to allow a Sikh student to wear a ceremonial dagger (*kirpan*) at school sparked a vociferous response in some quarters. Later public discussions focused upon accommodations to block the windows of a gym from a neighbouring synagogue and other groups asked for gender segregation at local pools and prenatal classes. Likely the highest public profile reaction came from the passage of a declaration by the town council of Herouxville seeking to clarify town values as a means of pre-empting the need for accommodation. The declaration pointedly targeted certain kinds of practices held to be anathema to the townsfolk. The list progressed from extreme practices known in some areas of the world to more problematic issues in a pluralistic society, extending from public stoning and burning with acid to gender segregation in public places and carrying weapons to school.[54] The Herouxville Declaration spawned a broad counteroffensive among independent Muslim groups, in particular the Canadian Islamic Congress. An *ad hoc* delegation of Muslim women took a trip to the town to share their concern over the declaration, a trip that garnered positive media amid complaints from the town council that the affair had been overblown.[55] The picture of a busload of smiling Muslim women, bringing with them Middle Eastern desserts and a message of good will, played well in the media and appeared to have turned the incident into a public relations victory.

Not long afterward, in late February 2007, the same issues played out in Quebec, promising to muddy the waters further. Media reports surfaced that profiled Asmahan Mansour, a young girl from an Ottawa team, who was compelled by a referee to remove her hijab veil during a soccer match in Montreal. In protest, the girl's coach decided to pull the team out of the tournament, considering the treatment demeaning and unfair.[56] Soccer officials stated that the issue was one of safety and uniformity of dress. The publicity of the incident and the apparent spillover of disputes over accommodation to innocent sports matches gave another sympathetic image to the Muslim community, as parents countered that Asmahan had long been playing "without any complaint" from officials.[57] The affair had the markings of an inter-Muslim dispute as well, as the referee was also identified as a Muslim. The dispute had displayed both the internal challenges to Muslim unity and the external successes that Muslim groups had attained in bringing concerns to the public mind.

Thus the cases of the Herouxville Declaration and the hijab-clad soccer player each proved that Canadian Muslims could equally benefit by raising the profile of these divisive incidents. These issues of "reasonable accommodation" arose as lightning-rods in the ensuing March 2007 Quebec election and were credited by many as one of the keys to the electoral success of the Action Democratique du Quebec led by Mario Dumont.[58] But they also demonstrated that the Muslim community had acquired a high degree of sophistication in appealing to the broad audience of public opinion, displaying a mounting care for how they are portrayed in media reports. Likewise, Muslims were gaining visibility in the mainstream media. A high degree of national and international publicity greeted CBC television's January 2007 debut of a situation comedy surrounding the misadventures of a group of Muslims in a Canadian community with the derivative title of *Little Mosque on the Prairie*. The programme was created by Zarqa Nawaz, a Canadian Muslim filmmaker who had already cast an iconoclastic eye at Women in Islam in her documentary *Me and the Mosque*. The programme met mixed reviews but the controversy surrounding it sparked plenty of interest in the premiere, which garnered a massive audience of over 2 million.[59] Some reviewers complained both about poor production values and the overt stereotyping of ordinary townsfolk as uneducated and bigoted about the Muslim characters which were generally depicted in more sympathetic guise. The interest in Muslim characters on television sparked roustabout columnist Mark Steyn to quip that "Muslim is the new gay," even as he criticized the tropes purveyed by the series creator.[60] However, the production was undoubtedly successful in making Muslim society more approachable to the mainstream and it has remained a draw, even if it has lost the swell of interest that first accompanied it.

These successes were underscored by the release of a CBC-Environics poll in February 2007 on the subject of Muslims in the Canadian context. The poll was published under a heading that gushed, "Glad to be Canadian, Muslims say." It went on to report that Canadian Muslims were happy in Canada, 80% claiming to feel "broadly satisfied" with their status in Canada, as contrasted with lower levels in European contexts such as Britain and Germany.[61] The poll also went on to report singularities within the Muslim community: for example, 54% of Muslims claimed support for the federal Liberal party and an alarming 12% communicated that they felt that the planning of terror attacks could be "justified."[62] Nevertheless, the overall message coming out of the poll was of the overall contentment of Muslims in spite of any challenges they might feel in the Canadian context.

Conclusions

The emergence of a set of Muslim voices in Canadian public life in the wake of the attacks of September 11, 2001, and the ensuing debates surrounding security and the place of Muslims citizens highlights the adaptation of the Muslim population to the pluralist model of interest representation. On the whole, this has been a healthy development. The corporatist approach taken by many European states risks the creation of monopoly groups that may not fully reflect the diversity of opinion among Muslims while at the same time artificially marginalizing rivals who may well seek out more radical means to voice their concerns. While Canadian Muslims were not necessarily fully mobilized or represented in Canadian political life before 9/11, the event and its aftermath have paradoxically provided an impetus for Muslims to make contact with Canadian political institutions and culture. This has proceeded in a somewhat typically Canadian fashion, with the government seeking new inroads in the community and encouraging their participation in corporatist forums while civil society has responded in various ways that defy attempts to categorize the Muslim community as a united interest. The result is a cacophony of Muslim voices that might tentatively be divided between a secularizing and critical vision promoted by self-constituted societies of interested Muslims and a more parochial and traditional vision that promotes Muslim institutions and more conservative religious values.

In spite of the great strides that Muslim organizations and individuals have made in asserting themselves in Canadian politics, there remains a strong tendency for Muslims to remain isolated within their own communities. The tight ethnic, parochial, and sectarian ties that bind Muslims in their countries of origin continue to resonate in Canadian society, where there is relatively little understanding of the struggles of Muslims in their countries of origin and few interreligious networks to bring together people of different religious communities. Muslim organizations are largely modeled on the *de facto* corporatist organizations that obtain in majority Muslim countries where officially-sanctioned *muftis* and community-based personal status laws govern their daily affairs. The pluralist approach to interest representation which characterizes the Canadian approach to religion in public life is not always a natural fit. As a result, there is ample reason to question whether constructive pluralist responses such as the construction of Islamic financial institutions, discussion fora, Islamic schools, or the interaction of Islamic groups in policy communities is a straightforward contribution to the growth of social capital.

The struggle over *shari'a* in Ontario is but one indication of the dissonance between a common Muslim desire for communalist-corporatist institutions and the secular-pluralist mode of engagement in Canadian politics. While the secular-pluralist model is more comfortable to modernizing groups, even more traditional Muslims boast victories through autonomous assertion of their individual rights, as in the case of the Ecole de technologie superieure decision of 2006. At other times, some Muslims contend for the right to wear the veil while others seek to apply a more Western-style uniformity to their behaviour, as was indicated with a dispute over a girl wearing a hijab to a soccer match.

Overall, the involvement of Muslim individuals and groups identified here fit the prediction made by Eickelman and Piscatori about the spread of Muslim populations to Western societies when they stated that "[t]he new political geography, blurring conventional social distinctions, empowering new groups, and challenging governments, may in the long run facilitate the emergence of pluralism, even as some forces in society vigorously resist it." This observation was followed by a caveat: "In the sense that symbolic and political connections across national and other political boundaries may be encouraged, conventional understandings of "external" and "internal" appear doubtful."[63] Doubtless this underscores the chief concern for those observing Muslim participation in Canadian politics, the extent to which global divisions over issues of a religious and "civilizational" nature might erode Muslim identification with Canadian politics. Certainly this was one of the primary concerns reflected in the Report of the Standing Committee on Foreign Affairs and International Trade on Canada's relations with the Muslim world in 2004. As global controversies and incidents in the various Middle Eastern disputes continue to feed emotive feelings, the relative success of Muslim participation may come under more pronounced pressure.

If there is any substance to the claim that Canada has better integrated its Muslim population than other countries, it is likely in the extent to which Canada's pluralist model matches the diversity of opinion within the Muslim community. While the Canadian tradition of multiculturalism does not necessarily encourage the retention of traditional religious perspectives, it does encourage a role for the maintenance of cultural practices affected by those religions. Rather than falling into the trap of hardening religious identity into a communalist framework, Muslims have thrived within the democratic give-and-take of pluralist politics.

The experience of Canadian Muslims illuminates the strengths of the pluralist model as against the institutionalization of religious differences in government policy. In a larger sense, the pluralist model has allowed

Canadian government to respond in a flexible way to a malleable group of religious interests over the course of time. Today's religious networks may bear little resemblance to those of the past, either based on denominational affiliation or ideological underpinnings. The pluralist model allowed the government to respond as well to the major Christian religious movements of the past as it does to the Christian, Muslim, Hindu, or irreligious movements of the present. On the other hand, attempts to establish religious rights under constitutional caveats (as in the case of Roman Catholic and public school systems) have recently run up against calls for equal treatment by newly emergent groups provided unequal treatment. Likewise attempts to recognize sectarian interests through providing official government imprimatur, such as in the case of religious arbitration in Ontario, prove problematic to the sensibilities of a population that does not necessarily wish to be categorized by their religious affiliation. The fluidity and adaptability of the pluralist model is therefore more likely to provide a functional foundation for religious interactions in public life.

Notes

[1] Recent additions to the long list of scholarship on the topic include Gilles Kepel, *The War for Muslim Minds: Islam and the West* (Cambridge, MA: Belknap Press, 2004); Olivier Roy, *Globalized Islam: the Search for a New Ummah* (London: Hurst & Co., 2004); Graham E. Fuller, *The Future of Political Islam* (New York: Palgrave, 2003). See also Gilles Kepel's groundbreaking work *Allah in the West*, trans. Susan Milner (Stanford: Stanford UP, 1997).

[2] In using the term pluralism here, I refer to the model of interest representation in which groups are held to be autonomous and self-constituting, gathered among individual citizens who unite around a common cause of one sort or another. This is contrasted with the corporatist approach in which governing authorities seek to include groups in the structure of policymaking through constitutionally and officially-recognized representative groups. While all societies bear hallmarks of both systems, North American democracies have largely followed the pluralist approach while European democracies favour a corporatist one.

[3] Ted Jelen and Clyde Wilcox, *Religion and Politics in Comparative Perspective: the One, the Few and the Many* (Cambridge: Cambridge UP).

[4] Dale F. Eickelman and James Piscatori, *Muslim Politics* (Princeton: Princeton UP, 1996).

[5] Eickelman and Piscatori, *Muslim Politics*, 141-148.

[6] In the 1980s, scholars were discussing "survival strategies" for the small Muslim community in Canada. Baha Abu-Laban, "The Canadian Muslim Community: the Need for a New Survival Strategy", in Earle H. Waugh, Baha Abu-Laban, and

Regula B. Qureishi, eds., *The Muslim Community in North America*, (Edmonton: University of Alberta Press, 1983), 75-92.
[7] Canada boasts the first mosque built in North America, the Al-Rashid mosque, located in Edmonton, built in 1938.
[8] Baha Abu-Laban, "Canadian Muslim Community", 76-77.
[9] Ahmad F. Youssif, "Family Values, Social Adjustment and Problems of Identity: the Canadian Experience", *Journal Institute of Muslim Minority Affairs* 15, no.1&2 (January-July 1994): 114, 118.
[10] Youssif, "Family Values", 118.
[11] For example, Tomas Gerholm and Yngve Georg Lithman, eds., *The New Islamic Presence in Western Europe* (London: Mansell Publishing Limited, 1988), Gilles Kepel, *Allah in the West*, trans. Susan Milner (Stanford: Stanford UP, 1997).
[12] Baha Abu-Laban, "The Muslim Community in Canada" in Syed Z. Abedin and Ziauddin Sardar, eds., *Muslim Minorities in the West* (London: Grey Seal, 1995), 140.
[13] Figures come from Karim H. Karim, "Crescent Dawn in the Great White North: Muslim Participation in the Canadian Public Sphere," in Yvonne Yazbeck Haddad, ed., *Muslims in the West: From Sojourners to Citizens* (New York: Oxford UP, 2002), 263, and from Haddad and Jane I. Smith, eds., *Muslim Minorities in the West: Visible and Invisible*, vi.
[14] Shaheen Azmi, "Canadian Social Service Provision and the Muslim Community in Metropolitan Toronto," *Journal of Muslim Minority Affairs* 17, no.1 (1997): 159.
[15] *Adler v. Ontario* [1996] 3 SCR 609.
[16] Rima Berns-McGowan, *Muslims in the Diaspora: the Somali Communities of London and Toronto* (Toronto: University of Toronto Press, 1999), 228.
[17] Joe Matyas, "Remarks concern London Muslims," *London Free Press*, 27 May 1996.
[18] Kathy Rumleski, "Muslims will hold own march," *London Free Press*, 29 May 1996.
[19] Kathy Rumleski, "Muslims, Christians reconcile," *London Free Press*, 3 June 1996.
[20] Haddad, *Muslim Minorities in the West*, vii.
[21] T.Y. Ismael and John Measor, "Racism and the North American Media following 11 September: the Canadian Setting," *Arab Studies Quarterly* 25, no.1&2 (2003), 117.
[22] For example, "Somalis in Canada... encounter an attitudinal contradiction: respect for their right to be different and suspicion of the religion to which they adhere." Berns-McGowan, *Muslims in the Diaspora*, 232.
[23] See the profile provided by PBS for their documentary on the Khadr family, "Son of al Qaeda", http://www.pbs.org/wgbh/pages/frontline/shows/khadr/ [accessed 7 September 2007].
[24] Security Certificates are means by which the ministers of immigration and public security may detain non-citizens who are either foreign nationals or permanent residents who are deemed to be potential threats to Canadian security.

Erin Kruger, Marlene Mulder, and Bojan Korenic, "Canada after 11 September: Security Measures and "Preferred" Immigrants," *Mediterranean Quarterly*,15, no.4 (2004): 72-87.
[25] One such case involved future MP Omar Alghabra. See Rasha Mourtada, "A Climate of Fear", Canadian Business Online, http://www.canadianbusiness.com/article.jsp?content=20040329_59090_59090 [accessed 3 September 2006].
[26] Agha Saeed, "The American Muslim Paradox", in Haddad and Smith, *Muslim Minorities*, 39-40.
[27] "Facts About the CIC", *Canadian Islamic Congress* [online], http://www.canadianislamiccongress.com/cicfacts.php [accessed 31 August 2006].
[28] The Canadian Islamic Congress website provides ample evidence of the organizational resources of the group and among other things offers various donated resources in response to financial gifts. The organization employs a national executive director in Ottawa and stages regular fund-raising activities. See the website at www.canadianislamiccongress.com. Congress President Mohamed el-Masry is an outspoken and prolific critic of Israel, American foreign policy, and follows a fairly consistently polemic approach in his writing, generally featured in the Congress publication *Friday Magazine*. This has often brought him condemnation and may also have led to the group's recent marginalization. See Ezra Levant, "A Muslim leader worth ignoring," *National Post* 16 June 2006.
[29] Parliament of Canada, *Exploring Canada's Relations with the Countries of the Muslim World,* Report of the Standing Committee on Foreign Affairs and International Trade, Bernard Patry, Chair, March 2004, xxiii-xxiv.
[30] *Exploring Canada's Relations*, 30.
[31] "Military needs more Muslims, Hillier says," *CBC News*, 10 April 2006.
[32] Hussein A. Hamdani, Kamran Bhatti, and Nabila F. Munawar, "Muslim Political Participation in Canada: from Marginalization to Empowerment?," *Canadian Issues*, Summer 2005, 29-30.
[33] Commission des droits de la personne et des droit de la jeunesse (Quebec), Resolution COM-510-5.2.1, 20 March 2006, English translation.
[34] "Quebec group says school should find prayer space for Muslims," Canadian Press News Release, 22 March 2006.
[35] "Ontario Islamic Court should be welcomed, not feared," *Friday Magazine* [on-line], 3 September 2004. http://www.canadianislamiccongress.com/fb/friday_bulletin.php?fbdate=2004-09-03#2 [accessed 12 September 2006].
[36] Tarannum Kamlani and Nicholas Keung, "Muslim group opposes sharia law," *Toronto Star*, 28 August 2002.
[37] Canadian Council of Muslim Women, "Submission to Ms. Marion Boyd: Review of the Ontario Arbitration Act and Arbitration Processes, Specifically Matters of Family Law", http://www.ccmw.com/MuslimFamilyLaw/submission%20made%20to%20Ms%20Marion%20Boyd.htm [accessed 13 September 2006].

[38] Farzana Hassan-Shahid, "Shariah: Are Opponents of Shariah Anti-Islam?" *The American Muslim* [online], 8 February 2005. http://theamericanmuslim.org/tam.php/features/articles /shariah_are_opponents_of_shariah_anti_islam/ [accessed 17 September 2006].
[39] Marion Boyd, "Dispute Resolution in Family Law: Protecting Choice, Promoting Inclusion", December 2004. http://www.attorneygeneral.jus.gov.on.ca/english/about/pubs/boyd/ [accessed 13 September 2006].
[40] "McGuinty rules out use of shari'a law in Ontario", *CTV News* [online], http://www.ctv.ca/servlet/ArticleNews/story/CTVNews/1126472943217_26/?hub= TopStories [accessed 13 September 2006].
[41] "McGuinty rules out use of shari'a law in Ontario", *CTV News* [online], http://www.ctv.ca/servlet/ArticleNews/story/CTVNews/1126472943217_26/?hub= TopStories [accessed 13 September 2006].
[42] Daood Hamdani, *Engaging Muslim Women: Issues and Needs* (Toronto: Canadian Council of Muslim Women, 2006) 11.
[43] Anthony De Palma, "Six of 17 arrested in Canada's antiterror sweep have ties to mosque near Toronto", *The Globe and Mail* 5 June 2006, Alexandra Shimo, "Vandalism at mosque sparks fears of backlash," *The Globe and Mail* 5 June 2006.
[44] Alana Coates, "'Hateful' attack at mosque," *The Gazette,* 11 June 2006.
[45] One article by Christie Blatchford sparked particular controversy when the journalist made a point of criticizing the assumption that "faith and religion – *nothing*, you understand – to do with the alleged homegrown terrorist plot." Christie Blatchford, "Ignoring the biggest elephant in the room," *The Globe and Mail*, 5 June 2006. The controversy she sparked was picked up in Robert Fulford, "The Toronto Star's self-imposed blindness," *National Post* 8 June 2006.
[46] Robert Fisk, "How racism has invaded Canada," *The Independent* [online], 11 June 2006, http://news.independent.co.uk/world/fisk/article754394.ece [accessed 1 September 2006].
[47] "PMs meeting with Muslims may lead to study: MP," *CTV News* [Online], 11 June   2006, http://www.ctv.ca/servlet/ArticleNews/print/CTVNews/20060608/harper_meeting _060611 [accessed 11 June 2006].
[48] Tarek Fatah, "Keep politics out of our mosques," *Toronto Star,* 7 June 2006.
[49] Prithi Yelaja and Tabassum Siddiqui, "And who speaks for Muslims?," *Toronto Star*, 12 June 2006.
[50] Mohamed El-Masry, "'Smearing Islam and Bashing Muslims, Who and Why," *Friday Magazine* [online], http://www.canadianislamiccongress.com/fb/friday_bulletin.php?fbdate=2006-06-30 [accessed 1 September 2006].
[51] Sonya Fatah, "Fearing for safety, Muslim official quits," *The Globe and Mail*, 3 August 2006.
[52] Quoted in Sonya Fatah, "Moderate Muslim group splinters," *The Globe and Mail,* 25 August 2006

[53] Campbell Clark, "PM picks Liberal MP as adviser on Mideast," *The Globe and Mail*, 9 August 2006.

[54] Dene Moore, "Herouxville wants immigrants that fit in with its citizens," *National Post* [online], 29 January 2007. www.canada.com/nationalpost/story.html?id=ac491c78-76df-467b-ab58-2bc90e4bfb63&k=83142 [accessed 27 February 2007].

[55] Alison Hanes, "Quebec town lifts veil on Muslim stereotypes," *National Post* [online], 12 February 2007, www.canada.com/nationalpost/news/archives/story.html?id=594d5936-7ea2-4235-a113-7e32827e7566 [accessed 27 February 2007].

[56] Jon Willing, "Hijab-clad soccer girl turfed," *CNews* [online], 26 February 2007 [accessed 1 March 2007].

[57] Tu Thanh Ha, "Quebec soccer officials won't punt soccer rule," *The Globe and Mail* [online] 26 February 2007 theglobeandmail.com/servlet/story/RTGAM.20070226.whijab0226/BNStory/Natio nal/home [accessed 1 March 2007].

[58] Konrad Yakabuski, "Mario emerges as the Undisputed Winner," *The Globe and Mail* [online], 27 March 2007 www.theglobeandmail.com/servlet/story/RTGAM.20070327.wyakabuskiquebec03 17/ BNStory/National [accessed 31 March 2007].

[59] Antonia Zerbisias, "'Mosque' finds an Audience," *Toronto Star* [online], 11 January 2007 www.thestar.com/article/169952 [accessed 27 February 2007].

[60] Mark Steyn, "The Little Mosque that Couldn't," *Macleans* [online], 5 February 2007 www.macleans.ca/culture/entertainment/article.jsp?content=20070205_140131_14 0131 [accessed 1 March 2007].

[61] "Glad to be Canadian, Muslims say," *CBC News* [online], 13 February 2007, www.cbc.ca/canada/story/2007/02/12/muslim-poll.html [accessed 1 March 2007].

[62] *Calgary Sun* columnist Licia Corbella noted the proportion with alarm in an ensuing editorial in the *Calgary Sun*. The intimation of the rest of the findings, however, seemed to suggest that a few smaller group of Canadian Muslims would find such attacks justified than in other nations where such attacks had been launched. Licia Corbella, "Disturbing Reality Buried," *Calgary Sun* [online], 18 February 2007 calsun.canoe.ca/News/Columnists/Corbella_Licia/2007/02/18/3642930-sun.html [accessed 1 March 2007].

[63] Eickelman and Piscatori, *Muslim Politics*, 138.

CHAPTER FIVE

CONSENSUAL SHARI'A ARBITRATION AND LOCAL VALUES COMMUNITIES IN LIBERAL SOCIETY: SPLENDID ISOLATIONISM VERSUS THE SEARCH FOR MORAL REFERENTS

JOHN SOROSKI

In 1991, the government of Ontario introduced changes to the province's *Arbitration Act* which enhanced opportunities for individuals to make use of private, self-chosen dispute resolution bodies in legal conflicts. Representatives of a number of the province's religious groups used these opportunities to establish institutions and processes for arbitrating matters of family law—including decisions about the distribution of marital property upon divorce—using standards drawn from their religions' beliefs and values. These forms of arbitration were consensual, in the sense that they only became operative when authorized by both parties in a legal dispute, and they were alternative to the more general system of resolving such disputes in the province's courts using more neutral, public standards of value. The opportunities for consensual religious arbitration provided by the *Arbitration Act* were the source of little public interest or commentary until 2003, when a Muslim organization, the Islamic Institute of Civil Justice, proposed establishing a process using Islamic religious law—the shari'a[1]—as the basis of arbitration for those of its members interested in such a possibility. The proposal raised considerable controversy, and the cloisters on consensual religious arbitration in Ontario were suddenly lifted.

In June 2004, the Ontario government asked former Ontario Attorney-General Marion Boyd to conduct a public inquiry and to prepare a report concerning the religious dimensions of legal arbitration in the province. Three large concerns animated those critical of religiously-based arbitration. First, some commentators, like the Humanist Association of Canada, expressed what might be taken as a liberal concern that enabling religiously based arbitration had the effect of substituting religious standards of value for more legitimate public and secular standards.[2] Secondly, feminists, women's groups (including the Canadian Council of Muslim Women) and others argued that the patriarchal nature and values of some interpreters and some interpretations of the shari'a were likely to produce arbitration results which favored men over women in the form of inequitable distributions of marital property upon divorce.[3] Thirdly, and relatedly, concern was expressed that Muslim women might be persuaded through social pressure within their communities to authorize this inequitable shari'a arbitration even though it conflicted with their own interests.[4] Ultimately, the government of Ontario found these criticisms of shari'a tribunals persuasive, and in September of 2005 Premier Dalton McGuinty announced that the province would be eliminating religiously based family law arbitration for all faiths.[5] Despite this outcome, the dispute over consensual shari'a arbitration in Ontario is worth closer consideration. It represents an interesting example of an issue of contention in recent liberal thought. This is the question of the appropriate role in liberal polities for what might be called "local values communities"—ethnic, cultural, religious, and other groups embodying complex comprehensive (and often illiberal) value systems.

The debate here is to a great extent between those described as "comprehensive" or "autonomy" liberals, and their counterpart "political" or "diversity" liberals, a divide noted by John Rawls in *Political Liberalism*.[6] As liberals, both camps share two large related liberal ideas. They endorse a premissory characterization of persons as having a claim to goods such as autonomy, individuality, and mutual-independence. And they endorse, therefore, the idea that values such as rationality, neutrality, and equality ought to apply to and delimit the obligations of such individuals. What distinguishes political and comprehensive liberals is the extent to which these ideas are understood as informing ongoing, everyday individual and collective life as well as the institutions of the state.

The "political" version of the philosophy suggests that liberalism's premissory characterization of persons as mutually-independent individuals does not constitute a statement about the actual nature of humans or an aspirational goal. This theory of the person has instead the more abstract purpose of allowing us to define collectively justifiable or acceptable political ends. The claim here is not then a fundamental vision of human goals or ends, but a means of establishing political obligations in a world in which persons are in significant disagreement about such goals and ends. As such, the liberal values of rationality, neutrality, and equality are understood in this light as authoritative in the definition of political institutions and obligations, but not necessarily so as guides to our claims about how individuals should live their lives or arrange their social, familial, and other relationships. As Will Kymlicka suggests, political liberalism is premised on the idea that "people can be communitarians in private life, and liberals in public life."[7] Among those associated with the political or diversity liberal perspective are John Rawls and Stephen Macedo in their later works[8], Martha Nussbaum, William Galston, and Chandran Kukathas.[9]

Comprehensive liberalism is associated with a greater integration of liberalism's ideas with the whole of human life. For comprehensivists, the liberal conceptualization of persons as autonomous, individual, and mutually independent is seen (to a greater or lesser extent, depending on how comprehensive the vision is) as an actual human ideal. Comprehensivist claims often suggest a central valuation on free and independent individual self-construction and an idealization of individual independence understood as a way of life as well as a definer of political obligations. This is a notion aptly captured by William Galston's characterization of the comprehensivist John Stuart Mill as an advocate of the idea of "excellence as the full flowering of individuality."[10] As a consequence of its identification of these forms of human excellence, comprehensive liberalism suggests that the liberal values of rationality, neutrality, and equality might be expected to play an important or central place in defining individual choices and mutual obligations in the ethical, personal, and social realms as well as the political. Among those associated with the comprehensivist or autonomy perspective are Immanuel Kant, John Stuart Mill, and John Dewey,[11] John Rawls and Stephen Macedo in their earlier work, Don Herzog, and Susan Moller Okin (whose work I discuss later in this essay).[12]

The differences between comprehensive and political liberals are reflected in differences between the two schools of thought about the appropriate role of local values communities in liberal society. In his version of the political liberal thesis, John Rawls emphasizes the idea that liberalism is appropriately understood as a response to the reality of disagreement between individuals and groups about comprehensive claims.[13] Political liberalism suggests therefore that individual values and decisions might derive from reference to local communities of value, and that the state should be largely indifferent as to whether or not an individual's relationship to such communities does or does not conduce to particular individual outcomes. The "diversity" variant of political liberalism offers a stronger endorsement of cultural and other sources of personal value, suggesting among other things that such communities might be thought to play an important role in creating the conditions or background which make individual choice meaningful and valuable.[14]

The comprehensivist vision is, conversely, considerably more skeptical or at times even hostile to local values communities. Because communities of value like those embodied in tradition and religion often endorse inegalitarian belief systems, individual-constraining and irrationalist values, and forms of socialization which esteem self-limitation and denial rather than autonomous choice, comprehensivists often perceive them as impediments to the realization of the comprehensive liberal vision of individual excellence. While the liberalism of comprehensive liberals denies the legitimacy of outlawing such sources of value, it suggests that the claims of local values communities to special recognition, community rights, and other arrangements like those embodied in Ontario's shari'a proposal are reasonably rejected.

I attempt here to offer some clarification of this debate, primarily by suggesting that the conflict between comprehensive or autonomy and political or diversity liberals, and between opponents and proponents of consensual shari'a arbitration, can be understood in a larger sense as a debate about the meaning and background requisites of the liberal value of individual autonomy. This is a debate with particular resonance in the Canadian context. The emphasis on the idea of multiculturalism as a hallmark of the Canadian identity seems to be growing in strength in recent years, and it suggests the likelihood of more frequent calls for special forms of cultural accommodation in the future. The increasing importance of the *Charter of Rights and Freedoms* in deliberations about our public values also suggests the relevance of the autonomy debate. Arguably, a number of relatively recent and noteworthy Supreme Court decisions such as *R. v. Butler*, *R. v. Keegstra*, and *R. v. Sharpe* among others might be thought to have turned on the question of how our courts and Canadian society at large understand the good of autonomy.[15]

Comprehensive liberalism, at least in its broader forms, suggests an identification of autonomy with the now familiar idea of making "rational life plans" independently of the constraints of external systems of value like those expressed in traditions and cultures—in "splendid isolation" one might say. A consideration of political liberalism, in contrast, suggests its accord with the notion that autonomy is realized when one is able to live one's life according to one's own self-recognized system of moral or social imperatives, an idea which suggests that local values communities might be expected to play an important role in the individual's quest to identify those duties. I make use of this distinction between liberal autonomy interests in tracing out a response to the shari'a debate in Ontario.

In the first section of the paper, I briefly outline a liberal theory of justification for shari'a arbitration, in part as a response to arguments like those offered by the Humanist Association of Canada that such a program offends the liberal value of state neutrality by substituting religious standards of value for public and secular standards. My suggestion is that the requirement of neutrality represents only one of two norms of justification in liberalism. The second is consent. The consensual shari'a program represents an intriguing hybrid which relies partially on *both* norms.

This view is problematized by some critics of the shari'a program, however, who worry that many Muslim women might be pressured by their communities and religious leaders into accepting shari'a arbitration, a circumstance which they argue is inconsonant with the notion of real consent. These sorts of concerns about the relationship between women and their local communities of value are expressed more generally by liberal-feminist Susan Moller Okin. Like those critical of Ontario's shari'a program, Okin suggests that local values communities are potential sources of social pressure and socialization which undermine women's autonomy and encourage them to make disequalizing personal choices. Her answer to the titular question of her noted essay, "Is Multiculturalism Bad for Women?," seems to be yes, as she suggests the possibility that "women might be better off if the [traditional] culture into which they were born were ... to become extinct."[16] In the second section of the paper I discuss and respond to the comprehensivist-oriented critique by Okin and others of local values communities, which I suggest founds itself largely on a conception of autonomy as splendid isolationism. I argue that splendid isolationism represents an unrealistic theory of human decision-making.

While the arguments of the second section suggest that splendid isolationism is untenable, is it the case that the influence of local values communities is nonetheless a social ill, something regrettably borne and appropriately minimized, perhaps like the social equivalent of mosquitoes? In the third section, I make a more positive case for the political liberal defence of local values communities. These communities play a number of important roles in contributing to realizing the liberal value of autonomy, more particularly understood not simply as rational life planning, but also as incorporating the value of living one's life according to one's self-recognized duties.

I conclude by noting that despite my optimism about the liberal worth of local values communities, it is nonetheless possible to overvalue them. Liberalism presupposes a citizenry with the competencies necessary for autonomous decision-making. To the extent that individuals come to the table without these skills or are impeded in developing them by their local communities, those groups may indeed take on some of the characteristics of impediments to autonomy attributed to them by comprehensive liberals like Okin. The conflict between comprehensive and political liberals is one not readily resolvable by endorsing one side over the other. The dispute expresses what is perhaps better understood as an internal tension *within* liberalism rather than as a debate between two liberalisms. A valuation of local values communities and the idea of autonomy as living one's life according to one's self-recognized moral duties suggests that consensual shari'a arbitration is a defensibly liberal arrangement; a recognition of the liberal autonomy interest in rational life planning and the possibilities that some citizens may be under-equipped for this task suggest that it is one which is appropriately offered with some limitations and safeguards.

A Liberal case for Consensual Shari'a Arbitration

An initial obstacle to the claim that both comprehensive and political liberals ought to recognize the legitimacy of Ontario's shari'a arbitration process is the question of whether, as liberals, *either* should. The duties associated with the shari'a program were to have derived from a state imposed requirement (the Ontario *Family Law Act*) that spouses recognize an obligation to share marital property upon divorce, and the arrangements made under this requirement were enforceable through the public court system. Yet the standard by which such divisions of property were to be made in shari'a cases was a religious one. As the brief of the Humanist Association of Canada to the Boyd inquiry suggests, the arrangement would seem to affront our expectation that publicly imposed obligations derive from the sort of neutral and rational standards understood as legitimating obligation in a liberal state. Can a state imposed and enforced policy invoking religious standards be understood as compatible with even the most basic requirements of a liberal state?

I think our answer to this question must depend on our understanding of the source and nature of liberal claims about the legitimacy of our obligations in the state. While a variety of philosophical rationales of liberalism are available to us,[17] among the more influential are claims which suggest that we begin in our consideration of the institutions of the state with a recognition of the equal moral status of individual persons.[18]

This recognition of the individual in turn suggests that the state has an obligation in its imposition of public duties to ensure that such duties have their explanation or source in standards of value which are recognizable as capable of accounting for, applying to, and binding those who are to be obliged by them as well as those who seek to oblige them.[19] Perhaps the most obvious way to avoid the "failure of respect" (as Ronald Dworkin, for example, would describe it)[20] entailed in failing to meet this requirement is to ensure that public obligations derive from the neutral and rational standards of the sort the Humanist Association endorses; that is, from forms of justification which *everyone* in society can be expected (at least in theory) to recognize and understand.

But a second means of meeting the requirements of individual moral equality is also available to us. The obligations of the state can be understood as respecting the moral equality of individuals affected by them even when they are not rationalistically-derived, if they flow from a standard of value which the obligee himself recognizes. This is, of course, the liberal notion of *consent*. Neutrality critics of the shari'a proposal may perhaps have underestimated the possibility that the program might be understood as finding its legitimacy at least partly in this form of liberal justification rather than solely in the norm of neutral rationality.

While I think such an underestimation is a mistake, it is an understandable one. For a variety of reasons, liberalism's neutrality standard has come to be associated in our contemporary social imagination with the entirety of liberalism's justificatory possibilities in the public realm. Our higher courts' *Charter* invalidations of public prohibitions on abortion, same sex marriages, and "swingers' clubs" can be characterized in a broader sense as disqualifications of public policies which found themselves on religious and other forms of valuation that run afoul of the neutrality standard. The larger impression such (rightly decided, I believe) rulings leave is that the neutrality standard appropriately governs our collective and public obligations and the consent standard governs our private individual decisions about such things as lifestyles, career paths, life partners, and the like. And in fact, in a modern liberal society, for most matters of public policy this relationship holds true. As our courts' conclusions in much of our *Charter* jurisprudence implies, true collective individual consent to society-wide laws invoking non-neutral and a-rationalist standards is impossible to obtain in any diverse contemporary community.[21]

What distinguishes Ontario's proposed shari'a process from the sorts of public policies which must find their justifications in the neutrality standard is that it does not in its specific applications represent a society-wide law. The *Ontario Family Law Act's* requirement of a shared property settlement upon divorce *is* one of general application, and it must therefore find its justifications in rationalist, neutral, and egalitarian standards. The shari'a option element of the law, however, would apply only when the two parties in a divorce elected to invoke it. In effect, then, the set of those affected by the law in its specific application in such circumstances is not the entire society, but simply the two divorcing spouses involved in the dispute. By dramatically narrowing the set of those affected by it, the law makes possible a consent-based justification within the public law that would be impossible in any more broadly applicable regime.

A useful analogy here might be the idea of a communal meal. In their application, most laws are something like the equivalent of a dinner party in which every guest is served the same entrée. In such circumstances, the dish to be served must accord with the nutritional, dietary, and culinary requirements of all the diners. This is a requirement which is likely to necessitate a fairly bland choice—the "rubber chicken" served at many banquets; in our analogy, the public neutrality standard for divorce settlements. The Ontario religious arbitration option, on the other hand, is more akin to a dinner party in which a selection of dishes is available (as, for example, at a communal meal in a Chinese restaurant). While the "meal" itself is not optional, the particular dish the diners choose in participating in the meal is a matter of limited choice. Each guest in such a situation may select a dish which more fully satisfies his or her own requirements (including, in our analogy, the "rubber chicken" of the public neutrality standard if the religious option is unpalatable).

The larger suggestion, then, is that despite the concerns of its critics, the religious arbitration option proposed in Ontario need not be understood as falling short of the requirements of liberal justification. Its authority can be traced not to publicly neutral and rationalistic forms of justification, but to the norm of individual consent. Arguably, that standard may (when it is available) in fact represent a more compelling, more satisfying form of justification than the neutral alternative, in the same way that the availability of choice at a dinner party increases the likelihood of each participant's satisfaction with the meal. The availability of the religious option enables individuals to choose an evaluative standard for their property settlement which offers a better fit with their own conceptions of their values, duties, interests, and preferences than the one size fits all public standard.

"Splendid Isolationism," Consent, and Social Influence

A crucial difficulty for a consent based justification of shari'a arbitration comes in the form of concerns that authentic consent may be difficult or impossible to obtain or recognize in the context of the relationship of many Ontario Muslim women to their local values community. This is a concern expressed by many of the presenters at the Boyd inquiry. The Canadian Council of Muslim Women, who opposed the proposal, argued, for example, that "the 'voluntary' nature of the women's agreement [to arbitration] may be coloured by the coercion put upon her that she is being a 'good' Muslim by following some arbitrator's interpretation of Sharia/Muslim family law."[22] The Legal Education and Action Fund echoed this concern, pointing out that "some women may be called a bad adherent to a particular faith or even an apostate if they do not comply with arbitration," noting as well that "for some women there may be very strong pressures based on culture and/or religion, or fear of social exclusion."[23]

These worries are specific expressions of a larger concern about the relationship between women and local communities of value which has recently been raised by some feminist and liberal thinkers. They problematize multiculturalist deference to local values communities, suggesting that the social authority of such groups and their frequent association with forms of value which subordinate women create a social context that represents a serious impediment to female autonomy. In a more general critique of cultural values, Janet Halley argues, for example, that culture "systematically produces constraints" (including the value of "male superordination over women") "that it then hides as habit, assumption, worldview."[24]

Susan Moller Okin, who is perhaps most strongly associated with this view, argues that "discrimination against and control of the freedom of females are practiced ... especially by religious [cultures] and those that look to the past – to ancient texts or revered traditions – for guidance or rules about how to live in the contemporary world."[25] In considering recent liberal defences of cultural rights,[26] then, Okin suggests that a crucial question must be "*whether our culture instills in us and forces upon us particular social roles.*"[27] Okin is particularly concerned with the role of local culture as a socializer and transmitter of belief in the private realm. She notes that

> [t]hough they may not impose their beliefs or practices on others, and though they may appear to respect the basic civil and political liberties of women and girls, many cultures do not, especially in the private sphere,

treat them with anything like the same concern and respect with which men and boys are treated, or allow them to enjoy the same freedoms.[28]

The forms of valuation and socialization which concern Okin are widely documented in literature describing traditional cultural and religious belief systems. Charles Fonchingong, for example, notes that writings from the early phase of twentieth century African literature are replete with androcentric narratives trivializing and implicitly subordinating women, suggesting the prevalence of such orientations in the underlying culture. In Chinua Achebe's novel *Things Fall Apart*, for example, the protagonist proudly slaughters a goat to celebrate one of his wives' successful production of three sons in a row, while, Fonchingong notes, in Elechi Amadi's *The Concubine* the main character struggles to cope with his demoralization over his wife's inability to produce a male heir.[29] Commentary critical of the Catholic Church's conception of female gender roles in the family and the clergy, as well as the Church's teachings on issues of reproductive choice provides a similar example of culturally endorsed gender subordination in the western context.[30]

Okin's arguments suggest, as do those of the shari'a program's critics, that the culturally-delineated choices of women immersed in the culture of a local values community may not be freely adopted and authentic, but rather by-products of the male dominated belief systems endorsed and furthered by their local culture. As such, cultural rights, Okin argues, bring with them the potential to "substantially limit the capacities of women and girls of that culture to live with human dignity equal to that of men and boys, and to live as freely chosen lives as they can."[31]

In her response to Okin's critique of multiculturalism, Martha Nussbaum has suggested that Okin's views are reflective of the values of comprehensive liberalism—that is, of the notion that the "fostering of personal autonomy in all areas of life [is] an appropriate goal of the state."[32] I would suggest that we might similarly characterize the views of Janet Halley, LEAF, and perhaps of the CCMW as well. Intriguingly, however, the primary argument of these commentators does not seem to be that the state should limit multiculturalism because it impedes the development by individuals of a liberal and rationalist perspective on the world. The concern emphasized, rather, is that choices for the inegalitarian and a-rational alternatives embodied in illiberal values communities may not in fact be truly consensual.

What is striking about these concerns upon initial consideration is how frequently those offering them assimilate what would seem on first thought to be two different forms of social input in individual decision-making. That is, they appear to equate *coercion* with what seem to be normatively oriented social *influences*. For the Canadian Council of Muslim Women, for example, statements by members of the Muslim community that women are or are not being "good Muslims" are defined as coercive; for LEAF, free choice is vitiated by the existence of cultural or religious pressures. Halley identifies cultural "worldviews" with constraint (not with insight or guidance), and she provides cultural values with a rather dark colouring by suggesting that they "hide" these constraints. Okin condemns with equal force cultures which *instill* illiberal beliefs about social roles in their members and cultures which *force* those roles upon them, and she suggests that female autonomy is imperiled by cultural belief even when local values communities respect the basic civil and political liberties of their female members.

But surely there are significant differences between these forms of cultural pressure or influence and that which we would more objectively identify as coercion. The forms of cultural value identified in liberal endorsements of group rights and embodied in such things as the shari'a option are not coercive in the sense that those subject to them lack alternatives. For example, Muslim women unhappy with the shari'a option have, at their preference, the choice of the more neutral public standard available to them. The pressures associated with this sort of promulgation of local cultural norms are not coercive in encouraging those subject to them to recognize the motivations of self-preservation rather than conscience. They are not, for example, imposed via the sorts of peril and punishment we usually associate with coercion—fines, jail terms, or violence. And the norm-enforcing pressures identified by LEAF and the CCMW arise from and have influence presumably because the subject of the influence herself recognizes and authorizes them. No one fears that Muslim women will be pressured to adopt Christian or Jewish forms of divorce arbitration (or *vice versa*) because we recognize that these sources of value are unlikely to be authoritative for those outside of the faith. The norm-enforcing pressure the critics condemn would seem to derive from the subject's self-endorsed system of values, is exerted by a community whose values she presumably shares, and is expressed by authorities (like the local imam) who are authoritative only because and insofar as she herself recognizes their authority.

Without some additional explanation, then, it seems difficult to justify the equation here of what would seem to be legitimate forms of social influence and cultural valuation with more recognizably (and repugnantly) coercive forms of social input. Are these critics of multiculturalism identifying that which they themselves simply disapprove—the a-rationalist values about women's personal life choices embodied in local cultural values systems—with that which we all (or all liberals at any rate) must condemn: coercively imposed "choice"?

While this is a possibility, the antipathy of these comprehensivist critics to measures like the shari'a option seems in fact to be informed not simply by a valuation of liberalism as a cultural as well as political value. Arguably it has its source in a deeper underlying idea: the notion that realization of the liberal value of autonomy requires not simply the availability of choices, but the additional requisite of significantly unencumbered circumstances of choice as well.

Two requisites of autonomy are associable with this view. First, the comprehensivist equation of coercion and social influence suggests that authentic choice is choice made in reference fundamentally to the chooser and her own interests, independently of illiberal self-constraining cultural or religious inputs. Secondly, the theory seems also to suggest that autonomy is recognizable as authentic only if the content of individual choice is itself rationalist and self-referential. Halley's argument that social constraint "hides" itself as worldview implies the premise one thinks that individuals must be understood as unlikely to make self-limiting choices openly presented to them. Okin seems to deny that individuals could authentically endorse a values system which treats them differently on the basis of their gender. She depicts younger women as making such choices out of social pressure, and notes that "older women" are "often co-opted" into furthering gender differentiated cultural values.[33] The concerns of LEAF and the CCMW seem similarly to rest on doubts about whether a choice of the shari'a option could reasonably be understood as freely made. There seems little room here to conceive of anything but rationalist and self-referential choices as considered and authentic ones.

This vision offers a conception of autonomy which seems to emphasize something like an abstract version of John Rawls' idea of the making of a "rational life plan" as expressed in the conceptual apparatus of *A Theory of Justice*.[34] It is suggestive of a critical perspective on a-rationalist sources of value, and of a conception of the liberal state as having a duty to further autonomy in this form by minimizing the influence and social role of such sources. The central interest in autonomy for individuals in this vision is to be unfettered by the influences and valuations of sources external to themselves. This package of ideas might be referred to therefore as the idea of autonomy as "splendid isolationism".

In turn, our recognition of this comprehensivist conceptualization of autonomy suggests the possibility of an additional means of explaining the differences between comprehensivists and political liberals. The comprehensivist vision of autonomy might be contrasted with an alternative conception which I think readily finds a home within the values of political liberalism. In this conceptualization, autonomy is understood as attained not in splendid isolation, but through an individual's working out their own conception of their life path and duties with the aid, contribution, resources, and input of their society's diversity of sources of value, including those embodied in local values communities. The idea of autonomy as the "search for moral referents" suggests that local values communities are important contributors to autonomy in the liberal sense.

Before considering the claims of moral referent liberalism, however, we might more critically examine the implications of the splendid isolationist position. I offer two large criticisms of that perspective here. First, I suggest that the premissory conditions of true autonomy identified by splendid isolationists are unrealistically high. Few if any significant individual choices are made independently of social input in any society, and a vision of autonomy built therefore on the idea of decision-making independently of such influences is unrealistically optimistic. Secondly, the theory of splendid isolationism arguably relies on a largely untenable denial of the reality that individuals cannot avoid reliance on a-rationalist sources of value in making significant personal decisions.

Perhaps the central concern of those critical of culturally-delineated rights or choice options, and of the shari'a program in particular, is the idea that the local values communities associated with such rights encourage women to disadvantage themselves by making choices inauthentically, in light of social influences and pressures from their familial, ethnic and religious communities. The difficulty with this theory is that it seems to envision the existence of some more idealized circumstance of individual choice, in which individuals consult only themselves, free from the influences and input of others. But it is doubtful that such a realm actually exists. It is in fact difficult to think of any individual choice even in the most culturally open societies which might be said to be made independently of any social considerations or the influence and values of others. Trivial matters like one's style of personal dress or consumer choices[35] are, of course, frequently subject to social codes. But even much more significant choices are rarely made wholly free of external input and collective valuations. A great many adult children of church-going parents can relate tales of familial criticism for their decision to cease attending religious devotions. Numerous law, medical, and other students of professional careers choose their paths at least in part because of familial and cultural valuations of these choices, and devaluations of alternatives. And few individuals are likely to be able to claim that they received no input (if even only implicit and attitudinal) from their families and cultures in choosing their spouse or rearing their children. These realities of human life suggest that splendid isolationism's ideal of radically individualized choice is simply not sociologically viable. Human beings are social creatures: only hermits make decisions in a social vacuum. Indeed, families, communities, and societies which take no interest in the choices of their members would seem to evidence the traits of dysfunction rather than optimality.

This reality raises an important difficulty. To the extent that autonomous choice is identified with socially independent choice, the value or legitimacy of a whole range—perhaps *the* whole range—of choices associated with liberal society is called into question. Since any individual choice can be seen as constructed within the influences of social pressure, every choice in this light seems subject to the dangerous possibility of inauthenticity. Why then value or privilege the private status of any personal choice? In previous generations, western nations imposed public values on private choices within marriage by, for example, enforcing laws against birth control and various forms of sexual intercourse. Are the worries of advocates of splendid isolationism about inauthentic choice suggestive of new forms of this control—a marital code of conduct perhaps, or regulation of the allocation of duties and powers within the family? While one must be careful not to exaggerate the implications of the splendid isolationist position, the conceptualization of autonomy in its terms seems to validate a significantly increased role for state oversight of private choices. I recognize that it is perhaps no answer to the specifics of Okin's critical project to make this point: it is precisely such things as the influence of groups like the family which Okin condemns.[36] Nonetheless, from a *liberal* perspective, the implications of the premises of this critical project for the public/private divide are potentially troubling, particularly if what we are trying to protect is individual autonomy.

To these concerns, we might add a second category of criticism. There are, I would argue, some significant conceptual or epistemological difficulties associated with the splendid isolationist perspective. I have suggested that unlike moral referent liberalism, the splendid isolationist version of liberalism identifies autonomy with decision-making independent of reference to a-rationalist sources of value external to the individual. There is, however, an argument to be made that the very conceptualization of an individual making life plans independently of reference to some external set or sets of values is incoherent or at least question begging.

For surely if an individual's life plan is to consist of something beyond a dog-like list of appetites prioritized by their relative strengths for the chooser, some reference to a larger set of values suggesting a higher set of priorities is required. In his noted work on autonomy, Harry Frankfurt has suggested that we can identify two orders of human desire. "First order" volitions are immediate desires and preferences. "Second order" volitions are our desires about what we would want to desire; that is, our considered conclusions about what we would want to make of our lives and how, therefore, we order, and enhance or suppress our various first order volitions.[37] The question the splendid isolationist view of autonomy begs, then, is this. From whence comes our life plan, our higher individual ordering of first level preferences, if not from some theory or theories beyond our own first order volitions which defines for the chooser some larger value or values, or, to put it in the time honoured phraseology of political philosophy, some theory of the good life? The larger argument in response to Okin and other advocates of isolationist theories of autonomy, then, is that there can be no splendid isolation because all meaningful individual choice relies, if even implicitly, on some reference to extrinsic moral or idealistic theories of value of the sort embodied in a-rationalist sources like culture and religion.

It is worth noting that this reality is perhaps somewhat obscured by the values embodied in rationalist claims like Okin's. The splendid isolationist theory seems to suggest that we *can* envision such a thing as a life plan constructed independently of a-rationalist theories of value. Okin's critique of multiculturalism and the related criticisms of Ontario's shari'a option suggest that we identify autonomous choice with the rationalist, egalitarian, and self-interested standards which govern public liberalism. There is some initial appeal to this notion. If public liberalism's neutral standard of egalitarian self-interest is not reliant on a-rationalist valuations (and while this may be among liberalism's more controversial claims, I believe that it is not), then surely the same standard applied at the individual level represents a standard of personal choice which is also *not* reliant on reference to a-rationalist values. If this is so, the problematic frameworks of meaning associated with potentially illiberal local values communities might be safely abandoned, because a more rational alternative is available to us all. This conclusion, or some version of it, would arguably seem to inform many comprehensivist visions of liberal life.

The problem with such claims, however, is that something more than a purely rational form of insight is necessary in order for one to endorse public liberalism's standards of rational self-interest as the guide for one's individual choices. To choose to live by the light of such directives is to implicitly conclude that the proper ordering of one's life and obligations to others is achieved by rationally (cold-bloodedly a critic might suggest) calculating what would, within the laws of society, most fully maximize one's self-interest and individual well-being. The theory denies that one might seek to give more than one gets, to live one's life for some larger social rather than individual goal, to immerse oneself in one's social ties, or to act spiritually rather than self-interestedly. My point is not that this theory of value is necessarily condemnable, but that it *is* a theory of value, one which relies not simply on rationality (although that is its *content*), but on a theory of the ends and values of human life which is not itself fundamentally "rational".

The larger problem with splendid isolationism's identification of autonomy not only with rationalist circumstances of choices but with rationalist *choices* then is that it implies the substitution of one particular a-rationalist theory of the goods and ends of human life for the multiplicity of possible choices otherwise available to individuals. As Robert Post notes in his assessment of Okin's critique of multiculturalism, the more comprehensively that feminist-oriented liberalism comes to invoke "objective and external criteria" in condemning what would otherwise seem to be freely chosen life patterns by women immersed in multicultural communities,

> . . . the more it loses its status as a general set of constraints on permissible gender roles and becomes a full-blown articulation of a particular vision of gender roles defined by measurable standards of equality. Not only would such an articulation naturally resist the competing visions of gender roles exemplified by multiculturalism, but it would also be more controversial and difficult to defend within our own culture.[38]

In this view, then, Okin's theory does not imply an identification of liberalism solely with the singular autonomy interest of rational life planning in splendid isolation, but the stipulation or imposition upon society of the second order theory of value which Okin and other comprehensivists prefer—what we might call *cultural liberalism*—as the standard which ought to determine individual as well as public choices. One reason this sort of vision is likely to be controversial and difficult to defend within the larger culture of our society is that it represents a form of totalizing valuation, suggesting that all aspects of human life are appropriately delimited within the terms of a singular model of the good or ideal.[39] Not only is this sort of ambitiousness difficult to reconcile with the very value of autonomy invoked by the supporters of the splendid isolationist viewpoint, it is also likely to meet resistance in any open and liberal society.

Local Values Communities and Autonomy as the Search for Moral Referents

My critique of splendid isolationism to this point would seem to suggest that we recognize the a-rationalist influences on individual choice of local values communities as what might be seen as a necessary evil. I have argued that virtually all choice is to at least some extent socially influenced, and therefore that isolationism's identification of autonomy with socially independent choice is sociologically implausible. And I have argued that significant human choices rely to an extent under-recognized by isolationists on necessarily a-rationalist beliefs about such things as human or individual ends. To this largely negative defence of local values communities might be added a more positive set of claims.

The splendid isolationism of comprehensive liberalism can be contrasted to an alternative theory of autonomy which I think makes sense from within the perspective of political or diversity liberalism. Like the isolationist vision, this theory proceeds from an understanding of individuals as having as their fundamental goal the project of a self-constructed plan of life. Unlike the isolationist vision, the alternative suggests that such a project might find its direction not simply in isolated or fundamentally self-referential decision-making, but in reference to a theory or theories of value which provide moral or social guidance to the chooser. The alternative implies the possibility of understanding the liberal individual as actively engaged, if he or she chooses to be, in attempting to construct and live a moral life which transcends his or her own particular and immediate interests. In turn, this vision is suggestive of a conception of autonomy defined as a life lived according to one's own self-recognized system of moral or social imperatives. At least three important roles for local values groups in liberal society can be identified with this ideal. Local communities of value contribute to making available the very options of choice which liberalism's valuation of autonomy esteems, they make available complex systems of valuation which contribute to individual decision-making, and they act as participants in public debate about social and personal values, encouraging individuals to consider alternative possibilities which might otherwise be unrecognized.

The first important role local values communities might be thought to play in this vision is as the very options of choice themselves. It is emblematic of a circumstance of real choice that there is a meaningful difference in outcomes depending on what we choose. Perhaps the very paradigm of non-autonomous choice is the meaningless choice: the option given to toddlers to go to bed now or fifteen minutes from now, or the slate of party-approved candidates in communist electoral systems. Intriguingly, then, in modern societies like our own which are ever more dominated by the values of cultural liberalism, there is some argument to be made that the availability of meaningful alternatives of choice is increasingly narrowed not by the *presence* of illiberal local communities of value, but by their *disappearance*. If real choice suggests the necessity of real alternatives, what we need in largely liberal societies is perhaps more, rather than fewer illiberal possibilities of individual choice. As Richard Falk has observed, "societal diversity enhances the quality of life by expanding cultural resources."[40] So too does the expansion of cultural resources increase the resources of *choice* and, thereby, of meaningful autonomy.

Arguably, then, the sort of choice made available by religious arbitration of such things as divorce settlements is a means of providing real choice in this area. In opposition to the culturally dominant values in our society of self-interested self-assertion valorized in the neutral standard of the state would stand the sort of alternative embodied in opposed visions like those of the Islamic shari'a, which suggest that religious duty must be first and foremost in the life of the chooser. The self-disadvantage for Muslim women associated with this option is, certainly, difficult to endorse or appreciate for those who stand outside the Islamic point of view, but surely we fail to respect autonomy when we substitute our own considered assumptions of value for those of the chooser herself. Meaningful choice requires meaningfully different alternatives. In a liberal society, it may often be illiberal alternatives which provide that sort of difference.

The second important contribution made by local values communities in a liberal polity is not simply as a source of choices, but as providers of what Joel Anderson and Axel Honneth call "semantic space"[41]—carriers or expressions of belief complexes which bring with them not only direction, instruction, or constraint in life choices, but relatively elaborated systems of value with their own fundamental premises, justificatory schemata, and means of reasoning and deliberating about those choices. Interestingly, this is a conceptualization of local values communities expressed both in communitarian criticisms of liberalism, and, increasingly, in more recent theories of liberalism itself.

Communitarian Alasdair MacIntyre argues, for example, that "theories of justice and practical rationality" (that is, claims about how we live our lives)

> . . . confront us as aspects of traditions, allegiance to which requires the living out of some more or less systematically embodied form of human life, . . . each with its own canons of interpretation and explanation, . . . each with its own evaluative practices.[42]

This point is perhaps most notably embraced within liberal terms in the work of Will Kymlicka. In *Multicultural Citizenship*, Kymlicka argues that "access to a societal culture" is an essential requisite of meaningful individual choice. "People make choices about the social practices around them, based on their beliefs about the value of these practices," Kymlicka argues,

> [a]nd to have a belief about the value of a practice is, in the first instance, a matter of understanding the meanings attached to it by our culture.[43]

Kymlicka's defence of a range of special "cultural rights" flows from this recognition of the centrality of culture to the valuations of choice available to individuals, and thus to individual autonomy. His concern is that our dominant majority culture may be alien to those of minority cultures, and thus incapable of providing a meaningful background of valuation for the choices of such persons. His suggestion therefore is that it is both necessary and valuable within liberal terms to provide means by which minority cultures might attempt to preserve themselves from assimilation, because such cultures provide contexts of choice and valuation which are essential to individual autonomy.[44]

Kymlicka is especially concerned to ensure the protection of contexts of choice for "national minorities" like aboriginal peoples, through mechanisms such as the Canadian reserve system and aboriginal self-government. Aboriginal scholars share this recognition of the importance of cultural space for groups like Canadian natives. Mary Ellen Turpel-LaFond, for example, has emphasized in her work the oppositional nature of European valuations of individualism and aboriginal orientations to values such as "caring and sharing."[45]

The larger suggestion of the arguments offered by Kymlicka and communitarians like MacIntyre is that individual choice cannot reasonably be understood as taking place outside of or apart from the larger systems of valuation embodied in and carried by culture. Whether one's cultural source is something like the "great traditions" of Aristotelianism or medieval Christianity identified by MacIntyre as the paradigms of cultural sources of value[46], or the dominant culture of our contemporary society, individual choice of necessity relies not just on alternative possibilities, but on the more complex premissory, explanatory, and justificatory values embodied in the complexes of culture. The importance of local values communities in this theory, then, is that they provide the intellectual resources upon which individuals might draw in working out their own theory of the good. Whether or not one endorses the communitarian view that one by necessity reasons incrementally from whatever values perspective one already inhabits[47], clearly few of us are Aristotle or Aquinas (or even John Rawls!); we are not in a position, nor are we likely to be equipped to work out our own entirely unique comprehensive theory of value from scratch. If we are to live a coherent and sensible moral life, we need access to the resources of systems of value like those embodied in cultural localities.

I hasten to point out that despite the communitarian overtones of my arguments here, I am making what I believe to be a liberal rather than communitarian claim. My suggestion is not that individuals are somehow trapped within a singular community of value, as communitarian theories sometime seem to suggest. It is, rather, that our very esteem for autonomous choice suggests the value of having available to us the range and diversity of justificatory theories embodied in a multiplicity of local values communities rather than simply the cultural liberal model seemingly endorsed by splendid isolationism, and, increasingly, by our society's larger culture. A liberal society which values diversity makes possible not just the monolithic and undifferentiated choices available within a uni-cultural society, but more complex mixtures of possibility. There is, for example, such a thing as a "Catholic liberal" in Canadian society[48], and, indeed, there is such a thing as Islamic feminism, as the shari'a critique of the Canadian Council of Muslim Women would seem to indicate. This need not be taken as evidence of the incoherence or solipsism of liberal society as communitarians sometimes like to suggest[49], but an expression of the liberal conception of each individual as engaged in reasoning not just about his rational life plans, but about the philosophy which ought to guide his or her decisions about those matters. The argument, then, is that our valuation of choice would seem to suggest the merit of having available to us a range of *theories* of choice (like those embodied in the moral systems of local communities of value) as well as simply the choices themselves.

While the first two characterizations of the contribution of local values communities to the liberal life I offer here suggest a relatively passive role for those communities–as sources of choice and the embodiments of systematic values systems, the third contribution we might note suggests a more active role for such groups. To the extent that local values communities merely provide a choice among possibilities and a theory about choosing, their role in liberal life would be relatively limited, and the choices they endorsed relatively uncompelling. The alternative choices and systems of value they embody would be lifeless and stale—a dead library of bookish choices rather than something more akin to the life and dynamism of a public bazaar. However, such communities can also be understood as playing a more active role in liberal choice: as participants themselves in public debate about the nature of individual life and obligation. They are in this sense, evangelists of alternatives, Socratic disturbers of social consensus, constructors and carriers of value, and not simply museum-like repositories of it. In this form, local values communities represent and make possible for the liberal chooser active engagement, debate, criticality, and the competition of ideas and values— the complex of values John Stuart Mill, for example, associated with the "search for truth".

These attributes are exemplified in such things as public debate around abortion. While public liberalism's values of neutrality and rationality legitimately deny the validity of state restrictions on access to abortion, we need not take this as constituting a definitive statement about the merit of *individual* choices on abortion. Local communities of value like those embodied in Christian churches and organizations have made an arguably important contribution to public debate on this issue by putting forward the idea that while abortion may be a right, it is nonetheless a right that individuals should refrain from using. Whether or not one agrees with this view, its availability seems a useful contribution to the liberal citizen's efforts to actively identify and construct his or her own theory of moral imperatives.

The same might be said about the public disagreement around consensual shari'a. Those, like the members of the Islamic Institute of Civil Justice, who endorse the shari'a program assert that the duties they recognize derive from the dictates of God, recognized through their faith. Those opposed to shari'a arbitration point out that the duties imposed by Islam on those undergoing divorce treat the genders unequally, and they seem therefore to imply a devaluation of women. The conflict represents an opportunity for those with opposing views to engage in public debate about the merit of their claims about the values of human life. Clearly, Islam's apparent theory about male and female social roles is likely to find few takers in our culture outside of those who have felt the call of faith, but the availability of those views arguably contributes to the process by which individuals in our society clarify their own views on these subjects.

Perhaps more importantly, the debate represents an opportunity for those who *have* felt the call of faith to evaluate their own beliefs. A number of the shari'a proposal's critics, including the Canadian Council of Muslim Women, have noted that some Islamic clerics have suggested that the failure to make the shari'a choice were it available would represent apostasy. While the identification of failure to partake in shari'a arbitration with apostasy has been criticized for its "coercive" influence, does it perhaps in fact simply represent the considered evaluation by the religion's authorities of Islamic duties? If so, then the unwillingness of Muslim women critical of the proposal to recognize these duties might be thought to appropriately raise some questions—for the critics themselves—about the strength or sincerity of their faith. It may also suggest to some of them that Islam is perhaps less compelling than they may have originally believed. The conflict between faith and moral values identified through other sources is, of course, an age old one, and one which any believer seeking to identify his or her moral imperatives as part of their course in life must negotiate. But these are ends arguably served more fully by exposing such conflicts through public debate rather than evading them through limitations on the role of local values communities.

Liberalism's Autonomy Interests and Consensual Shari'a Arbitration

My argument to this point suggests that we can connect two different liberal theories of autonomy to two different conceptions of the role of local communities of value in our society. If we understand autonomy as having its realization in a life lived according to individually transcendent but nonetheless self-recognized moral imperatives, we are likely to see the merit in making available space for local values communities to contribute to our personal deliberations about those imperatives. If, on the other hand, we understand autonomy as realized through a primarily rationalistic process of independent self-construction, as in splendid isolationism, we are likely to see local values communities as potentially dangerous impediments to that process.

Is this, then, simply a debate between two liberalisms, between those who endorse one ideal versus those who endorse its contrary? Both William Galston and Jacob Levy have suggested that, despite the relatively recent provenance of the "comprehensivist-political" phraseology of John Rawls and others, the divide between liberals endorsing greater and lesser roles for local values communities is a much older one. Galston identifies the historic debate as one between "Enlightenment" and "Reformation" liberals;[50] Levy, as between "rationalist" and "pluralist" liberals.[51] The divide, then, is one which liberalism has both lived with for a very long time, and has seemingly been unable to transcend.

Levy suggests that the divide represents an enduring and unavoidable tension within liberalism, an expression of an inherent Berlinian conflict between potential liberal goods. As he notes:

> A complete embrace of the local, the traditional, and the communal makes for a conservative communitarian; a complete rejection of them makes for a Jacobin. This means that no liberal thinker or style of thought is going to be purely pluralistic or purely rationalistic; the dedication to freedom, if taken seriously, will require *some* thought about the kinds of threats to freedom that each view worries about.[52]

I think this an apt conclusion. As the case for the notion of autonomy as the search for moral referents suggests, reference by individuals to a variety of a-rationalist external values system is unavoidable, and, indeed necessary to the liberal individual's project of self-definition. They are the ore which individuals mine in constructing their own self-authorized theory of morality, which in turn informs and directs their decision-making and choices about their life plans. But the unavoidability of reference to external or a-rationalist sources of value creates a tension or paradox. To the extent that any particular local community of value is or becomes too authoritative for an individual chooser, it raises the risk of impeding his or her ability to stand back from and recognize at least the possibility of alternatives; it becomes totalizing and oppressive. This is the sort of problem raised by autonomy/comprehensivist liberals like Okin, and by many of the critics of consensual shari'a. On the other hand, if the role of local communities of value is too delimited, individuals will not have access to the moral and intellectual resources necessary to adequately flesh out a morally-informed, meaningful, and self-chosen life, or they will of necessity be thrown back on the rather singular vision of such a life embodied in something like cultural liberalism. These are the sorts of concerns emphasized by diversity/political liberals.

Arguably, then, this is a tension or paradox which cannot readily be evaded by the expedient of endorsing one form of liberal autonomy at the expense of the other. This would seem to suggest the necessity of some caution in considering measures like Ontario's consensual shari'a program. The option does represent a means by which individuals might if they see fit, better adapt their own life choices to their own system of moral value. But it also raises the possibility that by making this option available to Muslim women in Ontario the government could be exposing them to what might be for some a too pervasively authoritative local values community, one which may impose subtle or not so subtle pressures to make a choice which is not authentic. To the extent that such women are trapped in a values community which too monolithically embodies a singular system of moral valuation, there is the danger too that their very reasoning about alternatives may be delimited or constrained to an extent incompatible with truly autonomous decision-making. These realities prompt a number of observations.

First, in considering the potential peril here, we should be careful not to exaggerate the extent to which we characterize the local community of value which Islamic women in Ontario inhabit as a monolith, or moral ghetto. Downtown Toronto is not the Taliban's Afghanistan, and individual choosers within the Canadian context arguably have available to them a multiplicity of cultural and moral resources which problematize and undercut the valuations of fundamentalist Islam.[53] The debate which has arisen around the shari'a option would seem evidence of the availability of such resources. The weight of the shari'a critique before the Boyd Commission was not carried by those living outside of the Islamic community, but by the Canadian Council of Muslim Women, a fact which seems to suggest that Muslim women in Canada are not constrained to the recognition of a singular choice of values systems in their moral deliberations.

On the other hand, the fact that many Canadian Muslim women can be identified with an independence from fundamentalist Islam does not necessarily imply that all can act so freely. Some question has been raised in the debate around consensual shari'a about whether Islamic-Canadian women who are recent immigrants have come to Canada properly equipped to make autonomous and authentic choices. Many such women will have been raised, socialized, and educated (or in the case of Taliban Afghanistan, *not* educated) within a cultural context where the skills and forms of reasoning associated with liberal autonomy are not valued or inculcated.

Nor are these sorts of problems necessarily unique to women from Canada's Muslim immigrant community. Western Canada's Hutterite community is an endogenous population in which young women may not only be encouraged or commended for adopting traditional subservient gender roles, but also, because of the significant self-segregation of such communities from the outside community, denied access to resources of understanding which would make their preferences for such roles

informed ones. The polygynous practices of groups identifying themselves
as "fundamentalist Latter Day Saints" (FLDS) in Canada may also have
their foundations in circumstances of uninformed and uneducated choice.
Bountiful, British Columbia, the centre of Canada's FLDS church, is a
community made up almost entirely of adherents to this sect, whose
members have also traditionally controlled the town's school board and
other institutions of local government.[54] Young men and women of the
FLDS Church are therefore brought up almost entirely within a society in
which polygynous marriage is the unquestioned norm and church
expectations of female submission to masculine authority are
comprehensively observed in everyday practice. The existence of
communities like those of the Hutterites and that of Bountiful raises
concerns about the principle of accommodating such groups through
measures like religion specific legal systems. Can "choice" be authentic
and autonomous for women from these communities given the implicit
limitations here on their ability to develop the skills of choice usually
associated with more open societies?

   It is worth noting that the debate between autonomy and diversity
liberals has been conducted to a great extent in the American context
between those endorsing publicly-mandated education for children aimed
at equipping them with the critical skills of rationality associated with
liberal thought, and those seeking to evade such requirements in the name
of preserving diversity (often, the diversity represented by the preservation
of their own local community of value from the corrosive effects of
younger members' re-evaluations of its claims).[55] While my intention here
is not to review that debate, the argument that real autonomy requires that
liberal citizens be equipped with the skills of criticality, rationality, and the
like seems from the perspective I am endorsing here a fairly evident one.
To the extent that liberalism in any of its forms values autonomy, it would
seem difficult from within that perspective to endorse something like the
educational equivalent of a consensual shari'a option for the children of
Islamic Canadians (or, for that matter, similarly limited forms of education
for the children of Bountiful or of Canada's Hutterite communities). An
educational regime in this form would seem to preclude the development
of the necessary skills required for real autonomy (including among them
the awareness of alternative possibilities), and it would therefore imply the
authorization of the very sort of totalizing scheme of value which the
liberal esteem for autonomy requires we reject.

   The reality, though, that many Islamic women will have been products
of exactly this sort of system of socialization complicates the question of
consensual choice here. In the specifics of our fact situation, is the shari'a

option compelling, or one better avoided because of the specific nature of the likely choosers here? Without wishing to evade the complexity raised by this sort of question, I would argue that the peril here might to a great extent be mitigated through measures aimed at enhancing the authenticity of the choice made by potential participants. Surprisingly, some inspiration might be drawn in this regard from one of the practices of what is generally seen as a religiously traditional and insular culture: the Amish. While the Amish share in a general sense both the quasi-self-segregation and the traditional views about gender roles of groups like the shari'a Muslims, the FLDS, and the Hutterites, their practice of *rumspringa* represents, I would argue, a means within their unique cultural context of making significant decisions about religiously delimited forms of life authentic ones.

The *rumspringa*, or "running around" period occurs in late adolescence for the Amish, in the time before individuals must expressly and publicly commit to the religious values of their society. During the running around years adolescents are expected to "sow their wild oats," and some degree of flirtation with the outside world is the norm. Depending on the rebelliousness of the particular youth, the *rumspringa* may include departing from the traditional Amish dress code, smoking, drinking, participating in youth parties, and listening to modern music. More extreme *rumspringa* experiences include getting one's driver's licence and working and living away from the community (often with a group of other Amish young) in the outside world.[56] The theory of the *rumspringa* is that its experiences will serve to make each young person aware of the possibilities of the real world, and through so doing, make his or her ultimate choice of the Amish life a real and unregretted one.

In turn, it might be suggested that the principle of authentic choice endorsed by liberalism and evident in the *rumspringa* might be achieved within the context of the shari'a option too. A properly drafted program might perhaps require that those wishing to choose the shari'a option consult a lawyer (whose fiduciary duty would require him to inform the chooser of the downside of the shari'a choice as well as of the available alternative of the neutral state standard) or attend a seminar aimed at highlighting some of the issues of choice in play here. Such an approach would preserve the option for choosers while enhancing their ability to consider their choice in a critical light.[57]

There is, of course, little doubt that the sorts of choices involved in possibilities like the shari'a option are likely to be difficult for women intimately connected to a local community of value like fundamentalist Islam. Clearly, the more self-segregated communities of this type are, as in the case of Canada's Hutterites and Fundamentalist Latter Day Saints, the more problematic will be the claim that choices for religiously delimited public laws rather than liberal alternatives really are authentic. In such circumstances it will be considerably more difficult to justify within liberal terms the provision of these kinds of options, and considerably more important if they are provided to include mechanisms aimed at making such choices considered and authentic ones.

In a larger sense, however, the nature of the challenge posed by the shari'a option for Islamic women in Canada is not entirely dissimilar to that faced by any individual in a liberal society. If we wish to be autonomous and to live a meaningful and self-chosen life, it is necessary to develop the skills and predispositions associated with making authentic and self-authorized choices in the face of conflicting options and the influence of family, friends, society, and our own and others' local communities of value. As John Stuart Mill has argued,

> The human faculties of perception, judgment, discriminative feeling, mental activity, and even moral preference, are exercised only in making a choice. . . . to conform to custom, merely as custom, does not educate or develop in [one] any of the qualities which are the distinctive endowment of a human being.[58]

The liberal valuation of autonomy rests in no small part on a respect for individual moral integrity. It may be that that capacity requires for its attainment both the circumstances of freedom *and* some degree of personal courage by those who seek it.

Works Cited

Achebe, Chinua. *Things Fall Apart*. Oxford: Heinemann, 1958.
Ackerman, Bruce A. *Social Justice in the Liberal State*. New Haven, Connecticut: Yale University Press, 1980.
Amadi, Elechi. *The Concubine*. Oxford: Heinemann, 1966.
Anderson, Joel and Axel Honneth, "Autonomy, Vulnerability, Recognition, and Justice." In *Autonomy and the Challenges to Liberalism: New Essays*, ed. Joel Anderson and John Christman, 127–149. Cambridge: Cambridge University Press, 2005.
Anderson, Joel and John Christman, eds. *Autonomy and the Challenges to Liberalism: New Essays*. Cambridge: Cambridge University Press, 2005.

Bellah, Robert N. *et al*. *Habits of the Heart: Individualism and Commitment in American Life*. Los Angeles: University of California Press, 1985.

Blais, Andre. "Accounting for the Electoral Success of the Liberal Party in Canada: Presidential address to the Canadian Political Science Association." *Canadian Journal of Political Science* 38(4) (2005): 821–40.

Boyd, Marion. "Dispute Resolution in Family Law: Protecting Choice, Promoting Inclusion: Review on the Use of Arbitration in Family and Inheritance Cases." Toronto: Attorney-General of Ontario, 2004.

Canadian Council of Muslim Women (CCMW). "Position Statement on the Proposed Implementation of Sections of Muslim Law [Sharia] in Canada", 2004, Canadian Council of Muslim Women, http://www.ccmw.com/Position/%20Papers/Position_Sharia_Law.htm (accessed July 11, 2006).

Dworkin, Ronald. *Taking Rights Seriously*. Cambridge, Massachusetts: Harvard University Press, 1977.

Falk, Richard. "The Rights of Peoples (In Particular Indigenous Peoples)". In *The Rights of Peoples*, ed. James Crawford, 17–37. Oxford: Oxford University Press, 1988.

Flathman, Richard. *Political Obligation*. New York: Atheneum, 1972.

Fonchingong, Charles. "Unbending Gender Narratives in African Literature." *Journal of International Women's Studies* 8(1) (2006): 134-142.

Foucault, Michel. *Power/Knowledge*. New York: Pantheon Books, 1980.

Frankfurt, Harry. *The Importance of What We Care About*. New York: Cambridge University Press, 1988.

Fried, Charles. *Right and Wrong*. Cambridge, Massachusetts: Harvard University Press, 1978.

Galston, William. *Liberal Purposes: Goods, Virtues, and Diversity in the Liberal State*. Cambridge: Cambridge University Press, 1991. "Two Concepts of Liberalism." *Ethics* 105(3) (1995): 516-534.

Gill, Emily. *Becoming Free: Autonomy and Diversity in the Liberal Polity*. Lawrence, Kansas: Kansas University Press, 2001.

Graham, Karen. "Submission to the Review on the Use of Arbitration in Family and Inheritance Cases on behalf of the Humanist Association of Canada." Unpublished, 2004.

Gutmann, Amy. *Democratic Education*. Princeton, New Jersey: Princeton University Press, 1987.

Gutmann, Amy and Dennis Thompson. *Democracy and Disagreement*. Cambridge, Mass.: The Belknap Press of Harvard University Press, 1996.

Halley, Janet. "Culture Constrains." In *Is Multiculturalism Bad forWomen?*, Susan Moller Okin. Ed. Joshua Cohen, Matthew Howard, and Martha Nussbaum, 100-104. Princeton: Princeton University Press, 1999.

Herzog, Don. *Happy Slaves: A Critique of Consent Theory*. Chicago: University of Chicago Press, 1989.

Kant, Immanuel. *Fundamental Principles of the Metaphysics of Morals*, ed. Thomas K. Abbot. Indianapolis: Bobbs-Merrill, 1949 [1785].

Krakauer, Jon. *Under the Banner of Heaven: A Story of Violent Faith*. New York: Anchor Books, 2003.

Kraybill, Donald. *The Riddle of Amish Culture* (Baltimore: Johns Hopkins University Press, 2001.

Kukathas, Chandran. "Can a Liberal Society Tolerate Illiberal Elements?" *Policy* 17(2) (2001): 39-45.

Kymlicka, Will. *Multicultural Citizenship*. Oxford: Clarendon Press, 1995.
"Liberal Complacencies." In *Is Multiculturalism Bad for Women?*, Susan Moller Okin. Ed. Joshua Cohen, Matthew Howard, and Martha Nussbaum, 31-34. Princeton: Princeton University Press, 1999.
Contemporary Political Philosophy (2d ed.). Oxford: Oxford University Press, 2002.

Levy, Jacob. "Liberalism's Divide, After Socialism and Before." *Social Philosophy & Policy* 20(1) (Winter 2003): 278–297.

Macedo, Stephen. *Liberal Virtues*. Oxford: Clarendon Press, 1990.
"Liberal Civic Education and Religious Fundamentalism: The Case of God v. John Rawls". *Ethics* 105(3) (1995): 468–96.
Diversity and Distrust: Civic Education in a Multicultural Democracy. Cambridge, Massachusetts: Harvard University Press, 2000.

MacIntyre, Alasdair. *Whose Justice? Which Rationality?* Notre Dame, Indiana: University of Notre Dame Press, 1988.

Manning, Christel J. "Women in a Divided Church: Liberal and Conservative Catholic Women Negotiate Changing Gender Roles." *Sociology of Religion* 58 (4) (1997): 375–390.

Mill, John Stuart. *On Liberty*. In *Utilitarianism, On Liberty, Considerations on Representative Government*. Ed. Geraint Williams. Rutland, Vermont: Charles E. Tuttle, 1994 [1859].

Nafisi, Azar. *Reading Lolita in Tehran*. New York: Random House, 2004.

Nussbaum, Martha. "A Plea for Difficulty." In *Is Multiculturalism Bad for Women?*, Susan Moller Okin. Ed. Joshua Cohen, Matthew Howard, and Martha Nussbaum, 105-114. Princeton: Princeton University Press, 1999.

Okin, Susan Moller. *Is Multiculturalism Bad for Women*? Ed. Joshua Cohen, Matthew Howard, Martha Nussbaum. Princeton: Princeton University Press, 1999.

"Is Multiculturalism Bad for Women?" In *Is Multiculturalism Bad for Women*?, Susan Moller Okin. Ed. Joshua Cohen, Matthew Howard, and Martha Nussbaum, 7-24. Princeton: Princeton University Press, 1999.

Popper, Karl. *The Open Society and its Enemies*. Princeton, New Jersey: Princeton University Press, 1966.

Post, Robert. "Between Norms and Choices." In *Is Multiculturalism Bad for Women*?, Susan Moller Okin. Ed. Joshua Cohen, Matthew Howard, and Martha Nussbaum, 65-68. Princeton: Princeton University Press, 1999.

Rawls, John. *Political Liberalism*. New York: Columbia University Press, 1993.

A Theory of Justice. Cambridge, Massachusetts: The Belknap Press of Harvard University Press, 1971.

R. v. Butler [1992] 1 *S.C.R.* 452.

R. v. Sharpe [2001] *1 S.C.R.* 45.

R. v. Keegstra [1990] 3 *S.C.R.* 697.

Richards, David A. J. *The Moral Criticism of Law*. Encino, California: Dickenson Publishing, 1977.

Schacht, Joseph. *An Introduction to Islamic Law*. Oxford: Oxford University Press, 1963.

Stolzenberg, Nomi. "'He Drew a Circle that Shut Me Out': Assimilation, Indoctrination, and the Paradox of a Liberal Education." *Harvard Law Review* 106 (1993): 581–667.

Taylor, Charles. *The Malaise of Modernity*. Concord, Ontario: House of Anansi Press, 1991.

Turpel-LaFond, Mary Ellen. "Aboriginal Peoples and the Canadian *Charter*: Interpretive Monopolies, Cultural Differences." *Canadian Human Rights Yearbook* 6 (1990): 3-45.

Women's Legal Education and Action Fund (LEAF). "Submission to Marion Boyd in Relation to Her Review of the Arbitration Act– September 17, 2004." Unpublished: 2004.

Notes

---

[1] The shari'a is a body of Islamic law drawn from religious sources such as the Quran and the hadith (the record of the actions and statements of the Prophet Mohammed), which has been set out and elaborated in the juridical writings of Islamic scholars. Islam does not recognize the liberal distinction between the church and the state, and the shari'a is therefore understood as applying to both realms (Joseph Schacht, *An Introduction to Islamic Law* (Oxford: Oxford University Press, 1963), 5).

[2] The shari'a is a body of Islamic law drawn from religious sources such as the Quran and the hadith (the record of the actions and statements of the Prophet Mohammed), which has been set out and elaborated in the juridical writings of Islamic scholars. Islam does not recognize the liberal distinction between the church and the state, and the shari'a is therefore understood as applying to both realms (Joseph Schacht, *An Introduction to Islamic Law* (Oxford: Oxford University Press, 1963), 5).

[2] Karen Graham, "Submission to the Review on the Use of Arbitration in Family and Inheritance Cases on behalf of the Humanist Association of Canada" (unpublished, 2004), cited by Marion Boyd, *Dispute Resolution in Family Law: Protecting Choice, Promoting Inclusion: Review on the Use of Arbitration in Family and Inheritance Cases* (Toronto: Attorney-General of Ontario, 2004), 47.

[3] Boyd, 42.

[4] Women's Legal Education and Action Fund (LEAF), "Submission to Marion Boyd in Relation to Her Review of the Arbitration Act – September 17, 2004" (unpublished, 2004), cited by Boyd, 50.

[5] Critics might be forgiven for suggesting that the Ontario government adroitly sidestepped the issue. One of the interesting difficulties for the government here was that other religious communities in the province (Christians and Jews) had had the opportunity to make use of consensual religious arbitration for quite some time. An attempt by the government to prohibit the disequalizing perils of specifically shari'a based religious arbitration by forbidding Islamic arbitration would perhaps have been expected to run afoul of the *Charter*'s guarantee of equality in section 15. Deciding perhaps that discretion was the better part of valour, the government opted to eliminate all forms of religious arbitration rather than attempting to preserve the less controversial Christian and Jewish forms while denying the Islamic proposal.

[6] John Rawls, *Political Liberalism* (New York: Columbia University Press, 1993), xxxix.

[7] Will Kymlicka, *Contemporary Political Philosophy* (2d ed.) (Oxford: Oxford University Press, 2002), 236.

[8] Rawls, *Political Liberalism*; Stephen Macedo, *Liberal Virtues* (Oxford: Clarendon Press, 1990). Arguably, both Rawls and Macedo can be understood as having turned to a more diversity oriented liberalism from previously more comprehensively oriented positions. Rawls acknowledges this in his case in *Political Liberalism* (xvii). Macedo amends the more comprehensively oriented

theory of liberalism he offers in the 1990 work *Liberal Virtues* in "Liberal Civic Education and Religious Fundamentalism: The Case of God v. John Rawls" (*Ethics* 105(3) (1995), 468 – 96). He notes there that he "would now more clearly circumscribe the direct authority of the state, allowing it to promote autonomy and critical thinking in politics but not in, e.g. religion" (n39).

[9] Martha Nussbaum, "A Plea for Difficulty," in *Is Multiculturalism Bad for Women?*, Susan Moller Okin, ed. Joshua Cohen, Matthew Howard, and Martha Nussbaum (Princeton: Princeton University Press, 1999), 105 – 114; William Galston, "Two Concepts of Liberalism." *Ethics* 105(3) (1995): 516 – 534; Chandran Kukathas "Can a Liberal Society Tolerate Illiberal Elements?" *Policy* 17(2) (2001): 39 - 45.

[10] William Galston, *Liberal Purposes: Goods, Virtues, and Diversity in the Liberal State* (Cambridge: Cambridge University Press, 1991), 230.

[11] Kant and Mill are almost universally offered as examples of comprehensive liberalism, although the focus of those offering this characterization is primarily on the comprehensiveness of these authors' theory of human value rather than on their perceptions of local values communities (see Rawls, *Political Liberalism*, 37; but see also Nussbaum, "A Plea for Difficulty," 109).

[12] John Rawls, *A Theory of* Justice (Cambridge, Massachusetts: The Belknap Press of Harvard University Press, 1971), noted in Rawls, *Political Liberalism*: xviii; Macedo, *Liberal Virtues*, noted in Stephen Macedo, "Liberal Civic Education and Religious Fundamentalism: The Case of God v. John Rawls." *Ethics* 105(3): 468 – 96; Don Herzog, *Happy Slaves: A Critique of Consent Theory* (Chicago: University of Chicago Press, 1989); Susan Moller Okin, "Is Multiculturalism Bad for Women?" in *Is Multiculturalism Bad for Women?*, Susan Moller Okin, ed. Joshua Cohen, Matthew Howard, and Martha Nussbaum (Princeton: Princeton University Press, 1999), 7 - 24.

[13] Rawls, Political Liberalism, xl.

[14] Will Kymlicka has argued, for example, that the valuations individuals place on their choices derive from the meanings attached to those choices by a culture. Those of minority cultures are in a sense dispossessed of meaningful referents of value when they find themselves immersed in a majority culture alien to them. In this view, since meaningful choice requires access to a societal culture, it is the liberal valuation of autonomy itself which suggests the merit of at least some recognition of local values communities in any society (Will Kymlicka, *Multicultural Citizenship* (Oxford: Clarendon Press, 1995), 83).

[15] *Butler* (*R. v. Butler* [1992] 1 *S.C.R.* 452) concerned *Criminal Code* provisions outlawing forms of pornography which degraded women; *Sharpe* ([2001] *1 S.C.R.* 45), the possession of child pornography; and *Keegstra* ([1990] 3 *S.C.R.* 697), hate speech involving claims that Jews were part of an evil and manipulative global conspiracy. In each case, the Supreme Court of Canada upheld at least in part restrictions on freedom of speech on the grounds that the restricted expression brought with it the danger of creating condemnable attitudes in individuals exposed to the expression in question. The Court's conclusion in each case that autonomous and authentic decision-making was imperiled by exposure to negative

messages is arguably largely consistent with the anti-multi-cultural orientations of
the comprehensivist side of the debate in consideration here.
[16] Okin, "Is Multiculturalism Bad for Women?," 22.
[17] Bruce Ackerman, *Social Justice in the Liberal State* (New Haven, Connecticut:
Yale University Press, 1980), 369.
[18] As seen, for example, in the works of Immanuel Kant (Immanuel Kant,
Fundamental Principles of the Metaphysics of Morals, ed. Thomas K. Abbot
(Indianapolis: Bobbs-Merrill, 1949 [1785])), John Rawls (*A Theory of Justice*),
Ronald Dworkin (Ronald Dworkin, *Taking Rights* Seriously (Cambridge,
Massachusetts: Harvard University Press, 1977)), and David Richards (David
Richards, *The Moral Criticism of Law* (Encino, California: Dickenson Publishing,
1977)).
[19] Amy Gutmann and Dennis Thompson offer a version of this notion when they
endorse the idea of "reciprocity" as one of the concomitants of public debate in
liberal societies, a requirement expressed in the aspiration that citizens employ "a
kind of political reasoning that is mutually justifiable" (Amy Gutmann and Dennis
Thompson, *Democracy and Disagreement* (Cambridge, Mass.: The Belknap Press
of Harvard University Press, 1996), 53).
[20] Dworkin, *Taking Rights Seriously,* 227.
[21] Richard Flathman makes the same point in regard to consent theory more
generally (Richard Flathman, *Political Obligation* (New York: Atheneum, 1972),
209).
[22] Canadian Council of Muslim Women (CCMW), "Position Statement on the
Proposed Implementation of Sections of Muslim Law [Sharia] in Canada"
(Canadian Council of Muslim Women, 2004), http://www.ccmw.com/
Position/%20Papers/Position_Sharia_Law.htm   (accessed July 11, 2006).
[23] LEAF; cited by Boyd, 50.
[24]Janet Halley, "Culture Constrains" in *Is Multiculturalism Bad for Women?*, Susan
Moller Okin, ed. Joshua Cohen, Matthew Howard, and Martha Nussbaum
(Princeton: Princeton University Press, 1999), 99–104, at 101.
[25] Okin, "Is Multiculturalism Bad for Women?," 21.
[26] Like that offered by Will Kymlicka in *Multicultural Citizenship*, for example
(see note 14 above).
[27]Okin, "Is Multiculturalism Bad for Women?," 22 (italics in original).
[28] Okin, "Is Multiculturalism Bad for Women?," 21.
[29] Charles Fonchingong, "Unbending Gender Narratives in African Literature."
Journal of International Women's Studies 8(1) (2006): 134–142, at 135, citing
Chinua Achebe, Things Fall Apart (Bonn: Heinemann, 1958) and Elechi Amadi,
The Concubine (Bonn: Heinemann, 1966).
[30] Christel Manning ("Women in a Divided Church: Liberal and Conservative
Catholic Women Negotiate Changing Gender Roles." *Sociology of Religion* 58 (4)
(1997): 375–390) notes for example the following characterization of the Catholic
Church by a disaffected female member:

Catholicism is very, very man-based. Like my daughter couldn't serve as an altar-boy or altar-girl or whatever because they said it's just not done. . . . Because men run the church, the Pope is a man, the cardinals, the bishops, the priest is a man, everybody is a man! I think we're all here to work together as equals, not men up there judging women down here. (379)

[31] Okin, "Is Multiculturalism Bad for Women?," 21.

[32] Nussbaum, "A Plea for Difficulty," 108.

[33] Okin, "Is Multiculturalism Bad for Women?," 24.

[34] Rawls, *A Theory of* Justice, 408.

[35] In the 1960s, for example, purchasing a non-American car was a consumer choice made in conflict with social attitudes that suggested the decision was, at best, eccentric; at worst, unmanly. Similarly, decisions about consumer purchases and fashion are also driven, of course, by advertising invoking cultural authorities, authoritative symbolism, and other tools of influence in the marketer's arsenal.

[36] Okin, "Is Multiculturalism Bad for Women?," 12.

[37] Harry Frankfurt, *The Importance of What We Care About* (New York: Cambridge University Press, 1988), 16. Emily Gill offers a helpful gloss on Frankfurt's ideas. "Even addicts", she suggests, "experience second-order volitions when they are unwilling addicts. . ." (Emily Gill, *Becoming Free: Autonomy and Diversity in the Liberal Polity*. Lawrence, Kansas: Kansas University Press, 2001), 22) meaning, of course, that even those most driven by appetite nonetheless might be expected to recognize something beyond those appetites as appropriately defining their priorities.

[38] Robert Post "Between Norms and Choices" in *Is Multiculturalism Bad for Women?*, Susan Moller Okin, ed. Joshua Cohen, Matthew Howard, and Martha Nussbaum (Princeton: Princeton University Press, 1999), 63–7, at 66.

[39] Michel Foucault has described one of the goals of his post-modernist philosophy as being the identification of "hegemonies of truth." Arguably, the implications of splendid isolationism are suggestive of the "tyranny of globalizing discourses" (Michel Foucault, *Power/Knowledge* (New York: Pantheon Books, 1980), 83) which Foucault contends are antithetical to freedom. Karl Popper's condemnation in *The Open Society and its Enemies* of Plato's systematic integration of all aspects of human life in *The Republic* is also suggestive of the sorts of concerns raised by theories of social life which attempt to stipulate too much (Karl Popper, *The Open Society and its Enemies* (Princeton, New Jersey: Princeton University Press, 1966), 169).

[40] Richard Falk, "The Rights of Peoples (In Particular Indigenous Peoples)" in *The Rights of Peoples*, ed. James Crawford (Oxford: Oxford University Press, 1988), 23, cited by Kymlicka, *Multicultural Citizenship*, 121.

[41] Joel Anderson and Axel Honneth, "Autonomy, Vulnerability, Recognition, and Justice," in *Autonomy and the Challenges to Liberalism: New Essays*, ed. Joel Anderson and John Christman (Cambridge: Cambridge University Press, 2005), 127–149, at 138.

---

[42]Alasdair MacIntyre, *Whose Justice? Which Rationality?* (Notre Dame, Indiana: University of Notre Dame Press, 1988), 391. In his communitarian works like *The Malaise of Modernity* (Concord, Ontario: House of Anansi Press, 1991), Charles Taylor similarly suggests that individual choice is not meaningful, not articulable, outside of some individually transcendent framework of value. As he succinctly notes, individuals cannot ". . . determine what is significant, either by decision, or perhaps unwittingly and unwillingly by just feeling that way. This is crazy. I couldn't just decide that the most significant action is wiggling my toes in warm mud. Without a special explanation, this is not an intelligible claim." (36)
[43] Kymlicka, *Multicultural Citizenship*, 83.
[44] While this claim might be thought to identify Kymlicka as a political rather than comprehensive liberal, it is likely that he would reject that categorization. Kymlicka suggests, for example that the political-comprehensive distinction is "overvalued" (Kymlicka, *Contemporary Political Philosophy*, 239), and his own position is a nuanced one. In *Multicultural Citizenship*, he endorses what seems to be a comprehensivist conception of the foundations of liberalism, proclaiming the central value of an ongoing revision of one's conceptions as part of life in a liberal society (Kymlicka, *Multicultural* Citizenship, 82). And in "Liberal Complacencies" he in fact accepts Okin's comprehensivist concern that local values communities might be thought to impede women's autonomy even in the context of societies which publicly protect civil liberties (Will Kymlicka, "Liberal Complacencies," in *Is Multiculturalism Bad for Women?*, Susan Moller Okin, ed. Joshua Cohen, Matthew Howard, and Martha Nussbaum (Princeton: Princeton University Press, 1999), 28–34, at 32). While this would seem to imply the validity of greater state intervention within multicultural communities on behalf of liberal values, Kymlicka has also suggested that liberals cannot "impose their principles on groups that do not share them" (Kymlicka, *Multicultural* Citizenship, 165), an argument which is consistent with the more extreme versions of political liberalism offered by writers like Chandran Kukathas (who has argued that liberalism ought be characterized as a "federation of liberty"—that is, an aggregation of potentially illiberal groups—rather than a "union of liberty", where intra- as well as extra-group life is delimited by liberal values (Kukathas, 45).
.[45] Mary Ellen Turpel-LaFond, "Aboriginal Peoples and the Canadian *Charter*: Interpretive Monopolies, Cultural Differences." *Canadian Human Rights Yearbook* 6 (1990): 3–45, at 29.
[46]MacIntyre, 349.
[47] See, for example, MacIntyre, 91.
[48] Andre Blais, "Accounting for the Electoral Success of the Liberal Party in Canada: Presidential address to the Canadian Political Science Association," *Canadian Journal of Political Science* 38(4) (2005): 821–40.
[49] Robert Bellah, for example, associates the idea of self-constructed systems of morality with a rather vapid solipsism he emblematizes in the new age beliefs of Sheila Larson, who has created for herself a faith she calls "Sheilaism". She defines her faith this way: "it's just try to love yourself and be gentle with yourself. You know, I guess, take care of each other. I think He would want us to take care

of each other" (Robert Bellah and others, *Habits of the Heart: Individualism and Commitment in American Life* (Los Angeles: University of California Press, 1985), 220-1.
[50] William Galston, "Two Concepts of Liberalism." Ethics 105(3) (1995): 516–534, at 526.
[51] Jacob Levy, "Liberalism's Divide, After Socialism and Before." Social Philosophy & Policy 20(1) (Winter 2003): 278–297.
[52] Levy, 291.
[53] Nor is it clear that we need picture Muslim women as quite so vulnerable or unimaginative as the critics of multiculturalism would seem to suggest. In *Reading Lolita in Tehran* (Azar Nafisi (New York: Random House, 2004)), Azar Nafisi recounts the story of a group of Muslim women who set out covertly to read a variety of western classics while living under the fundamentalist Shi'ite regime of contemporary Iran. If Muslim women living within such an order can envision and grasp these possibilities, can consider these sorts of alternative modes of valuation even in the face of the very real coercion of state violence, it would seem to be an undervaluation of their Canadian counterparts to assume that they might not have the means and character to recognize such possibilities in our own much more open and less oppressive circumstances.
[54] Jon Krakauer, *Under the Banner of Heaven: A Story of Violent Faith* (New York: Anchor Books, 2003), 34.
[55] Nomi Stolzenberg suggests, for example, that minority demands for exemption from liberally-oriented public primary education are compelling because such processes threaten cultural survival (Nomi Stolzenberg, "'He Drew a Circle that Shut Me Out': Assimilation, Indoctrination, and the Paradox of a Liberal Education." *Harvard Law Review* 106 (1993): 581–667, at 583). Charles Fried defends such exemptions on the ground of parents' individual rights (Charles Fried, *Right and Wrong* (Cambridge, Massachusetts: Harvard University Press, 1978), 152). William Galston also suggests limitations on liberal oriented public education (William Galston, *Liberal Purposes: Goods, Virtues, and Diversity in the Liberal State* (Cambridge: Cambridge University Press, 1991), 254). Amy Gutmann takes a more middle ground position (Amy Gutmann, *Democratic Education* (Princeton, New Jersey: Princeton University Press, 1987), 42), while Stephen Macedo defends the role of public schools in equipping children with the "liberal virtues" (Stephen Macedo, *Diversity and Distrust: Civic Education in a Multicultural Democracy* (Cambridge, Massachusetts: Harvard University Press, 2000), 164).
[56] Donald Kraybill, *The Riddle of Amish Culture* (Baltimore: Johns Hopkins University Press, 2001), 145–6; 184–5.
[57] In her concluding recommendations following the Ontario public inquiry on the matter, Marion Boyd endorsed a variety of safeguards for those opting for shari'a arbitration. Among them was the suggestion that "[r]egulations in the *Arbitration Act* or the *Family Law Act* should require arbitration agreements in family law and inheritance cases to contain either a certificate of independent legal advice of an explicit waiver of independent legal advice" (Boyd, 135).

---

[58] John Stuart Mill, *On Liberty*, in *Utilitarianism, On Liberty, Considerations on Representative* Government, ed. Geraint Williams (Rutland, Vermont: Charles E. Tuttle, 1993 [1859]), 126.

CHAPTER SIX

FREEDOM OF RELIGION
AND TERRORISM IN CANADA

BARRY COOPER

The context for these reflections on the broad question of freedom of religion and Canadian democracy is shaped by Islamist terrorism and the connection of this political and ideological movement to Islam and to associated questions of significance for the Islamic community in Canada. The threat posed by Islamist terrorists is military and political, and it can be understood and analyzed using the relatively straightforward concepts of political science. The relationship between, for example, al-Qaeda and Canadian mosques staffed by salafist imams or mullahs is more complex. Some guidance can be found in the experience of Australia, the US, and the UK as well as from analyses of it by observers in those countries, matters that I consider briefly at the end of this chapter.

I begin, however, with an account of the character and evolution of Islamist terrorist organizations, specifically of al-Qaeda and its affiliates. The intramural arguments among salafists over the priority to be accorded the "near" versus the "far" enemy, fascinating as they may be in other respects, can for the present topic be ignored.[1] For the time being Canadian democracy is numbered among the "far" enemies but like other western countries it also provides rich recruitment possibilities, so it is not entirely a "far" enemy even in salafist usage.

Regarding the character of Islamist and indeed other terrorists we can be brief. In *New Political Religions,*[2] I described the consciousness shared by salafists and other terrorists who used religious symbols to give meaning to their actions as being pneumopathological; that is, such actions are evidence of a spiritual disease. The term was borrowed from Eric Voegelin, who borrowed it from Schelling. Voegelin used it to analyze first the National Socialist revolutionaries and then the international socialists who claimed to be following the teachings of Marx. It is a theoretically adequate concept but it is rather removed from common discourse and commonsense.

Christopher Hitchens, who is nothing if not commonsensical, described Islamist consciousness as an amalgam of self-righteousness, self-pity and self-hatred. The first attribute dates from the time of the Prophet; the second is from the thirteenth century when the Mongol Khan, Hülagu executed the Caliph (according to legend) by using ponies to stomp him to death; and the last is a twentieth-century experience and has been attributed to the inability of the Muslim community, the ummah, to resist modernity. Martin Amis was even more straightforward:

> We respect Islam – the donor of countless benefits to mankind, and the possessor of a thrilling history. But Islamism? No, we can hardly be asked to respect a creedal wave that calls for our own elimination. More, we regard the Great Leap Backwards as a tragic development in Islam's story, and now ours. Naturally we respect Islam. But we do not respect Islamism, just as we respect Muhammad and do not respect Muhammad Atta.[3]

Those who are more comfortable with psychological language can look to accounts of a typical example of a salafist intellectual such as Sayeed Qutb and his strange anxieties about western women whom he found both threatening and tempting in Greeley, Colorado, of all places, in 1949, when Greeley was dry. Or there is the testimony of Azar Nafisi whose *Reading Lolita in Tehran* discusses the problem of "temporary marriage" as a response to "men's needs."[4] Since the 1979 Revolution, such marriages can be consummated with nine-year old girls. On the other hand, Nafisi also reports on the problem of "illegal dreams" experienced by a ten-year old boy, of being at the seaside and witnessing, in the dream, men and women kissing. He did not know what to do. The language of sex also informs Islamist politics. As Bernard Lewis observed in *The Crisis of Islam,*[5] the Great Satan, first identified with the United States by the Ayatolla Khomeini, is the "insidious tempter who whispers into the hearts of men from among the jinn and men" (*Koran,* cxiv). The language of temptation and seduction seems to come naturally and unbidden. The problem with it is that the United States and, more broadly, the West is not engaged in seduction. The West may be attractive to Muslims, and immigration data would bear this out, but to pretend that the purpose of the West is to tantalize and tempt pious Muslims to sin says more about their kind of piety than about the West and its many vulgar and sexualized faults.

It is important to bear in mind from the start that Islamists, and especially suicide-mass murderers, are neither ordinary criminals nor honourable soldiers who would find useful employment in the genuine anti-Crusader armies of the great Saladin. In this respect, whether they are described as pneumopaths, psychopaths, or merely sex-obsessed narcissists, is secondary. However characterized, they are a problem to be analyzed, not a partner in conversation about God or anything else. Moreover, in this respect it is secondary whether the analysis is undertaken by a psychologist, a literary critic, a historian or a political scientist.

The arrest in June of 2006 of seventeen men in the Toronto area for planning a terrorist attack on several symbolic targets was important for what it said about al-Qaeda and its affiliates as well as for what it said about the operational success of CSIS and the RCMP against so-called home-grown Islamists. We will consider first what the Toronto arrests say about the evolution of the terrorist network identified with al-Qaeda.[6]

Over the years al-Qaeda has been organized in a number of different modes. During the early 1990s, it was focused almost exclusively on Osama bin Laden and his "Afghan Arabs," the veteran mujahadeen who, in their own minds, had defeated the Red Army for the first time in Soviet history. This first organization was minimally trained and supported in camps in Afghanistan and then dispatched abroad to conduct terrorist or other militant operations.[7] The most audacious action undertaken by this first al-Qaeda group, which we may call AQ-1, was the 1993 attack on the World Trade Center organized by Abdel Basit, aka Ramzi Yousef. Basit is thought by some analysts to have had ties to Iran. Other successful operations of the 1990s included attacks on the American embassy in Yemen and against USAF personnel in Aden. Operation Bojinka, which targeted a dozen or so trans-Pacific flights, and Basit's other attempts to kill the Pope and Bill Clinton, did not work out.

Later in the 1990s, the links between al-Qaeda and its agents became more obvious to Western security and counterterrorism agencies. The 1998 bombings of the US embassies in Dar-es-Salaam and Nairobi left a trail that led almost directly to al-Qaeda, as did the so-called "millennium bomber," Assad Ressam, who was arrested after disembarking from the MV *Coho* in Port Angeles. Ressam had supported himself for several years in Montreal and had his sights on LAX. Perhaps after a tip from CSIS, he was arrested after panicking when questioned by an American customs officer – a woman, as it happened. The last attack by this mode of al-Qaeda was the 2000 attack that nearly sunk USS *Cole*. Looking back, AQ-1 enjoyed mixed success and, because bin Laden did not claim responsibility, it maintained a relatively low profile.

The 9/11 attack announced a new mode: AQ-2. This large team was carefully selected and very well trained. Despite a few lapses, they maintained good operational security. And they were spectacularly successful. They were dispatched under the direct control of bin Laden, though at first he denied responsibility as if it were an operation undertaken in an earlier mode. The advantage of AQ-2 was its tight command-and-control; the disadvantage was that it was resource-intensive and, despite the ability to hide from security forces, it left enough traces to ensure that it was, if not a one-time attack, a mode of operation that was very difficult to repeat.

Even so, the success of 9/11 in influencing the consciousness of the salafist-inclined members of the ummah would be hard to exaggerate. Specifically it introduced and provided an opportunity to recruit "home-grown" jihadists precisely because the actions of counterterrorist organizations made a follow-on attack using the 9/11 model unlikely. A third variant, AQ-3, may be understood as a response to the new conditions created by Western and allied security forces after 9/11. This new mode uses local cells and local leadership, not foreign-trained and centrally commanded terrorists undertaking operations on foreign soil. These terrorists may have spent some time abroad for training or may have fought in foreign parts such as the Balkans, but by and large they have only been inspired, not commanded, by the al-Qaeda leadership. The members are at home in the target societies and conduct their operations only in the places they live.

Examples of this mode include al-Qaeda in Arabia or Tawhid wa al-Jihad in Egypt, which carried out the attacks on tourist sites in Sinai. The July 2005 attack on the London transit system falls into this category as well, though the leader, Mohammed Siddique Khan, is also thought to have been in touch with the al-Qaeda leadership in Pakistan. Likewise, the Madrid attack appears to have been conducted in this mode, as was the attack in Mumbai in July, 2005, which was likely carried out by Lashkar-e-Taiba (LeT), the first time an attack of such sophistication was carried out outside Kashmir. In contrast, al-Qaeda in Iraq, which might arguably fall into this category as well, can be better understood in the context of the Iraq insurgency rather than that of the evolution of terrorist activity.

In this mode, as noted, the terrorists are not effectively directed by the al-Qaeda leadership nor are they dispatched abroad by them. Recruits are also not as competent as AQ-2; several plots have been disrupted and arrests made–for example, the August, 2006 airline plot was stopped by British and American counterterrorism authorities, and a month later two attacks aimed at oil facilities in Yemen were prevented. Both of these latter two operations, like the successful London subway bombing, are likely to have had some remote direction from the al-Qaeda leadership, which underlines the relative weakness of the AQ-3 operatives.

The evolution of AQ-1 to AQ-3 has been described as the devolution of "al-Qaeda, the group" to "al-Qaeda, the movement."[8] The expectation is that the later modes are more like franchises than centrally-directed corporate entities. One of the implications of this development is that the later modes will be less skillful in conducting clandestine activities among hostiles without exposure–what intelligence professionals and John Le Carré call "tradecraft." The 7/7 bombers in London, for instance, were videotaped together on closed circuit television getting on a train in Luton a week before the attack, presumably for a practice run. This violates an elementary rule of tradecraft. Similar security lapses allowed American counterterrorist officials to plant a mole in the Liberty City, Florida cell.[9] Members of this group, called "Seas of David," wanted to get in touch with al-Qaeda but in fact contacted an FBI informant, which resulted in their arrest. Their exaggerations about blowing up the Sears Tower in Chicago did not mean that the Florida group could not do some serious damage if ever they made contact, as the 7/7 terrorists apparently did, with capable individuals actually in or associated with al-Qaeda. Similarly, the 2007 plot to blow up jet fuel tanks at JFK airport in New York might have succeeded had the plotters been more competent. We must constantly bear in mind that, notwithstanding their lax operational security, the London bombers succeeded in their attack.

In this context, the Toronto group, which operated in what we may call an AQ-4 mode, appears to have been organized on a basis that is significantly more sophisticated than the AQ-3 model. The Toronto jihadis, as with AQ-3, were home-grown and may also have had a loose connection to the al-Qaeda leadership. In addition, however, they had regular and password-protected communication to both American and British groups. AQ-4 is, by comparison to AQ-3, much more internationally connected, which opens the possibility of simultaneous attacks, say, in Toronto, New York, and London. This might have been possible for AQ-2, if it still existed, but not for a grassroots network operating, if not independently, then without the close operational control of the central leadership.

The big change from AQ-3 to AQ-4 seems to have been the use made of the Internet.[10] For several years the Internet has been a source of technical information and a means of communication for aspiring terrorists. There are, quite literally, thousands of websites containing information on timing devices, recipes for mixing explosives for IEDs, and for biological and chemical toxins. Much of this information is not entirely accurate, which has the happy consequence that amateurs mixing up a batch of a volatile explosive such as TATP are likely to blow themselves up in the process. Elsewhere, websites such as Azzam.com are useful for fundraising, recruiting and PR. Al-Qaeda in Iraq, when led by the late Abu Musab al-Zarqawi, made daily use of the Internet to publicize their policy statements. Videos of suicide operations, ambushes, eulogies for suicide murderers, and, most brutal of all, the videos of the decapitation of captives, all ensured that Zarqawi became a household name. Generally speaking, the Web has been a major enabler of the transition of al-Qaeda from group to movement, from cadre to network. The Internet has also been used as an effective tool in conducting information warfare in order to maintain esprit de corps on the side of the terrorists and to try to break the will of their opponents.

Aside from Web-based technical information and cyberwar, the key to the success of a terrorist operation is, at the end of the day, the ability to avoid detection when the police and counterterrorist agents are looking for such activities. Tradecraft is complex and subtle; it can be learned only in the real world where many sparrows fall and many amateurs are arrested. In this respect, terrorism (and counterterrorism) is like brain surgery: you cannot learn it on the Internet. Both the individual terrorist and the network must be skilled and, as with counterterrorist officers, the skills can be learned only with practice no matter how sophisticated the technology of communication. For example, on-line instructional materials tell would-be terrorists what kinds of information is needed for success but do not, because they cannot, explain how to get it without detection. The arrest of Ahmed Ressam resulted directly from his inability to fight what intelligence people call the "burn syndrome," the fear that the person observing you, such as a front-line customs official, knows you have a trunk full of explosives. In consequence of his fear, whether the Americans had been tipped off or not, Ressam acted suspiciously and then tried to run away.

Perhaps the most significant fact in all this is that the terrorists from AQ-1 to AQ-4 seem unable to learn from their mistakes. Even the elite AQ-2 squad made major errors, any one of which could have resulted in failure. In this respect the mistakes of coalition intelligence agencies have apparently been easier to deal with, much to the surprise of many analysts. It might be more accurate to say more cautiously that in the balance between failures in tradecraft and failures in intelligence analysis, *so far* the intelligence agencies seem to have learned more than the terrorists. The future decentralization of al-Qaeda means a future decline in tradecraft, notwithstanding such things as the very practical training in

IED construction, for example, available to jihadists in Iraq and Afghanistan. After all, fighting an insurgency is as different from a clandestine operation as a counter-insurgency is from a Clausewitzian war between regular armies. Learning to fire an RPG will not help you glide invisibly through the back streets of London. On balance, therefore, it would seem that the devolved modes of al-Qaeda, AQ-3 and AQ-4 can again be, as they have been, significantly interrupted by coalition intelligence agents.

To return to the Toronto cell, which I argued followed the AQ-4 mode: clearly, Internet chat rooms enabled this group to communicate internationally. But that enabler is also a two-edged sword or, switching metaphors, an Achilles heel. On-line people are not always the same as they appear in person: ask anyone who has had an unhappy experience with web-mediated dating. Likewise, just as investigators can monitor and sometimes meet pedophiles by impersonating children, CSIS or MI-5 or the FBI can do the same with jihadist networks. The Toronto group was penetrated by Mubin Shaikh, a self-proclaimed "sharia activist" and devout Muslim in the pay of CSIS and the RCMP.[11] Shaikh received a good deal more training by his handlers in the Canadian security organizations than he did from the target group. Indeed, the "Toronto 17" were so deficient in tradecraft that, even after three of their colleagues in the international network had been arrested quite publicly in the UK, the US and Bangladesh, they still continued to prepare for their attack. Elementary prudence would have told them to keep their heads down until the pressure from law-enforcement and intelligence officers was reduced.

The conclusion I would draw from this account of the evolution of the modes of al-Qaeda is that operational security in AQ-4 is no better than AQ-1. Of course, some AQ-4 bumblers could get lucky and pull off a major attack, which means that counterterrorism officers will not be out of work any time soon. More importantly, several analysts have made the point that many AQ-3 and AQ-4 recruits, notwithstanding their incompetence in operational security to date, are well educated and intelligent. Eventually some of them will figure out what their chief weakness is and take steps to fix it.

A second conclusion, which leads to the second general point I would like to make, is that AQ-4, of which the Internet-savvy amateurs of Toronto are an early example, are also *young* men. They are too young to have fought in Bosnia or Afghanistan and, while such men might make a pilgrimage to Pakistan for some rudimentary training as terrorists or insurgents, this would not be of much help in bringing down the CN Tower. On the one hand, their experience is limited. On the other, these

Gen-Y jihadists became Islamists after the spectacular success of AQ-2 on 9/11. The same sort of radicalization seems to have affected the 7/7 bombers in London operating in mode AQ-3. In this context, the great success of 9/11 for terrorists was not just in the large-scale killings that day but also in allowing them to recover the purpose of their nineteenth-century predecessors: propaganda by deed. One can conclude, I think, that for the "Toronto 17" and other potential Gen-Y jihadists, both 9/11 and the American-led coalition response to it have been received as reasons to act. The AQ-2 attack; the invasion of Iraq and the almost effortless military occupation of the seat of the Caliphate, Baghdad; the on-going Israeli-Palestinian conflict; the nuclear stand-off with Iran–all these events have been interpreted as a call to jihadis to do something about what is seen as an attack on the ummah led by the Great Satan. That is, the ideologically inspired AQ-4 terrorists are also not likely to fade away any time soon.

However that may be, al-Qaeda, in AQ-4 mode, is rapidly approaching the status of what Walter Laqueur called "nuisance terrorism."[12] They are not a strategic threat and may be seen more as cheerleaders than order-givers. One measure of the current status of al-Qaeda is the reliance placed on the media. Of course, the al-Qaeda leadership has been in the business of media-spin from the start – first by silence, then by low-grade but carefully scripted video or audio recordings. Much of this production has been examined, in the spirit of Kremlinology, to see who says what, how bin Laden or al-Zawahiri looks, and so on. In recent years, however, several things have changed. To begin with, over the summer of 2006 the production values of As-Sahab, "The Cloud" in Arabic, which is the media arm of al-Qaeda, have improved. This means they now have access to better equipment and perhaps even to a production studio.[13]

Second, al-Qaeda has since early 2006 been able to release video and audio productions directly and in record numbers through the Internet. This allows them to maintain full control over the message rather than having to rely on commercial broadcasters such as al-Jazeera. It is also less risky. At the very least, this new marketing tool reflects the increased availability of high-speed Internet connections in Pakistan and the technical competence of the As-Sahab IT team. It does not, however, reflect growing strength. For example, when in July of 2006 bin Laden issued two videos in as many days, he was responding to the crisis in Iraq precipitated by the betrayal and death of al-Zarqawi. At the time it looked like a negotiated settlement in Iraq was possible but the al-Qaeda leadership did their best to head it off. The best shot al-Qaeda had available was a press release, not a wave of bomb attacks. A media blitz, however, is a long way from a *Blitzkrieg*. Accordingly, one may conclude that, in the absence of major attacks, video releases by As-Sahab are the only way to get the al-Qaeda message to market. Indeed, in some respects it is the only reliable way the al-Qaeda leadership has to communicate with the outside world.

Granted then that the al-Qaeda leadership cannot mount a strategic attack as in mode AQ-2, AQ-4 can still pose a threat to Canada if groups such as the "Toronto 17" improve their tradecraft, which on the face of it does not seem to be a particularly difficult problem. The reason for this potential threat and what the Government of Canada can do about it engages the central theme of this discussion.

The "Toronto 17" did not emerge from the woodwork and plan to attack CSIS, the Toronto Stock Exchange, the TTC and so on because Canadians and their government sought to suppress them, to attack their religion or to do anything else that normal or commonsense observers would think wrong. On the contrary, they planned their attack because of what Canada did and does right: it allows individuals to live full and responsible lives, to worship God as they wish or not to worship at all. These considerations lead us to the ever-sensitive problem of Canadian multiculturalism and its associated mythologies. Clearly, normal counterterrorist precautions, including an agent on the inside of a terrorist group, are useful, but the real question of prevention must include the communities from which groups such as the "Toronto 17" spring.

Before indicating the range of responses available to the Canadian government, let us be clear about the nature of the problem. Terrorist conspiracies are prosecuted in court more or less along the lines of ordinary criminal conspiracies such as drug gangs. To be convicted, each person charged must be shown to have "adhered" to the object of a conspiracy and to have acted in its furtherance. It seems to me that, so far as communities that shelter terrorists in their midst are concerned, the legal burden of proof may be too high.

The argument is straightforward: the first priority of government is to protect citizens, not prosecute offenders after the fact in order to obtain convictions. Even the ever so politically correct editors of the *Harvard Law Review* (February, 2002) did not think issuing an arrest warrant for bin Laden was an appropriate response to 9/11. The traditional paradigm of punishing someone who commits a harm cannot work when the harm-doer is a suicide mass murderer. This is why, whatever the rhetorical problems associated with the term "war on terror," it is correct at least in its use of the term war. Salafist-inspired suicide-terrorists are conducting an ecumenic asymmetric war rather than widespread criminality.

During the last formal war fought by Canada, the *War Measures Act* was in effect. It would be an understatement to say that ordinary civil liberties were curtailed. It also seems true that if Canada is engaged in asymmetric war at home as well as in Afghanistan, it will be necessary to introduce preventative or anticipatory measures as well as rely on the existing criminal code. Such measures carry with them considerable threats to civil liberties. Even the existing anti-terrorist legislation proved controversial; preemptive counterterrorism laws, we can be confident, would prove even more so, especially if they were seen to impinge upon, or were intended to curtail, freedom of religion and associated liberties regarding speech and assembly.

It seems to me, however, that notwithstanding the problems–indeed, because of them–it is necessary to discuss the question of adapting our old approaches to the problem of religious freedom to the new realities of which AQ-4 is the most relevant constituent. To state the matter as starkly as possible, there is a difference between evidence useful for criminal prosecution and intelligence useful in counterterrorism operations. Accordingly, interrogation designed to gain evidence is not the same as interrogation designed to gain intelligence. The difference is, moreover, one of principle: it is better for ten guilty defendants to be wrongly acquitted than for one innocent defendant to be wrongly convicted. Hence the presumption of innocence at trial. The opposite is true in counterterrorism intelligence: better to follow ten false leads than to overlook one true one.

I am not unmindful of the legal and political difficulties imposed by the new reality introduced by AQ-4. Leaving the legal questions aside for the moment, it seems to me that, if the burden of proof of adhering to a criminal conspiracy is too high, as I have suggested it is, there may be another question, and a political remedy. It is not a particularly obnoxious moral argument to hold that members of any ethnic or religious community who are aware that terrorists live among them have an obligation to turn them in. If the community and especially its leadership knowingly do nothing, they may be considered "guilty by association" with terrorists. Now, the notion of guilt by association is an anathema to ordinary criminal law. At the same time, associating with terrorists, which may be less than "adhering" to a terrorist criminal conspiracy, does seem to describe adequately an important dimension of AQ-4 operations.

So there is no misunderstanding, the "Toronto 17" were arrested not for undertaking a lot of wild talk in Internet chat rooms or even for shooting paintballs in the Ontario bush but because they had begun the transition from *conspiring* to act in a criminal manner to *furthering* their conspiracy, not in the cyber world but in the real world. In the "Toronto 17" case, the action of furthering the conspiracy came when the potential terrorists tried to purchase large amounts of ammonium nitrate that was to be used for bomb construction. At that point, the RCMP said, they posed a real and unacceptable threat. Early in the fall of 2006 Danish police arrested nine men at this same transition phase.[14]

The problem I would like to consider is somewhat different than the conventional procedures for interrupting terrorist activity–surveillance, the use of wiretaps, moles and so on. It concerns the thorny matter of "guilt by association," and is best approached indirectly.[15] Shortly after the Toronto arrests, Imam Aly Hindy of the Salaheddin Islamic Centre in the suburb of Scarborough complained, "We are being targeted not because of what we've done, but because of who we are and what we believe in."[16] On the contrary, he and his congregants were targeted because what they believe in led to what they did. The problem is not whether the good Imam is a bit of a fundamentalist, as he is, but that he is part of a community that tolerated and harboured terrorists. To put the matter bluntly, Imam Hindy had a duty to report the likes of the "Toronto 17" to the police. Rants against *kufrs* and *jahiliyya* are the opposite of helpful. If Father O'Malley or Rabbi Goldstein were hiding Irish or Jewish terrorists in their church or synagogue, the same rules would apply.

Tarek Fatah of the moderate and secular Muslim Canadian Congress explained the reluctance of Muslims to turn in extremists as resulting from "a sense of community patriotism where people automatically don't want to wash their dirty linen in public." Practically speaking, he said that "the doors of debate are sealed by the cement of orthodoxy, but Muslims can't go on behaving as if everything is normal. We can't sit by quietly while fascist death cults secretly try to take control of our mosques."[17] This statement of the problem seems to me to be accurate.

The British government has had to deal with similar but more pressing problems. For example, British citizens of Pakistani heritage have been recruited to serve with the Taliban against British troops.[18] Moreover, Peter Clarke, head of the anti-terrorism branch of Scotland Yard, told the BBC of the existence of a "pipeline" to assist young British Muslims to travel to Iraq, join the insurgency there, and perhaps also kill British troops. Over the years organizations such as al-Muhajiroun (The Immigrants) with branches in Pakistan, the US, the UK and Canada have been involved in arranging transportation for young men to Pakistan for training. Following the dissolution of al-Muhajiroun in 2004, other groups such as the Islamic Thinkers Society in New York or al-Ghurabah (The

Strangers) and Firqah al-Najiyah (The Sacred Sect) in London have taken
its place.[19]

A second dimension of the problem lies in the general support for the
Taliban or the Iraqi insurgency as well as AQ-3 and AQ-4 modes of
terrorism found in the Muslim community in the UK.[20] The Pew Global
Attitudes Project found that British Muslims in general have far more
negative views of the West than their counterparts in Europe or North
America. This 2006 poll confirmed a YouGov poll from the previous year
that showed 6% of British Muslims, over 100,000 individuals, considered
the 7/7 attacks justified; 24% said they would be prepared to help the
terrorists, and 1% – 16,000 people – said they would be willing to join a
terrorist operation in the name of Islam.

Finally, there is the question of community leadership. As Amir
Taheri, wrote in the *Wall Street Journal*, most have adopted a posture
described as "yes-but-however."[21] It starts with a yes: mass murder of
innocent people is a terrible crime. It proceeds to a but: the terrorist killers
have legitimate grievances that have not been addressed by the
government, which therefore shares the blame for the killing. It goes then
to however: if the government does not change its policies, especially its
foreign policies, there will be further attacks.

In 2006, the British Home Secretary, John Reid, experienced the
effects first hand when he addressed a Muslim audience in North London
about the danger to the British Muslim community posed by
"fanatics...looking to groom and brainwash children, including your
children, for suicide bombings." He was vocally contradicted by several
members of the audience, some of whom had to be ejected. Among his
hecklers was the notorious Islamic militant, Anjem Choudary [22]

The British also enacted some effective anti-terrorism legislation. *The
Prevention of Terrorism Act 2005* contemplates the preemptory use of
"control orders" that can prohibit individuals from using the Internet, for
example, or associating with named individuals and groups. They may
also be used to impose curfews or restrictions on movement. The Secretary
of State can impose such orders if it is considered "necessary for purposes
connected with preventing or restricting involvement by that individual in
terrorism-related activity." The latter involves the commission, preparation
or instigation of terrorist acts, as one would expect, but also conduct that
"facilitates" or gives "encouragement" or "support or assistance" to
individuals involved in terrorism-related activity. The 2006 *Antiterrorism
Act* makes it a crime to glorify political violence in general.[23]

These two acts were enforced for a time. Abu Hamza, a cleric at the
well-known Finsbury Park mosque, was jailed for seven years last

February for soliciting murder. They were used to prevent the plot to blow up several trans-Atlantic airliners in 2005 and were invoked directly as the basis for acting against the recruitment of potential terrorists about which John Reid warned his audience. In short, the British government has given itself the authority to thwart the radicalization process before there is any threat to public safety. Unfortunately, the use of control orders and other anti-terrorism acts, procedures and regulations have not withstood litigation.[24]

    In contrast, American courts especially in the wake of the 2006 Hamdan v. Rumsfeld decision, which overturned procedures advocated by the Bush administration for using military commissions to try persons currently residing in Guantanamo Bay, have largely ruled against the government, usually on First Amendment grounds. The direction of American jurisprudence has prompted a strong response from Judge Richard A. Posner of the US Court of Appeals, Seventh Circuit, in a book the title of which echoes a famous remark by Justice Robert H. Jackson: *Not a Suicide Pact: The Constitution in a Time of National Emergency*.[25] The argument is clear: "[R]ooting out an invisible enemy in our midst might be fatally inhibited if we felt constrained to strict observance of civil liberties designed in and for eras in which the only serious internal threat (apart from spies) came from common criminals." Such robust commonsense seems regrettably rare among judges in the US, the UK and Canada.[26]

    In the context of enabling liberal constitutional regimes to defend themselves, mention has already been made of the *War Measures Act*; similar Presidential orders were issued to aid in the prosecution of World War II by the United States. There is no reason to think, therefore, that legislation akin to that initially passed in the UK is a threat to a constitutional regime. Indeed, all regimes stand for something, which means that no regime tolerates everything. This is why, for example, an Australian MP and Parliamentary Secretary for Immigration, Andrew Robb, told a meeting of local imams that they should conduct their sermons in English.[27] By so doing they would be taking responsibility before their fellow-citizens for their stand against extremism, and would not be able to claim, as many have done, that their allegedly jihadist sermons have been mistranslated.

    In the Canadian context, either official language would no doubt be acceptable, but the principle is sound. Likewise one can anticipate the routine banning of visits by radical clerics from foreign countries as well as a re-examination of immigration policy, multicultural policy and even welfare policy. At the end of the day, however, it is not the introduction of what might be termed prophylactic measures that will make a difference. As Thomas Friedman wrote in the *New York Times* following 7/7, "If it's a Muslim problem, it needs a Muslim solution."[28] This is undoubtedly true. We should not, however, underestimate the difficulties.

The response of the Toronto Muslim leadership when Mubin Shaikh was identified as the CSIS mole who provided intelligence on the "Toronto 17" was anger and outrage, not praise for his understanding of the danger terrorists pose both to his community and to his non-Muslim fellow-citizens. Instead his motives were questioned by moderate and secular Muslim leaders alike. Conservative, which is to say salafist, leaders denounced Shaikh as a traitor. Two weeks later the moderate and secular Tarek Fatah himself resigned as leader of the Canadian Muslim Congress citing threats to him and his family.[29] The problems within the Toronto Muslim community point to a principle that Canadians have ignored for the past several decades: the duty of immigrants is to learn to cherish the principles of the Canadian regime; the duty of Canadians is to ensure they do. Among other things, this double duty would entail some serious readjustment of the place of religion in Canadian politics. If Canadians, Muslim and non-Muslim alike, do not reach an understanding on these matters then we will be turned into spectators in the on-going game between AQ-4 and the security agencies, which has its own dangers to civil liberties as noted above.

Notes

[1] See however Fawaz A. Gerges, *The Far Enemy: Why Jihad went Global* (Cambridge: Cambridge University Press, 2005).
[2] Barry Cooper, *New Political Religions, Or an Analysis of Modern Terrorism* (Columbia, University of Missouri Press, 2004).
[3] Quoted in Martin Amis, "The Age of Horrorism," *The Observer*, 10 September 2006.
[4] Azar Nafisi, *Reading Lolita in Tehran: A Memoir in Books* (New York: Random House, 2004).
[5] Bernard Lewis, *The Crisis of Islam: Holy War and Unholy Terror* (New York: Modern Library, 2003), 81.
[6] For details see Stewart Bell, Adrian Humphries, Chris Wattie, "Terror Plot Called for Two Attacks," *The Calgary Herald*, 6 June 2006, sec. A1; Stewart Bell, "Homemade Bombs Require only 'Kitchen Chemistry,'" *The National Post*, 10 June 2006, sec. A6.
[7] Accounts of the evolution of al-Qaeda are cited in *New Political Religions*. In addition, see Bruce Hoffman, *Inside Terrorism*, rev. ed. (New York: Columbia University Press, 2006); Lawrence Wright, *The Looming Tower: Al-Qaeda and the*

Road to 9/11 (New York: Knopff, 2007). See also the series of analyses available from *Stratfor.com*: Fred Burton, "Al Qaeda in 2006: Devolution and Adaptation, "3 January, 2006; Anon, "Al-Zawahiri Tape: Key Insights into Al Qaeda Prime," 31 January 2006; Burton, "Al Qaeda: The Next Phase of Evolution?" 7 June, 2006; Burton, "The Web of Jihad: Strategic Utility and Tactical Weakness," 13 July 2006; Anon, "Saudi Arabia: Al Qaeda's Many Layers," 14 June 2004. Also David Blair, "Al-Qaeda Prepares for a New Wave of Terror," *The Telegraph*, 31 May 2007; Lawrence Wright, "The Master Plan," *The New Yorker*, 11 September 2006; Jason Burke, "Al-Qaeda, The Second Coming," *The Observer*, 11 March 2007.
[8] For example, Stratfor.com, Fred Burton, "Al Qaeda in 2007: The Continuing Devolution," 27 December 2006.
[9] For details, see reports on Stratfor.com: Fred Burton, "Beware of 'Kramer': Tradecraft and the New Jihadists," 18 January 2006; Anon, "U.S.: Miami's 'Kramer' Jihadists," 23 June 2006; Burton, "The 'Miami Seven': Disrupting a Network," 28 June 2006.
[10] See Sebastian Rotella, "A World Wide Web of Terrorist Plotting," *Los Angeles Times*, 17 April, 2007; ITAC Presents: Trends in Terrorism Series, *A Framework for Understanding Terrorist Use of the Internet*, Carleton University, The Norman Patterson School of International Affairs; Magnus Ranstorp, "The Virtual Sanctuary of Al-Qaeda and Terrorism in an Age of Globalization," in Johan Eriksson, Giampiero Giacomello, eds., *International Relations and Security in the Digital Age* (London, Routledge, 2007), 58-74; Bruce Hoffman, *The Use of the Internet by Islamist Extremists* CT-262-1 (May 2006), Testimony presented to the House Permanent Select Committee on Intelligence on 4 May 2006; Nicolien de Boer, "Terror Sites Increasing as Never Before," Radio Netherlands International, 17 January 2007; Sean O'Neill, "Al Qaeda's 'British Propagandists," *The Times*, 24 April 2007 ; Stewart Bell, "Terror Suspects in Canada, UK Made Plans Online," *National Post*, 26 April 2007.
[11] Michelle Shephard, "Mounties Had Mole in Alleged Terror Cell," *Toronto Star*, 13 July 2006, sec. A1; Sonya Fatah, Greg McArthur, Scott Roberts, "The Making of a Terror Mole," *The Globe and Mail*, 14 July 2006, sec. A4.
[12] Laqueur, "Postmodern Terrorism," *Foreign Affairs* 75,no. 5 (1996): 81-96.
[13] See Hassan M. Fattah, "Al Qaeda Increasingly Reliant on Media," *New York Times*, 30 September 2006; Michael Scheuer, "The Western Media's Misreading of al-Qaeda's Latest Videotape," *Terrorism Focus* 34 (6 September 2006). From Stratfor.com, see: Anon, "Osama bin Laden: Spreading the Word, Not the Image," 30 June 2006; Fred Burton, "Al Qaeda's Media Blitz," 6 July 2006; Burton, "Al Qaeda Recordings: Semantic Noise and Signals," 23 August 2006; Anon, "As-Sahab: Al Qaeda's Nebulous Media Branch," 8 September 2006; Lawrence Pintak, "Al-Zawraa and Egypt's On-air Ambiguity," *The Daily Star*, 8 January 2007; Michael Scheuer, "Al-Qaeda's Media Doctrine: Evolution from Cheerleader to Opinion-Shaper," *Terrorism Focus* 4, no.1 (22 May 2007).
[14] Jan Olsen, "Arrests in Denmark Said to Thwart Terror Attack," *Washington Times*, 5 September 2006

[15] Quotes given below and other facts are taken from: Isabel Vincent, "The Imam Who Wouldn't Condemn the Attacks," *National Post*, 30 July 2005; Kelly Patrick, "We Have to Make Fund for the Defence," *National Post*, 10 June 2006; Tom Blackwell, "We Need to Develop in them Love for Society," *National Post*, 10 June 2006; Peter Goodspeed, "Defenders of Islam," *National Post*, 10 June 2006.

[16] Quoted in Anthony De Palma, "Six of 17 Arrested in Canada's Antiterror Sweep Have Ties to Mosque Near Toronto," *New York Times*, 4 June 2006.

[17] Quoted in Peter Goodspeed, "Defenders of Islam," *National Post*, 10 June 2006.

[18] Michael Smith and Ghulam Hasnaim Karachi, "UK Muslims join Taliban to fight against British Troops," *Sunday Times*, 3 September 2006.

[19] Stratfor.com, "US Muslim Youths and Militant Islam," 16 June 2006.

[20] For details see Amir Taheri, "Muslim Matryushka," *Wall Street Journal*, 7 July 2006; Diana West, "Appeasing Jihadists," *The Washington Times*, 7 July 2006.

[21] Taheri, "Muslim Matryushka."

[22] See Philip Johnston, "Reid Meets the Furious Face of Islam," *Daily Telegraph*, 21 September 2006.

[23] See Souad Mekhennet and Dexter Filkins, "British Law Against Glorifying Terrorism Has Not Silenced Calls to kill for Islam," *New York Times*, 21 August 2006.

[24] See Clare Dyer, "Terror Suspects' Control Orders face New Court Challenge," *The Guardian*, 8 January 2007.

[25] Richard A. Posner, *Not a Suicide Pact* (New York: Oxford University Press, 2006).

[26] See Editorial, "Terrorism and the Courts," *The Washington Times*, 18 August 2006; Alan Dershowitz, "How to Protect Civil Liberties," *The Spectator*, 28 August 2006.

[27] Sara Price and Kerry-Anne Walsh, "Use English and Combat Extremism, Muslims Told," *Sydney Morning Herald*, 17 September 2006.

[28] Thomas Friedman, July 8, 2005, "If It's a Muslim Problem, It Needs a Muslim Solution," *New York Times,* 8 July 2005.

[29] Sonya Fatah, "Fearing for Safety, Muslim Official Quits," *Globe and Mail*, 3 August 2006.

APPENDIX A

I. Subjective Religiosity

Question 1:
(v9) Indicate how important it is in your life Religion: 1: Very important, 2: Rather important, 3: Not very important, 4: Not important at all.

Type of Society	1999-2000
Advanced Industrial	Austria (n=1507); Belgium (n=1889); Britain (n=980); Canada (n=1924); Denmark (n=1013); Finland (n=1028); France (n=1601); Iceland (n=967); Ireland (n=993); Italy (n=1978); Japan (n=1193); Luxembourg (n=1194); Netherlands (n=1002); Spain (n=1203); Sweden (n=1009); U.S.A. (n=1196); West Germany (n=1021)
Industrial	Argentina (n=1272); Belarus (n=951); Bulgaria (n=962); Chile (n=1191); Croatia (n=976); Czech (n=1882); Estonia (n=967); Greece (n=1124); Hungary (n=997); Latvia (n=999); Lithuania (n=962); Malta (n=996); Mexico (n=1527); Montenegro (n=1038); Philippines (n=1200); Poland (n=1085); Portugal (n=994); Romania (n=1138); Russia (n=2407); Slovakia (n=1307); Slovenia (n=1002); South Korea (n=1199); Turkey (n= 3395); Ukraine (n=1126); Venezuela (n=1197)
Agrarian	Bangladesh (n=1494); China (n=940); Egypt (n=3000); El Salvador (n=1248); India (n=1961); Indonesia (n=1000); Iran (n=2489); Jordan (n=1222); Morocco (n=1250); Nigeria (n=2019); South Africa (n=2994); Tanzania (n=1070); Uganda (n=1001); Vietnam (n=968); Zimbabwe (n=1001)

Question 2:
(v196) How important is God in your life? Please use this scale to
indicate: 10: means very important and 1: means not at all
important.

Type of Society	1999-2000
Advanced Industrial	Austria (n=1501); Belgium (n=1881); Britain (n=962); Canada (n=1917); Denmark (n=1001); Finland (n=988); France (n=1581); Iceland (n=952); Ireland (n=1009); Italy (n=1951); Japan (n=1194); Luxembourg (n=1174); Netherlands (n=999); Spain (n=1188); Sweden (n=994); U.S.A. (n=1198); West Germany (n=1011)
Industrial	Argentina (n=1264); Belarus (n=905); Bulgaria (n=965); Chile (n=1178); Croatia (n=986); Czech (n=1849); Estonia (n=959); Greece (n=1123); Hungary (n=984); Latvia (n=968); Lithuania (n=925); Malta (n=1002); Mexico (n=1516); Montenegro (n=993); Philippines (n=1199); Poland (n=1079); Portugal (n=987); Romania (n=1124); Russia (n=2395); Serbia (n=1161); Slovakia (n=1276); Slovenia (n=980); South Korea (n=1198); Turkey (n=3385); Ukraine (n=1098); Venezuela (n=1194)
Agrarian	Bangladesh (n=1491); Egypt (n=3000); El Salvador (n=1243); India (n=1885); Indonesia (n=1000); Iran (n=2511); Jordan (n=1218); Morocco (n=1245); Nigeria (n=2022); South Africa (n=2961); Tanzania (n=1155); Uganda (n= 989); Vietnam) (n=954); Zimbabwe (n=993)

Question 3:
(v186) Independently of whether you go to church or not, would you say you are: 1: A religious Person, 2: Not a religious person, 3: A convinced atheist, 9: Don't know.

Type of Society	1999-2000
Advanced Industrial	Austria (n=1435); Belgium (n=1841); Britain (n=897); Canada (n=1896); Denmark (n= 945); Finland (n=954); France (n=1541); Iceland (n=948); Ireland (n=979); Italy (n=1938); Japan (n=1186); Luxembourg (n=1104); Netherlands (n= 992); Spain (n=1179); Sweden (n=966);U.S.A.(n=1180); West Germany (n=967)
Industrial	Argentina (n=1225); Belarus (n=933); Bulgaria (n=914); Chile (n=16); Croatia (n=940); Czech (n=1782); Estonia (n=860); Greece (n=1071); Hungary (n=976); Latvia (n=930); Lithuania (n=887); Malta (n=1000); Mexico (n=1494); Montenegro (n=904); Philippines (n=1190); Poland (n=1070); Portugal (n=977); Romania (n=1093); Russia (n=2293); Serbia (n=1100); Slovakia (n=1252); Slovenia (n=926); South Korea (n=1198); Turkey (n=3320); Ukraine (n=1067); Venezuela (n=1184)
Agrarian	Bangladesh (n=1374); China (n=930); Egypt (n=2993); El Salvador (n=1247); India (n=1890); Indonesia (n=822); Iran (n=2195); Jordan (n=1207); Nigeria (n=2015); South Africa (n=2923); Tanzania (n=1111); Uganda (n=993); Vietnam (n=947); Zimbabwe (n=986)

II. Religious Involvement

Question 1:

(v185) Apart from weddings, funerals and christenings, about how often do you attend religious services these days? 1: More than once a week, 2: Once a week, 3: Once a month, 4: Only on special holy days, 5: Once a year, 6: Less often, 7: Never, practically never.

Type of Society	1999-2000
Advanced Industrial	Austria (n=1515); Belgium (n=1887); Britain (n=989); Canada (n=1925); Denmark (n=1017); Finland (n=1032); France (n=1608); Iceland (n=965); Ireland (n=1006); Italy (n=1983); Japan (n=1343); Luxembourg (n=1176); Netherlands (n=1002); Spain (n=1198); Sweden (n=1013); U.S.A. (n=1198); West Germany (n=1030)
Industrial	Argentina (n=1280); Belarus (n=990); Bulgaria (n=995); Chile (n=1181); Croatia (n=996); Czech (n=1887); Estonia (n=987); Greece (n=1131); Hungary (n=995); Latvia (n=981); Lithuania (n=1004); Malta (n=1002); Mexico (n=1530); Montenegro (n=1060); Philippines (n=1200); Poland (n=1090); Portugal (n=997); Romania (n=1136); Russia (n=2477); Serbia (n=1199); Slovakia (n=1327); Slovenia (n=989); South Korea (n=1198); Turkey (n=3327); Ukraine (n=1182); Venezuela (n=1192)
Agrarian	Bangladesh (n=1500); China (n=992); Egypt (n=3000); El Salvador (n=1253); India (n=2001); Indonesia (n=1000); Iran (n=2442); Jordan (n=1221); Morocco (n=1249); Nigeria (n=2022); South Africa (n=2998); Tanzania (n=1159); Uganda (n=1002); Vietnam (n=1000); Zimbabwe (n=1002)

Question 2:
(v40) Do you belong to religious or church organizations? 1: Belong,
2: Not mentioned.

Type of Society	1999-2000
Advanced industrial	Austria (n=1511); Belgium (n=1912); Britain (n=1000); Canada (n=1931); Denmark (n=1016); Finland (n=1038); France (n=1615); Iceland (n=968); Ireland (n=1007); Italy (n=2000); Japan (n=1362); Luxembourg (n=1211); Netherlands (n=1003); Spain (n=1209); Sweden (n=1015); U.S.A. (n=1200); West Germany (n=1036)
Industrial	Argentina (n=1280); Belarus (n=1000); Bulgaria (n=1000); Chile (n=1200); Croatia (n=1003); Czech (n=1903); Estonia (n=1005); Greece (n=1142); Hungary (n=1000); Latvia (n=1013); Lithuania (n=1018); Malta (n=1002); Mexico (n=1535); Montenegro (n=1060); Philippines (n=1200); Poland (n=1095); Portugal (n=1000); Romania (n=1146); Russia (n=2500); Serbia (n=1200); Slovakia (n=1331); Slovenia (n=1006); South Korea (n=1200); Venezuela (n=1200)
Agrarian	Bangladesh (n=1500); China (n=1000); El Salvador (n=1252); India (n=2002); Morocco (n=1251); South Africa (n=3000); Tanzania (n=1171); Uganda (n=1002); Vietnam (n=1000); Zimbabwe (n=1002)

Question 3:
(v184) Do you belong to a religious denomination, if yes which one?
0: No, not a member, 2: Roman Catholic, 3: Protestant,
4: Orthodox (Russian/Greek/etc.), 5: Jewish, 6: Muslim, 7: Hindu,
7: Buddhist, 8: Other, 9: No answer.

Type of society	1999-2000
Advanced Industrial	Austria (n=1491); Belgium (n=1897); Britain (n=838); Canada (n=1899); Denmark (n=1012); Finland (n=1038); France (n=1612); Iceland (n=964); Ireland (n=1010); Italy (n=1991); Japan (n=1267); Luxembourg (n=361); Netherlands (n=1002); Spain (n=1194); Sweden (n=1015); U.S.A. (n=1136); West Germany (n=1023)
Industrial	Argentina (n=1216); Belarus (n=478); Bulgaria (n=997); Chile (n=1103); Croatia (n=999); Czech (n=1891); Estonia (n=1004); Greece (n=1138); Hungary (n=992); Latvia (n=1008); Lithuania (n=1011); Malta (n=1002); Mexico (n=1477); Montenegro (n=1047); Philippines (n=1193); Poland (n=1094); Portugal (n=883); Romania (n=1135); Russia (n=2492); Serbia (n=1181); Slovakia (n=1331); Slovenia (n=1002); South Korea (n=1196); Turkey (n=3391); Ukraine (n=1153); Venezuela (n=1195)
Agrarian	Bangladesh (n=1499); China (n=990); Egypt (n=2999); El Salvador (n=1254); India (n=1974); Indonesia (n=999); Iran (n=2525); Jordan (n=1222); Morocco (n=1251); Nigeria (n=2019); South Africa (n=2909); Tanzania (n=1162); Uganda (n=990); Vietnam (n=996); Zimbabwe (n=859)

III. Prayer

Question 1:
(v198) Do you take some moments of prayer, meditation or
contemplation or something like that?) 1: Yes, 2: No, 3: Don't Know.

Type of society	1999-2000
Advanced Industrial	Austria (n=1484); Belgium (n=1869); Britain (n=951); Canada (n=1915); Denmark (n=1008); Finland (n=994); France (n=1586); Iceland (n=959); Ireland (n=1005); Italy (n=1947); Japan (n=1229); Luxembourg (n=1159); Netherlands (n=1002); Spain (n=1192); Sweden (n=1002); U.S.A. (n=1197); West Germany (n=983)
Industrial	Argentina (n=1264); Belarus (n=951); Bulgaria (n=959); Chile (n=1191); Croatia (n=980); Czech (n=1855); Estonia (n=941); Greece (n=1098); Hungary (n=989); Latvia (n=966); Lithuania (n=908); Malta (n=997); Mexico (n=1524); Montenegro (n=909); Philippines (n=1199); Poland (n=1069); Portugal (n=988); Romania (n=1129); Russia (n=2417); Serbia (n=1111); Slovakia (n=1300); Slovenia (n=984); South Korea (n=954); Ukraine (n=1129)
Agrarian	Bangladesh (n=1374); India (n=1963); South Africa (n=2954); Tanzania (n=1155); Uganda (n=991); Vietnam (n=971); Zimbabwe (n=993)

Question 2:
(v199) How often do you pray outside of religious services? Would you
say... 1: Every day, 2: More than once a week, 3: Once a week, 4: At
least once a month, 5: Several times a year, 6: Less often, 7: Never,
9: Don't know.

Type of society	1999-2000
Advanced Industrial	Austria (n=1023); Belgium (n=1158); Britain (n=462); 17); France (n=628); Ireland (n=846); Italy (n=1526); Japan (n=484); Luxembourg ¿den (n=513); U.S.A. (n=1069); West Germany (n=574)
Industrial	Argentina (n=964); Belarus (n=662); Bulgaria (n=320); Chile (n=979); Croatia (n=720); Czech (n=718); Estonia (n=448); Greece (n=658); Hungary (n=586); Latvia (n=602); Lithuania (n=518); Malta (n=913); Mexico (n=1318); Montenegro (n=467); Philippines (n=1160); Poland (n=912); Portugal (n=735); Romania (n=1050); Russia (n=826); Serbia (n=623); Slovakia (n=855); South Korea (n=547); Ukraine (n=571)
Agrarian	Bangladesh (n=1304); India (n=1716); South Africa (n=2687); Tanzania (n=1121); Uganda (n=920); Vietnam (n=284); Zimbabwe (n=907)

Question 3:
(v197) Do you find that you get comfort and strength from religion?
1: Yes, 2: No, 3: Don't Know.

Type of society	1999-2000
Advanced Industrial	Austria (n=990); Belgium (n=1113); Britain (n=439); Canada (n=1526); Denmark (n=475); Finland (n=639); France (n=602); Iceland (n=504); Ireland (n=810); Italy (n=1481); Japan (n=374); Luxembourg (n=605); Netherlands (n=686); Spain (n=546); Sweden (n=406); U.S. (n=1055); West Germany (n=525)
Industrial	Argentina (n=955); Belarus (n=551); Bulgaria (n=301); Chile (n=929); Croatia (n=682); Czech (n=678); Estonia (n=389); Greece (n=645); Hungary (n=565); Latvia (n=541); Lithuania (n=486); Malta (n=889); Mexico (n=1307); Montenegro (n=463); Philippines (n=1149); Poland (n=861); Portugal (n=726); Romania (n=984); Russia (n=798); Serbia (n=599); Slovakia (n=768); Slovenia (n=423); South Korea (n=490); Ukraine (n=526)
Agrarian	Bangladesh (n=1269); India (n=1659); South Africa (n=2643); Tanzania (n=1109); Uganda (n=898); Vietnam (n=259); Zimbabwe (n=886)

IV. Beliefs

Question 1:
(v191) Do you believe in god? 1: Yes, 2: No, 3: Don't Know.

Type of society	1999-2000
Advanced Industrial	Austria (n=1447); Belgium (n=1778); Britain (n=835); Canada (n=1863); Denmark (n=921); Finland (n=926); France (n=1470); Iceland (n=882); Ireland (n=992); Italy (n=1880); Japan (n=907); Luxembourg (n=1122); Netherlands (n=978); Spain (n=1144); Sweden (n=884); U.S. (n=1181); West Germany (n=933)
Industrial	Argentina (n=1266); Belarus (n=871); Bulgaria (n=872); Chile (n=1185); Croatia (n=976); Czech (n=162); Estonia (n=802); Greece (n=1051); Hungary (n=950 Latvia (n=893); Lithuania (n=801); Malta (n=999); Mexico (n=1530); Montenegro (n=904); Philippines (n=1198); Poland (n=1082 Portugal (n=964); Romania (n=1090); Russia (n=2118 Serbia (n=1086); Slovakia (n=1220); Slovenia (n=959); Turkey (n=3376); Ukraine (n=1030)
Agrarian	Bangladesh (n=1494); Egypt (n=3000); El Salvador (n=1250); India (n=1975); Indonesia (n=1000); Iran (n=2518); Jordan (n=1221); Nigeria (n=2020); South Africa (n=2981); Tanzania (n=1161); Uganda (n=998); Vietnam (n=935); Zimbabwe (n=997)

Question 2:
(v192) Do you believe in life after death? 1: Yes, 2: No, 3: Don't Know.

Type of society	1999-2000
Advanced Industrial	Austria (n=1308); Belgium (n=1660); Britain (n=751); Canada (n=1736); Denmark (n=857); Finland (n=831); France (n=1389); Iceland (n=841); Ireland (n=879); Italy (n=1686); Japan (n=846); Luxembourg (n=1030); Netherlands (n=921); Spain (n=977); Sweden (n=858); U.S. (n=1116); West Germany (n=898)
Industrial	Argentina (n=1132); Belarus (n=760); Bulgaria (n=782); Chile (n=1111); Croatia (n=881); Czech (n=1559); Estonia (n=725); Greece (n=890); Hungary (n=904); Latvia (n=704); Lithuania (n=650); Malta (n=910); Mexico (n=1370); Montenegro (n=801); Philippines (n=1132); Poland (n=949); Portugal (n=780); Romania (n=867); Russia (n=1768); Serbia (n=944); Slovakia (n=1106); Slovenia (n=923); Turkey (n=3332); Ukraine (n=859)
Agrarian	Bangladesh (n=1441); Egypt (n=3000); El Salvador (n=1190); India (n=1810); Indonesia (n=997); Iran (n=2459); Jordan (n=1219); Nigeria (n=1987); South Africa (n=2760); Tanzania (n=1087); Uganda (n=965); Vietnam (n=922); Zimbabwe (n=921)

Question 3:
(v193) Do you believe people have a soul? 1: Yes, 2: No, 3: Don't Know.

Type of society	1999-2000
Advanced Industrial	Canada (n=1854); Japan (n=962); Spain (n=1023); U.S. (n=1177)
Industrial	Argentina (n=1213); Chile (n=1135); Mexico (n=1494); Montenegro (n=827); Philippines (n=1175); Serbia (n=934); Turkey (n=3342)
Agrarian	Bangladesh (n=1490); Egypt (n=3000); El Salvador (n=1233); India (n=1849); Indonesia (n=995); Iran (n=2427); Jordan (n=1221); Nigeria (n=1999); South Africa (n=2905); Tanzania (n=1127); Uganda (n=920); Vietnam (n=923); Zimbabwe (n=954)

IV. Beliefs (continued)

Question 4:
(v194) Do you believe in hell? 1: Yes, 2: No, 3: Don't Know.

Type of Society	1999-2000
Advanced Industrial	Austria (n=1375); Belgium (n=1741); Britain (n=796); Canada (n=1801); Denmark (n=939); Finland (n=846); France (n=1458); Iceland (n=897); Ireland (n=874); Italy (n=1703); Japan (n=774); Luxembourg (n=1054); Netherlands (n=970); Spain (n=1004); Sweden (n=944); U.S. (n=1144); West Germany (n=933)
Industrial	Argentina (n=1179); Belarus (n=756); Bulgaria (n=762); Chile (n=1114); Croatia (n=868); Czech (n=1645); Estonia (n=769); Greece (n=898); Hungary (n=918); Latvia (n=754); Lithuania (n=559); Malta (n=939); Mexico (n=1456); Montenegro (n=836); Philippines (n=1134); Poland (n=944); Portugal (n=813); Romania (n=911); Russia (n=1751); Serbia (n=993); Slovakia (n=1061); Slovenia (n=930); Turkey (n=3352); Ukraine (n=846)
Agrarian	Bangladesh (n=1484); Egypt (n=3000); El Salvador (n=1236); India (n=1809); Indonesia (n=998); Iran (n=2411); Jordan (n=1219); Nigeria (n=1998); South Africa (n=2814); Tanzania (n=1089); Uganda (n=930); Vietnam (n=906); Zimbabwe (n=918)

Question 5:
(v195) Do you believe in heaven? 1: Yes, 2: No, 3: Don't Know.

Type of Society	1999-2000
Advanced Industrial	Austria (n=1388); Belgium (n=1742); Britain (n=804); Canada (n=1832); Denmark (n=907); Finland (n=857); France (n=1447); Iceland (n=858); Ireland (n=913); Italy (n=1717); Japan (n=794); Luxembourg (n=1053); Netherlands (n=953); Spain (n=1023); Sweden (n=907); U.S. (n=1156); West Germany (n=941)
Industrial	Argentina (n=1210); Belarus (n=756); Bulgaria (n=763); Chile (n=1128); Croatia (n=878); Czech (n=1635); Estonia (n=770); Greece (n=911); Hungary (n=920); Latvia (n=750); Lithuania (n=578); Malta (n=948); Mexico (n=1474); Montenegro (n=817); Philippines (n=1177); Poland (n=963); Portugal (n=832); Romania (n=917); Russia (n=1738); Serbia (n=967); Slovakia (n=1074); Slovenia (n=929); Turkey (n=3350); Ukraine (n=842)
Agrarian	Bangladesh (n=1488); El Salvador (n=1229); India (n=1823); Indonesia (n=1000); Iran (n=2420); Jordan (n=1219); Nigeria (n=2010); South Africa (n=2894); Tanzania (n=1073); Uganda (n=958); Vietnam (n=909); Zimbabwe (n=951)

V. Confidence in Religious Institutions

Question 1:
(v147) How much confidence do you have in churches: 1: A great deal of confidence, 2: Quite a lot, 3: Not very much confidence, 4: Not at all.

Type of Society	2000
Advanced Industrial	Austria (n=1503); Belgium (n=1871); Britain (n=942); Canada (n=1912); Denmark (n=949); Finland (n=1019); France (n=1564); Iceland (n=962); Ireland (n=1003); Italy (n=1975); Japan (n=1264); Luxembourg (n=1160); Netherlands (n=993); Spain (n=1195); Sweden (n=991); U.S. (n=1194); West Germany (n=975)
Industrial	Argentina (n=1267); Belarus (n=905); Bulgaria (n=953); Chile (n=1194); Croatia (n=972); Czech (n=1877); Estonia (n=871); Greece (n=1123); Hungary (n=983); Latvia (n=943); Lithuania (n=892); Malta (n=998); Mexico (n=1516); Montenegro (n=1018); Philippines (n=1197); Poland (n=1077); Portugal (n=982); Romania (n=1134); Russia (n=2319); Serbia (n=1115); Slovakia (n=1252); Slovenia (n=989); South Korea (n=1145); Turkey (n=3326); Ukraine (n=1116); Venezuela (n=1200)
Agrarian	Bangladesh (n=1495); Egypt (n=2988); El Salvador (n=1251); India (n=1922); Indonesia (n=985); Iran (n=2373); Jordan (n=1186); Morocco (n=1249); Nigeria (n=2020); South Africa (n=2919); Tanzania (n=1135); Uganda (n=978); Vietnam (n=956); Zimbabwe (n=988)

Question 2:
(v187) Generally speaking, do you think that the churches in your country are giving adequate answers to the moral problems and needs of the individual life? 1: Yes, 2: No, 3: Don't know.

Type of Society	1999-2000
Advanced Industrial	Austria (n=1354); Belgium (n=1664); Britain (n=785); Canada (n=1751); Denmark (n=817); Finland (n=853); France (n=1502); Iceland (n=772); Ireland (n=912); Italy (n=1785); Japan (n=812); Luxembourg (n=1012); Netherlands (n=840); Spain (n=1022); Sweden (n=778); U.S. (n=1140); West Germany (n=965)
Industrial	Argentina (n=1174); Belarus (n=774); Bulgaria (n=802); Chile (n=1141); Croatia (n=857); Czech (n=1536); Estonia (n=689); Greece (n=1048); Hungary (n=834); Latvia (n=699); Lithuania (n=648); Malta (n=935); Mexico (n=1471); Montenegro (n=793); Philippines (n=1160); Poland (n=911); Portugal (n=918); Romania (n=1012); Russia (n=1953); Serbia (n=935); Slovakia (n=1079); Slovenia (n=842); South Korea (n=937); Ukraine (n=935)
Agrarian	Bangladesh (n=999); Egypt (n=2964); India (n=1475); Indonesia (n=962); Iran (n=2121); Jordan (n=1135); Morocco (n=1186); Nigeria (n=1977); South Africa (n=2631); Tanzania (n=1083); Uganda (n=916); Vietnam (n=887); Zimbabwe (n=946)

Question 3:
(v188) Generally speaking, do you think that the churches in your country are giving adequate answers to the problems of family life?
1: Yes, 2: No, 3: Don't know.

Type of Society	1999-2000
Advanced Industrial	Austria (n=1382); Belgium (n=1685); Britain (n=787); Canada (n=1760); Denmark (n=852); Finland (n=859); France (n=1517); Iceland (n=755); Ireland (n=936); Italy (n=798) ; Japan (n=837); Luxembourg (n=1046); Netherlands (n=795); Spain (n=1020); Sweden (n=794); U.S. (n=1157); West Germany (n=958)
Industrial	Argentina (n=1171); Belarus (n=779); Bulgaria (n=820); Chile (n=1154); Croatia (n=849); Czech (n=1531); Estonia (n=694); Greece (n=1036); Hungary (n=823); Latvia (n=760); Lithuania (n=666); Malta (n=960); Mexico (n=1477); Montenegro (n=811); Philippines (n=1175); Poland (n=944); Portugal (n=916); Romania (n=1032); Russia (n=1931); Serbia (n=956); Slovakia (n=1107); Slovenia (n=853)
Agricultural	Bangladesh (n=1026); Egypt (n=2967); India (n=1482); Indonesia (n=959); Iran (n=2086); Jordan (n=1143); Morocco (n=1201); Nigeria (n=1979); South Africa (n=2709); Tanzania (n=1100); Uganda (n=919); Vietnam (n=882); Zimbabwe (n=960)

V. Confidence in Religious Institutions (continued)

Question 4:
(v189) Generally speaking, do you think that the churches in your country are giving adequate answers to people's spiritual needs?
1: Yes, 2: No, 3: Don't know.

Type of Society	1999-2000
Advanced Industrial	Austria (n=1364); Belgium (n=1643); Britain (n=807); Canada (n=1777); Denmark (n=807); Finland (n=896); France (n=1486); Iceland (n=767); Ireland (n=922); Italy (n=1812); Japan (n=828); Luxembourg (n=994); Netherlands (n=772); Spain (n=1014); Sweden (n=787); U.S. (n=1148); West Germany (n=976)
Industrial	Argentina (n=1175); Belarus (n=798); Bulgaria (n=812); Chile (n=1151); Croatia (n=907); Czech (n=1537); Estonia (n=749); Greece (n=1044); Hungary (n=841); Latvia (n=798); Lithuania (n=659); Malta (n=956); Mexico (n=1479); Montenegro (n=829); Philippines (n=1178); Poland (n=970); Portugal (n=906); Romania (n=1006); Russia (n=1930); Serbia (n=999); Slovakia (n=1144); Slovenia (n=860); South Korea (n=924); Ukraine (n=913)
Agricultural	Bangladesh (n=1064); Egypt (n=2895); India (n=1413); Indonesia (n=956); Iran (n=2036); Jordan (n=1119); Morocco (n=1176); Nigeria (n=1974); South Africa (n=2739); Tanzania (n=1090); Uganda (n=943); Vietnam (n=891); Zimbabwe (n=938)

Question 5:
(v190) Generally speaking, do you think that the churches in your
country are giving adequate answers to social problems facing our
country today? 1: Yes, 2: No, 3: Don't know.

Type of Society	1999-2000
Advanced Industrial	Austria (n=1349); Belgium (n=1654); Britain (n=781); Canada (n=1721); Denmark (n=847); Finland (n=875); France (n=1509); Iceland (n=786); Ireland (n=907); Italy (n=1759); Japan (n=876); Luxembourg (n=1008); Netherlands (n=817); Spain (n=992); Sweden (n=804); U.S. (n=1132); West Germany (n=937)
Industrial	Argentina (n=1156); Belarus (n=739); Bulgaria (n=801); Chile (n=1148); Croatia (n=854); Czech (n=1511); Estonia (n=694); Greece (n=1037); Hungary (n=817); Latvia (n=727); Lithuania (n=518); Malta (n=923); Mexico (n=1436); Montenegro (n=784); Philippines (n=1151); Poland (n=859); Portugal (n=886); Romania (n=934); Russia (n=1763); Serbia (n=925); Slovakia (n=980); Slovenia (n=843); South Korea (n=853); Ukraine (n=792)
Agrarian	Egypt (n=2882); India (n=1411); Indonesia (n=923); Iran (n=1922); Jordan (n=1132); Morocco (n=1111); Nigeria (n=1948); South Africa (n=2556); Tanzania (n=1027); Uganda (n=869); Vietnam (n=833); Zimbabwe (n=899)

Religion and Politics

Question 1:
(v200) How much do you agree or disagree with each of the following:
Politicians who do not believe in God are unfit for public office: 1:
Agree Strongly, 2:Agree, 3: Neither agree or disagree, 4: Disagree, 5:
Strongly disagree.

Type of Society	1999-2000
Advanced Industrial	France (n=1574);Britain (n=958); W.Germany (n=988); Italy (n=1933); Netherlands (n=998); Denmark (n=992); Belgium (n=1862); Spain (n=1103);Ireland (n=972);U.S. (n=1190);Canada (n=1884); Japan (n=1328); Sweden (n=1010); Iceland (n=953); Finland (n=985); Austria (n=1469); Luxembourg (n=1112)
Industrial	Argentina (n=1209); Belarus (n=891); Bulgaria (n=881); Chile (n=1131); Croatia (n=933); Czech (n=1845); Estonia (n=941); Greece (n=1119); Hungary (n=940); Latvia (n=938); Lithuania (n=948); Malta (n=985); Mexico (n=1385); Montenegro (n=946); Philippines (n=1197); Poland (n=1033); Romania (n=1046); Russia (n=2270); Serbia (n=1089); Slovakia1(n= 1280); Slovenia (n=977); South Korea (n=1074); Turkey (n=3251); Ukraine (n=1040); Venezuela (n=1173)
Agrarian	Bangladesh (n=1420); Egypt (n=3000); India (n=1575); Indonesia (n=984); Iran (n=195); Jordan (n=1176); Morocco (n=1189); Nigeria (n=2001); South Africa (n=2825); Tanzania (n=1143); Uganda (n=972); Vietnam (n=865); Zimbabwe (n=948)

Question 2:
(v201) Religious leaders should not influence how people vote in elections: 1: Agree strongly, 2: Agree, 3: Neither agree or disagree, 4: Disagree, 5: Strongly disagree.

Type of Society	1999-2000
Advanced Industrial	France (n=1590); Britain (n=955); W.Germany (n=1000); Italy (n=1946); Netherlands (n=999); Denmark (n=1011); Belgium (n=1882); Spain (n=1101); Ireland (n=996); U.S. (n=1193); Canada (n=1894); Japan (n=1326); Sweden (n=1008); Iceland (n=958); Finland (n=997); Austria (n=1489); Luxembourg (n=1143)
Industrial	Argentina (n=1188); Belarus (n=910); Bulgaria (n=886); Chile (n=1153); Croatia (n=970); Czech (n=1855); Estonia (n=955); Greece (n=1125); Hungary (n=941); Latvia (n=948); Lithuania (n=978); Malta (n=997); Mexico (n=1399); Montenegro (n=1005); Philippines (n=1194); Poland (n=1079); Romania (n=1047); Russia (n=2268); Serbia (n=1126); Slovakia (n=1298); Slovenia (n=981); South Korea (n=1122); Turkey (n=3236); Ukraine (n=1066); Venezuela (n=1164)
Agrarian	Bangladesh (n=1392); Egypt (n=2920); India (n=1535); Indonesia (n=992); Jordan (n=1139); Morocco (n=1022); Nigeria (n=1994); South Africa (n=2860); Tanzania (n=1145); Uganda (n=972); Vietnam (n=879); Zimbabwe (n=952)

Question 3:
(v202) It would be better for (this country) if more people with strong religious beliefs held public office: 1: Agree strongly, 2: Agree, 3: Neither agree or disagree, 4: Disagree, 5: Strongly disagree.

Type of Society	1999-2000
Advanced Industrial	France (n=1570); Britain (n=921); W.Germany (n=978); Italy (n=1926); Netherlands (n=1000); Denmark (n=982); Belgium (n=1862); Spain (n=1098); Ireland (n=972); U.S. (n=1185); Canada (n=1882); Japan (n=1324); Sweden (n=1003); Iceland (n=942); Finland (n=980); Austria (n=1459); Luxembourg (n=1092)
Industrial	Argentina (n=1180); Belarus (n=841); Bulgaria (n=868); Chile (n=1135); Croatia (n=937); Czech (n=1825); Estonia (n=901); Greece (n=1103); Hungary (n=927); Latvia (n=911); Lithuania (n=940); Malta (n=988); Mexico (n=1371); Montenegro (n=936); Philippines (n=1197); Poland (n=1019); Romania (n=1040); Russia (n=2232); Serbia (n=1075); Slovakia (n=1258); Slovenia (n=971); South Korea (n=1028); Turkey (n=3221); Ukraine (n=1013); Venezuela (n=1165)
Agrarian	Bangladesh (n=1382); Egypt (n=2977); India (n=1473); Indonesia (n=989); Jordan (n=1146); Morocco (n=1059); Nigeria (n=2002); South Africa (n=2825); Tanzania (n=1137); Uganda (n=955); Vietnam (n=862); Zimbabwe (n=927)

Question 4:
(v203) Religious leaders should not influence government decisions: 1:
Agree strongly, 2: Agree, 3: Neither agree or disagree, 4: Disagree, 5:
Strongly disagree.

Type of Society	1999-2000
Advanced Industrial	France (n=1590); Britain (n=936); W.Germany (n=999); Italy (n=1936); Netherlands (n=1000); Denmark (n=1000); Belgium (n=1871); Spain (n=1095); Ireland (n=987); U.S. (n=1188); Canada (n=1882); Japan (n=1320); Sweden (n=996); Iceland (n=952); Finland (n=995); Austria (n=1475); Luxembourg (n=1119);
Industrial	Argentina (n=1182); Belarus (n=885); Bulgaria (n=886); Chile (n=1137); Croatia (n=950); Czech (n=1837); Estonia (n=928); Greece (n=1122); Hungary (n=928); Latvia (n=923); Lithuania (n=959); Malta (n=991); Mexico (n=1376); Montenegro (n=995); Philippines (n=1197); Poland (n=1052); Romania (n=1040); Russia (n=2235); Serbia (n=1113); Slovakia (n=1272); Slovenia (n=977); South Korea (n=1103); Ukraine (n=1011); Venezuela (n=1166);
Agrarian	Bangladesh (n=1385); India (n=1519); Morocco (n=941); South Africa (n=2823); Tanzania (n=1144); Uganda (n=970); Vietnam (n=876); Zimbabwe (n=948)

CONTRIBUTORS

Barry Cooper is Professor, Department of Political Science, at the University of Calgary.

Boris DeWiel is Associate Professor, Department of Political Science, at the University of Northern British Columbia.

Mebs Kanji is Assistant Professor, Department of Political Science, at Concordia University in Montreal.

Ron Kuipers is Assistant Professor of the Philosophy of Religion at the Institute for Christian Studies in Toronto.

Paul Rowe is Assistant Professor, Department of Political Studies and International Studies at Trinity Western University in British Columbia.

John Soroski teaches Political Science at Grant MacEwan College in Edmonton, Alberta.

John von Heyking is Associate Professor, Department of Political Science at the University of Lethbridge.

John Young is Associate Professor, Department of Political Science, at the University of Northern British Columbia.

INDEX

theocracy of relativism, 42
Thompson, Dennis, 142, 146
Tillich, Paul, 76, 86, 87
Tinder, Glenn, 59
tolerance, 1, 2, 7, 10, 39, 43, 55, 93
Toronto 17, 157, 158, 159, 160,
   161, 164
Toronto Star, 96, 103, 111, 112,
   113, 165
tradecraft, 155, 156, 157, 159
Trudeau, Pierre, 42, 50
Turgot, Anne-Robert-Jacques, 36
Turpel-LaFond, Mary Ellen, 132,
   148
Tuveson, Ernest, 87
Übermensch, 72, 75
umma, 89, 91, 104
United Church of Canada, 6, 8, 12
United Nations Human Rights
   Commission, 7
Universal Declaration of Human
   Rights, 50, 51
universality, 10, 68, 69
utopianism, 46
valuation, 116, 119, 120, 123, 124,
   125, 129, 130, 132, 133, 137,
   140, 145, 149
value spheres, 16
values, 2, 3, 9, 10, 34, 47, 48, 62,
   67, 105, 106, 107, 114, 115, 116,
   117, 118, 119, 121, 122, 123,

124, 125, 126, 127, 128, 129,
   130, 131, 132, 133, 134, 135,
   136, 137, 138, 139, 145, 148,
   158
Van Die, Marguerite, 55
Vaughan, Frederick, 57
Voegelin, Eric, 38, 48, 55, 57, 59,
   151
voluntarism, 64, 66, 68, 89
Walsh, David, 53, 59
Walsh, Kerry-Anne, 166
War Measures Act, 160, 163
Wattie, Chris, 164
Weber, Alfred, 68, 85
Weber, Max, 15, 16, 33, 34, 76, 87
West, Diana, 166
Wilcox, Clyde, 89, 109
Willing, Jon, 113
Winthrop, Delba, 55
Wittgenstein, Ludwig, 33
Wolin, Richard, 86, 87
World Values Survey, 15
Wright, Lawrence, 165
WVS, 14, 16, 17, 18, 34
Yakabuski, Konrad, 113
Yelaja, Prithi, 112
Yousef, Ramzi, 153
Youssif, Ahmad F., 110
Zeno, 62
Zerbisias, Antonia, 113